THE ROOTS OF FREEDOM

A CONSTITUTIONAL HISTORY
OF ENGLAND

By Bernard Schwartz

American Administrative Law
American Constitutional Law
The Code Napoleon and the Common-Law World (ed.)
A Commentary on the Constitution of the United States
    (Part I, The Powers of Government; Part II,
    The Rights of Property)
Le Droit Administratif Américain: Notions Générales
French Administrative Law and the Common-Law World
An Introduction to American Administrative Law
Law and the Executive in Britain
The Professor and the Commissions
The Reins of Power: A Constitutional History
    of the United States
The Roots of Freedom: A Constitutional History
    of England
The Supreme Court

THE ROOTS
OF FREEDOM

A CONSTITUTIONAL HISTORY
OF ENGLAND

by

Bernard Schwartz

HILL AND WANG · NEW YORK

Manufactured in the United States of America
by American Book–Stratford Press, Inc.

PREFACE

"HUMAN HISTORY," says H. G. Wells, "is in essence a history of ideas." To an American interested in constitutional history, the great theme in his country's development is the idea of law as a check upon governmental power. That idea has its source in the history of that people from whom our institutions have sprung. American dependence upon English constitutional development is, indeed, so great that it is virtually impossible to understand the history of the United States and the development of its governmental institutions without some knowledge of the constitutional conflicts that took place in pre-Revolutionary England. If Americans today live under a constitutional polity, it is only because we are the heirs of a successful struggle to bridle governmental power by the law of the land. All too few people in this country realize the extent to which our modern liberties are based upon the crucial battles waged against seventeenth-century Stuart tyranny.

But the men who secured the independence of the American nation and established our constitutional system were fully aware of the vital importance of the Parliamentary victory over the Crown. They considered themselves the direct heirs of those Englishmen who had met and mastered the Stuart efforts at absolutism. The Declaration of Independence and the Constitution itself were but the restatements in their day of the Parliamentary opposition to the claims of the Crown.

The present volume is intended to recall for Americans what too many of them have forgotten—that the roots of their freedom are to be found in English constitutional history. More than that, the struggle of Englishmen over the centuries to develop rep-

v

16567

resentative government and the rule of law was the indispensable *sine qua non* of our present-day rights and liberties. The American Constitution is thus a magic mirror, wherein we see reflected not only our own lives, but the constitutional development of England and all that "the Flood of British freedom" has meant. When one thinks on this majestic theme, his eyes dazzle. If only a part of his own feelings on the matter are communicated to the reader, the writer will be amply rewarded for his labors in preparing this volume.

BERNARD SCHWARTZ

CONTENTS

1

ROOT PRINCIPLE

"SUCH IS THE UNITY of all history," reads a famous passage of F. W. Maitland, "that any one who endeavours to tell a piece of it must feel that his first sentence tears a seamless web." This is particularly true of one who seeks to tell the history of an institution such as the British Constitution which has been, not so much the result of conscious acts of legislation, as the accretion of a people's history. If, as Gladstone put it in a celebrated passage, "the American Constitution is the most wonderful work ever struck off at a given time by the brain and purpose of man," so "the British Constitution is the most subtle organism which has proceeded from progressive history."

To an American interested in the development of the British Constitution (particularly as the source from whence his own constitutional institutions are derived), as good a starting point as any is that scene at Runnymede on June 15, 1215—since become one of the most famous in the history of the English-speaking peoples—when King John affixed his seal to what has ever since been known as the Great Charter.

One who looks at English history through the lenses of American constitutional experience is bound to feel a kinship with the document that resulted from the barons' rebellion against John. For in it he sees for the first time in English history a written organic instrument, exacted from a thitherto sovereign ruler by the bulk of the politically articulate community, which purports to lay down binding rules of law that the ruler himself may not violate. The tendency to consider Magna Charta as the starting point of English constitutional development is only natural in one who lives in a country in which governmental institutions may be finitely traced to the lines laid down in defined written constitutions.

If this approach is erroneous, the error is one that has been shared by countless Englishmen themselves. "The whole of the constitutional history of England," declares what is still considered the leading work on the subject, that by Bishop Stubbs, "is little more than a commentary on Magna Carta." If the present-day historian finds hyperbole in this sanguine statement, he should bear in mind that, in Maitland's words, "Magna Carta came to be reckoned as the beginning of English statute law; it was printed as the first of the statutes of the realm." When the time came for Englishmen to print their laws, Magna Charta (in the version issued in 1225) took its place at the beginning of the statute book—a place it still occupies in the modern *Statutes of the Realm.*

The Great Charter itself did not, to be sure, spring full grown from the collective head of King John's baronial opponents. On the contrary, if Magna Charta marks the beginning of a new period of English constitutional history, it also marks the culmination of all that had gone before—especially since the Norman Conquest.

Of course, English constitutional history, like other aspects of English history, does not commence with the invasion from Normandy. Before the Conquest, too, the English were developing into a nation—with its own institutions, laws, and traditions. Albeit slowly, the spirit of nationhood was maturing, fostered by strong kings like Ethelbert (with whom English law first began to speak), Alfred (considered by legend the first architect of the British Constitution), and Canute (under whom the Anglo-Saxon monarchy attained its apogee).

But the Anglo-Saxon polity at the time of Hastings had scarcely begun to develop, at least under modern conceptions of governmental power. In the means and processes of getting the public business performed, the Saxon government has been characterized as but little developed beyond the tribal state first organized in England after the original settlement. There was no effective provision for securing an adequate military force or public revenue. The national government (as distinguished from local institutions) was so rudimentary as to be almost primitive. George B. Adams, the leading American writer on English constitutional history, has gone so far as to assert that, "At the moment when the Saxon kingdom was overthrown, the outlook for the future development of national government was not promising." Certainly there is much to be said for that view during the days when the saintly but inane Edward sat upon the throne. Had Harold been given the time to develop into an effective king, perhaps it might have made a difference. Or perhaps not, in view of the lack of strong governmental institutions in Saxon England.

What we do know is that the Norman Conquest did make a difference—and a difference that was indeed fundamental. As any reader of *Ivanhoe* well knows, to the Saxons, the victory of William and his Norman invaders may have seemed a great catastrophe that befell England. From a broader perspective, however, the Conquest served as a catalyst to English constitutional development. The infusion of a race whose forte was law and administration brought to that development exactly what was needed to enable it to proceed along rapid and secure lines.

Since the time of the Norman Conquest, there has been a continuity in English law and institutions that has been unique in the Western world. For all the changes that have occurred— hardly a law remains unaltered—the essentials of the English system are the same as those that Blackstone described in the eighteenth century, Coke in the seventeenth, Littleton in the fifteenth, Bracton in the thirteenth, and Glanville in the twelfth. Eventful though the life of English law and institutions may have been in the near thousand years since 1066, it has been but a single life.

Despite what has been said, it would not be accurate to assume that the accession of William the Conqueror meant a complete break with the Anglo-Saxon past. William as the ruler of England was a conservative both by temperament and necessity. The Normans, as Winston Churchill has put it, were administrators and lawyers rather than legislators. They retained the best features of the Anglo-Saxon government and invigorated the old institutions by engrafting onto them efficient Norman practices.

William did not begin his rule by wiping the legal slate clean;

instead, he plainly meant his English subjects to keep their old laws. "I let you wit," he wrote in his celebrated charter which is still preserved by the City of London, that "I will that you . . . be worthy of all the laws that you were worthy of in King Edward's day." Yet, though we must not suppose that the Saxon system was swept away by the Normans, two vital changes— which metamorphosed the character and Constitution of the nation—were made by the Conquest: the establishment of a strong monarchy and the introduction of political feudalism.

If Canute had shown what the Saxon monarchy might one day have become, his vigorous reign was the rare exception in the century before the Conquest. Edward the Confessor, vested only with titular headship, was more the typical ruler of pre-Norman days. Merely duke in Normandy, William was going to be king in England. His military success in 1066 was so great that the country lay entirely at his disposal. William could be a true ruler of a centralized monarchy, as not even the greatest of the Anglo-Saxon kings could have been. Says the contemporary *Anglo-Saxon Chronicle:* "He was a very stern and violent man, so that no one dared do anything contrary to his will. . . . the good security he made in this country is not to be forgotten—so that any honest man could travel over his kingdom without injury with his bosom full of gold; and no one dared strike another, however much wrong he had done him."

Without the strong central government instituted by William, none of the legal and constitutional reforms instituted by his Norman and Plantagenet successors would have been possible. Moreover, the establishment of a tradition of firm government enabled the institutional framework of state machinery to develop upon which was to be built the British Constitution familiar to the modern observer.

The strength of the monarchy established by the Norman Conquest is strikingly shown in the monumental 1086 inquiry into the wealth of England known as *Domesday Book.* To refer again to the chronicler: "He ruled over England, and by his cunning it was so investigated that there was not one hide of land in England that he did not know who owned it, and what it was worth, and then set it down in his record." In minute detail, the land was described county by county, village by village, the owners and subtenants were recorded and their property valued

—even the livestock was listed—with a view to settle clearly the rights of the Crown and the taxable resources of the nation. Such a meticulous survey could scarcely have been carried out in any other country in western Europe and would have been unthinkable in Saxon England.

It has been said that the strong government set up by William the Conqueror was a wholly natural development. "He became all powerful in England," in the words of George B. Adams, "because he had been and was all powerful in Normandy." Yet, all powerful though the Norman Crown doubtless was, it was far from authoritarian in the modern sense. The absolutism of William and his successors was tempered by the peculiar institution we know as *feudalism*.

Countless scholars have engaged in erudite controversy over the extent to which feudalism—or something very akin to it—had developed in pre-Norman days. For our purposes, however, we may assume (with the majority of them) that feudalism, particularly in its political aspect, was essentially a Norman importation—that, as Stubbs said, "Feudalism in both tenure and government was, so far as it existed in England, brought full-grown from France." The introduction of the *feudum* has been well characterized as a step which created a revolution in the upper strata of social life in England and set new principles at work in its constitutional and political history.

What do we mean by feudalism?

With Maitland, we can say that feudalism may be described as a state of society in which public rights and duties are inextricably interwoven with the tenure of land, in which the whole governmental system—financial, military, judicial—is part of the law governing such tenure. In this kind of society, following Maitland again, the main bond is the relation between lord and man—a relation implying, on the lord's part, protection and defense; on the man's part, service and reverence, with the service including particularly service in arms. This personal relation is based upon a proprietary relation: the tenure of land. The man holds land of the lord, his service is a burden on the land, and the lord has important rights in the land. From the modern point of view, we may say that the full ownership of the land is parceled up between man and lord.

More than that, the organization of the nation itself is a system of these relationships: at the head stands the king as lord of all, below him are his tenants in chief, who themselves are lords of tenants, who again may be lords of tenants, and so on, down to the lowest possessor of land.

In the feudal society, personal freedom and political right have become bound up with the relations created by the possession of land. With the Norman Conquest, such had, in fact, become the state of the society in England. The *Domesday* survey shows us how the feudal system had already become consolidated; all the landowners of the kingdom had become, in one way or another, vassals—either of the king or of some tenant under him.

With the details of feudal tenure and its incidents, we need not be here concerned. Certainly, they were extremely technical and involved. One who finds it difficult to unravel the early law on the subject is left with Maitland's consolation in his great work on *Domesday Book:* "If we are puzzled by this labyrinth of soken, let us console ourselves with the reflection that the Normans also were puzzled by it."

The fundamental aspect of feudalism, for one concerned with its impact upon English constitutional history, is the relationship between lord and man. This relationship was basically contractural in nature; feudal tenure imported contractual rights and obligations—as between both lord and man. It is easy for us to understand this in its application to the holding of land, for we naturally analogize the lord-man relationship to that of landlord-tenant with which we are familiar. What is more difficult is to realize that, under feudalism, the political organization of the society itself was also based upon the same lord-man relationship.

In the feudal system, the obligations of public service that, under modern conceptions, the citizen owes to the State were not due to the State as such but were considered private obligations that one man owed to another as a return for land that he held of the other. The obligations of the citizen, particularly that of military service, are intimately connected with the holding of land. The tenant in respect of land owes some service to the lord; this is the return he makes to his lord for the land. But since, as *Domesday Book* assumes, all land was, in the last resort, held from the king, the same obligation was ultimately the basis for the performance of duties, such as that of national defense, which we should deem wholly political in nature.

To the modern mind, all of this is based upon an inextricable confusion of public with private law—the country's Constitution seems, to paraphrase Maitland, a sort of appendix to the law of real property.

It is, however, erroneous to think of the feudal relationship as entirely one-sided—as one that imposes only obligations upon the landholder in favor of his lord. On the contrary, the binding tie between lord and man was the swearing of homage, which involved rights and obligations on both sides. In the words of a contemporary statement, "such is the relation of homage that the lord owes as much to the tenant as the tenant to the lord, save only reverence." The condition of vassalage is, as J. E. A. Jolliffe, a leading modern constitutional historian of the period, tells us, fidelity and service on the one side and warranty and protection on the other. Either lord or man, by failing to perform his share of the contract and refusing redress, gives to the other the right to defy him and to coerce him with all the means in the other's power.

Implicit in the concept of feudalism just discussed was the limitation of the vassal's obligations to those which had been fixed in the agreement setting up the tenure or which had become customary. This meant, for the most part, military service plus a number of specified incidents: relief (paid on entry into the estate), wardship (control during the minority of a vassal's heir), and marriage (control over the marriage of a vassal's heiress), as well as three recognized aids (for the knighting of the lord's eldest son, the marriage of his eldest daughter, or the ransoming of his body from captivity).

As time went on, the principal obligation—actual military service—tended to give way to the obligation of making an equivalent commutation in the form of a money payment: so-called scutage. Thus, the tenant's obligation was essentially the payment of specified sums. The amounts involved were never, to be sure, fixed with anything like the kind of certainty that the modern fiscal expert would require. All the same, the vital notion was developed that the obligations of the tenant were limited by the feudal contract to those stated and could not be increased by unilateral action of the lord.

But it was also this notion that dominated the public law of post-Conquest England, permeated as it was with feudal conceptions. The relations between the king and his subjects, like those between the ordinary lord and vassal, were regulated by the same feudal contract which neither could alter without the consent of the other. The understanding that feudal custom had about the services of the barons and the rest of the nation to the king could not be changed at the latter's will.

It is true that (like the details of the feudal relation generally) the rules on the matter were very unsettled—throughout the period prior to Magna Charta, the king got what he could and often got a great deal. Yet there is always the concept of limit in the just and lawful claims fixed by the feudal contract. When this limit is transgressed, the feudal tie has been broken; the aggrieved baron is then within his rights in declaring his obligation of vassalage at an end and coercing the king by every means in his power to do him right. When Richard Marshal led a revolt in 1233, he justified his action by pointing to alleged unlawful measures by the king himself, saying: "So I was not his man (when I took arms against him), but stood absolved from his homage rightfully, and not by my own doing but by his."

The present-day American naturally sees in all this the germ of the doctrine that there are principles above the State, which the State—otherwise sovereign power that it is—may not alter: that the State itself is and must be below the law. It cannot be denied that such law is in its infancy; but its rudimentary principles can be worked out in more detail in succeeding ages.

The accidents of the succession in the Norman kings after William the Conqueror soon added another vital ingredient to the constitutional cauldron—that of the written charter guaranteeing established rights and liberties. The adherent of deterministic theories of history is bound to be disturbed at the course of English constitutional development following the death of William I. To notice just one of the hundred forces that play upon history, says Maitland, "we have but to suppose that the Conqueror, instead of leaving three sons, had left one only, and to ask whether in that case a charter of liberties would ever have been granted in England."

When the Conqueror died in 1087 (according to the chronicle of Ordericus Vitalis written almost half a century later) he made a deathbed statement of repentance for the acts of wrong done by him. In addition, he looked to the future and disposed of his dominions among his sons: Robert (the eldest), must have Normandy; William should have England; Henry (the youngest), he was sure, would have all in the end. And so it actually came to pass.

William Rufus succeeded to the throne, in compliance with the Conqueror's wish, though he was not the eldest son. Under such circumstances, he was willing to make any promise to obtain his inheritance. He swore to Lanfranc, the aged Archbishop of Canterbury, that if he were crowned he would preserve justice, equity, and mercy throughout the realm and would defend against all the peace, liberty, and security of the Church. When a majority of the barons rebelled on behalf of his elder brother Robert, he sought the aid of the people with the promise that he would make better laws and forbid unjust taxation. A third time, when he believed himself near death, he made even broader promises of good government, with "good and holy laws, inviolable observance of right, and a severe examination of wrongs such as would frighten others."

It is true that such promises hardly deterred William Rufus from the tyranny that is associated with his reign. When reminded of his oaths by Lanfranc, he asked in anger, "Who is there who can fulfill all that he promises?" But the mere fact that he made such promises at all (going beyond the traditional coronation oath of the Saxon kings) was itself an important precedent. And when, on Rufus' sudden death in a hunting accident in 1100, his youngest brother Henry seized the throne without even the shadow of hereditary right, he went one step further to obtain the support of the nation by the issuance of a written Charter of Liberties.

The traditional theory made Magna Charta the direct descendant of Henry I's Coronation Charter. Though this view has been challenged by more-modern historians, that hardly lessens the constitutional importance of the document issued by Henry as the price of support for his accession. In this document was set forth in detail for the first time a list of abusive practices that would be corrected by the new king. More than that, its benefits were not limited to those of a particular class. Of course, by the very nature of the society of the time, the detailed concessions were made to the barons and the Church, while those to the nation at large were few and vague. Still, of great significance is the fact that the corrections promised were not restricted to the tenants in chief: the barons themselves were expressly to be bound by the same limitations in regard to their men. Stubbs's famous contention that Henry, in his Charter, "definitely commits himself to the duties of a national king" has been severely criticized. Yet, in the perspective of history, it is not so far wide of the mark as some recent writers would have us believe.

The most important fact about the Coronation Charter is that it was issued in the form of a written charter, as a legally binding royal grant. It is the first of a long list of similar documents— from the Magna Charta itself to the colonial charters that were the direct antecedents of the constitutions that today govern Americans.

Henry's Charter begins with the declaration: "Know ye that by the mercy of God and the common counsel of the barons of the realm of England I have been crowned king of the same realm." When Henry died, his nephew Stephen, in defiance of the late king's wishes, usurped the Crown and had to bid even higher than Henry to obtain support. His second or Oxford Charter (1136), characterized by Stubbs as "the second of our great charters of liberties," was based upon recognition of his lack of legal right to the throne. It appeals, not to hereditary right, but to election—"I Stephen by the grace of God, elected as king of England, by assent of the clergy and people." As in the Charter of Henry I, the promises were, in the main, to the Church and barons. Yet, as was also true of the earlier document, there were clauses attempting to conciliate each of the three estates. The general promise of peace and justice was amplified by an undertaking to extirpate all exactions, unjust practices, and chicanery by sheriffs and others, and to maintain good laws and ancient and just customs.

After Stephen's weak rule, there was a definite reaction. The wide promises of Stephen gave way to the meager words of the charter granted by Henry II on his coronation. And neither of Henry's sons, at their crownings, granted any charter at all. But the precedent of the earlier charters, particularly that of the first Henry, was there to serve as a guide when the need arose to put legal bounds against abuses of the royal power.

All that was lacking was the misuse of the royal power to an extent that would unite the nation against its possessor. And that was supplied when John succeeded to the throne on the death of his brother Richard in 1199. To generations of historians, John has been one of the arch-villains of English history. The tradition in this respect started soon after John's death in the writings of the chroniclers Roger of Wendover and Matthew Paris. According to the latter, "John was a tyrant not a king, a destroyer instead of a governor, crushing his own people and favouring aliens, a lion to his subjects but a lamb to foreigners and rebels. . . . He was an insatiable extorter of money; he invaded and destroyed his subjects' property. . . . Foul as it is, Hell itself is defiled by the fouler presence of King John."

Some present-day historians have sought to give a more favorable picture of John, contending that his great failing was not so much his defective personal character as his misfortune to reign in an era when antiquated feudal custom and institutions were inadequate to the needs of a changing economic and social order. In the words of W. L. Warren's 1961 biography, John merely "reaped the whirlwind sown by his swashbuckling father and brother."

Such attempts to cast John in a more favorable light have scarcely altered the general attitude toward that monarch. "The terrible verdict of the king's contemporaries," declares J. R. Green's *Short History of the English People,* "has passed into the sober judgment of history."

John may well have been (and, in all likelihood, was) the unprincipled tyrant depicted by his contemporaries. Yet, paradoxical though it may sound, we are indebted much more to John's defects than to any merits that he might have possessed. In truth, Winston Churchill tells us, "when the long tally is added it will be seen that the British nation and the English-speaking world owe far more to the vices of John than to the labours of virtuous sovereigns; for it was to the union of many forces against him that the most famous milestone of our rights and freedom was in fact set up."

One may go further and assert that English constitutional history is far more obligated to its wicked, than to its righteous, monarchs. We need not necessarily agree with Lord Acton that great men are almost always bad men, but our constitutional law should clearly be based upon some such assertion. In fact, the Anglo-American organic structure has been erected upon the assumption that the king not only is capable of doing wrong but is more likely than other men to do wrong if he is given the chance. This assumption was derived from the experience of Englishmen during the reigns of evil kings like John. John, Richard II, Charles I, James II—their names form a list of the worst English monarchs. Yet it was precisely their misrule, and the popular reaction engendered thereby, that gave rise to the most fruitful developments in English constitutional history.

John himself came to the throne when the effective monarchy built by his father appeared unassailable. So solid, indeed, was the base upon which Henry II constructed his system of central-ized law and administration that it remained firm through the absentee rule of Richard I, the abuses of John, and the weak reign of his son, Henry III.

John did not, however, remain content with operating the strong governmental machine bequeathed by his father. Instead, like William Rufus before him, he sought to push the machine to its utmost limit of power. In the neat phrase of W. L. Warren, "He sought to fashion maximum security for the Crown out of the greatest possible insecurity for his subjects." To accomplish his ends, he used the royal power more ruthlessly than any of his predecessors (with the possible exception of William Rufus, about whose reign we do not have enough detailed knowledge to state a categorical comparative opinion). "No one in the land could resist his will in anything," says the contemporary chron-icler Gervase of Canterbury. "The king himself seemed alone to be mighty in the land and he neither feared God nor regarded men."

Perhaps, as already intimated, the traditional view of John's actions is somewhat unfair to that monarch. He found himself faced by needs, particularly financial ones, more pressing than those which had confronted his predecessors. Nascent French nationalism, carefully nurtured by one of the greatest rulers of France, Philip Augustus, rendered well-nigh inevitable the loss of the vast Continental domains that had come to John from his father. Added to this was John's misfortune to live in a period of monetary inflation, which shrank his real income just when he so badly needed every coin he could lay his hands on for the war with Philip.

John's constant need for revenue was the principal factor behind the exactions and abuses that were the primary cause of

Magna Charta. There was no system of taxation, in the modern sense, by which the pecuniary exigencies of the Crown could be satisfied. The only fiscal machinery available to John was that connected with the feudal system: the recognized feudal incidents and aids, as well as knight's service, which had, as already noted, come to mean so-called scutage—a money payment in commutation of the actual military service that had once been due.

To obtain the needed revenue, it was necessary to increase the customary feudal obligations. During John's reign, according to William S. McKechnie's standard treatise on Magna Charta, "the stream of feudal obligations steadily rose until the barons feared that nothing of their property would be saved from the torrent." This was particularly true of scutage, which John altered from a device reserved for emergencies into a regular source of revenue. The normal rate of scutage was raised and the frequency of its imposition increased, until, with the demand for a new scutage in 1214 at an unprecedented rate, the limit of the barons' endurance was reached and John was met with flat refusals to pay.

In addition, John sought to exercise his other feudal rights to their utmost limits, affecting his vassals on the point where they were most sensitive—their family interests—as well as to exact money by other means, such as efforts to impose a general property tax. His ingenuity in this respect is illustrated by the curious entry in the public record for Christmas 1204: "The wife of Hugh Neville promises the lord king two hundred chickens that she might lie one night with her husband."

At the beginning, John's efforts, extra-legal though they seemed to men bound by the customary feudal rules, may have appeared successful. Thus, the so-called Thirteenth (a tax of a shilling in the mark of property) of 1207 brought in more than twice the ordinary revenue for a year. Yet, in the phrase of the papal legate in Shakespeare's *King John,*

> 'Tis strange to think how much King John
> hath lost
> In this which he accounts so clearly won.

John's financial excesses led directly to the barons' rebellion that resulted in the Great Charter. "He was a pillager of his subjects," says the annalist who wrote at Barnwell priory shortly after John's death, and, for that reason, "they foresook him and, ultimately, little mourned his death." Well might John plaintively declaim, in the Shakespeare play, when his acts had united the nation against him,

> Our discontented counties do revolt;
> Our people quarrel with obedience.

The price of continued obedience was the fixing of the king's seal to the Charter at Runnymede.

What was it that converted the resistance to John from a petty attempt of the barons to preserve their feudal prerogatives into an epochal event in the history of freedom? The answer to this query is to be found in the very existence of the Great Charter itself. The end result of the rebellion against John was, not the mere death or deposition of a tyrant, but a written instrument laying down the fundamentals of good government as they were understood at the time. In this sense, Magna Charta is based directly upon the Coronation Charter of Henry I.

The derivation of Magna Charta from the Charter of Henry I is told dramatically in a famous tale of the contemporary chronicler Roger of Wendover. As he tells it, Archbishop Stephen Langton (whose role was crucial in the actual securing of the Great Charter), at a great service held in St. Paul's in 1213, made the theatrical gesture of producing the then-forgotten document of the first Henry, saying, "a charter of King Henry I has now been found by which you can, if you will, recover your long-lost liberties in their pristine condition." And, continues the chronicler, "when it had been read and understood by the barons, they rejoiced with exceeding great joy, and all swore, in the archbishop's presence, that they would fight for those liberties, if it were needful, even unto death."

Modern scholars consider this tale apocryphal. But it is clear that, some time in 1212, the emphasis of the opposition to John shifted from one of the king's deposition to one of a written document defining good government to be secured from the Crown. As W. L. Warren puts it, "in place of the conspiracy to murder John and set up a new king, which had been their one policy in 1212, they were now waving a charter." This was the crucial development, and it could scarcely have occurred had there not been the precedent of Henry I's Charter: it furnished both a safe standing-ground (for men who deemed existing custom practically immutable) and a precedent for a deliberate scheme of governmental reform.

Yet, if the Charter secured at Runnymede in 1215 may thus be said to be derived from the Henry I Charter, its importance is to be found in the fact that it goes far beyond that earlier document both in its wording and implications. Most significant were the differing circumstances in which the two charters were secured. As already seen, Henry issued his Coronation Charter to obtain support for his accession to the throne; but the instrument itself was plainly a unilateral act on the part of the monarch—a promise by the king given as a matter of grace and not as the result of any external coercion.

John's Charter also, it is true, is in terms only a grant by a sovereign to his subjects. "John, by the grace of God," it starts, and, after listing his titles and his formal greeting to his subjects, goes on to state, "Know that we . . . have . . . granted to all freemen of our kingdom, for us and our heirs forever, all the liberties written below, to be had and held by them and their heirs, of us and our heirs forever." And, after listing the different liberties granted, it concludes, with the traditional words of royal grant: "Given by our hand, in the meadow which is called Runnymede, between Windsor and Staines, on the fifteenth day of June, in the seventeenth year of our reign." The actual giving, by John's hand, was effected by the imprint of his great seal.

But if the Magna Charta was thus cast in the form common to royal charters of the period—announcing in the pious legal language of the day that the king has been pleased to make certain unilateral grants, by the advice of certain counsellors who are named—how different was its reality! In actuality, John's Charter was anything but a unilateral act of grace on the part of that monarch. The promises made at Runnymede were exacted by the united arms of most of the kingdom. The reasons stated for the grant of the Charter were quaintly paraphrased by Lord Coke four centuries later: "Here be four notable causes of the making of this great charter rehearsed. 1. The honour of God. 2. For the health of the King's soul. 3. For the exaltation of holy church, and fourthly, for the amendment of the Kingdom." But the real reason, William S. McKechnie tells us, is to be found in the army of the rebels. The true *quid pro quo* which John received for the grants made by him was the renewal by his opponents of the homage and fealty that they had solemnly renounced.

Seen in this light, what can we say is the true legal nature of the Great Charter? Here, once again, is a question on which countless scholars have disagreed. As already indicated, the document's form as a unilateral grant—a mere act of grace—on the part of the Crown does not give the answer. Bishop Stubbs's famous characterization of Magna Charta as "really a treaty between the King and his subjects" has been rejected by more-recent historians. Yet it is not so far from the truth as they suppose—if we bear in mind that, unlike the usual treaty between independent States, this was a concord worked out between ruler and subjects of the same State.

From the point of view of the modern American, such an agreement, drawn up by the different estates of the realm, and accepted by the king as the price for their continued obedience— setting limits to the powers of government—has many of the earmarks of the constitutional documents with which he is familiar. Even the charter form—a grant of franchises freely made— does not seem out of place to one cognizant of the constitutional role played by documents cast in a similar form in the American Colonies.

What is clear is that there took place at Runnymede what was essentially a bargain struck between the king and the nation. The result of this bargain was a document enumerating what were deemed the basic liberties of Englishmen of the day. This enumeration may strike us as brief, contained as it is in sixty-three short chapters; for its date, nevertheless, it is a rather lengthy document. It was natural for the men of the day to resort to the legal form invariably used for all irrevocable grants—the feudal charter authenticated by the grantor's seal. The analogy was that of a grant of land and much of the language employed was actually that appropriate to such a grant. If the substance of Magna Charta is the establishment of a framework of good government, its form, as McKechnie puts it, "is borrowed from the feudal lawyer's book of styles for conferring a title to landed estate."

In a provocative passage, Maitland asks, "Have you ever pondered the form, the scheme, the main idea of Magna Charta? If so, your reverence for that sacred text will hardly have prevented you from using in the privacy of your own minds some such words as 'inept' or 'childish,' etc." Certainly, Magna Charta is an unrewarding document for the nonspecialist. "If we set aside the rhetorical praise which has been so freely lavished upon the Charter," says Winston Churchill, "and study the document itself, we may find it rather surprising."

The Great Charter is drawn up as a feudal grant. It abounds in the technicalities of feudal law and, when these are out of the way, it seems to deal mainly with mundane and petty aspects of the relations between the king and his tenants in chief. There is in it no broad statement of principle or defined political theory. It is not what we would look for in a declaration of constitutional doctrine, but only a practical document to remedy current feudal abuses. Most surprising is that most of what we now consider the great safeguards of Anglo-American liberty are conspicuously absent from the first great charter of English liberties.

Yet if we analyze the Great Charter on its own terms, there is much that is notable. It is of great significance that the custom of feudal tenure is stated as a defined component of English law, with precise limits set to royal claims in strict terms of money, time, and space. The questions of scutage, feudal reliefs, wardship, and the like are regulated in legally enforceable terms against a king who had claimed to be all but a law unto himself. More important is the fact that, though Magna Charta is primarily a feudal document directed against specific feudal abuses committed by the king against his tenants in chief, its important provisions are cast in broader terms. This is of crucial consequence, for it means that the key chapters of the Charter have been capable of construction to fit the needs of later ages that sought precedents to justify establishment of the liberties we now deem basic.

The barons were concerned with their own grievances against John; but, when the original Articles of the Barons were being refined, the words "any baron" were changed, in important provisions, to "any free man" (*liber homo*). This change in phraseology may have seemed of minor significance at the time (certainly "free man" was a technical feudal term with a much more restricted meaning than we should assign to it), yet it turned out to be of momentous importance in giving the Charter the widest application in future centuries. The wrongs done to the barons may have been the direct cause of Magna Charta, but the language used was broad enough to protect the entire nation against governmental oppression.

This was particularly true of what history came to consider the two key provisions of the Great Charter: (1) Chapter 12, under which "No scutage or aid shall be imposed in our kingdom, unless by common counsel of our kingdom"; and (2) Chapter 39, which declares, "No free man shall be taken or imprisoned or disseised or exiled or in any way destroyed . . . save by the lawful judgment of his peers and by the law of the land."

The first of these may have been intended by the barons only as an assertion of their right not to have their feudal obligations unilaterally altered by the king, but, without undue stretching, it can readily be construed as an admission of the right of the nation to ordain taxation.

In addition, Chapter 14 specifies how the consent of the nation is to be given. To obtain the common counsel of the kingdom to the assessing of an aid or scutage, it states, "we will cause to be summoned the archbishops, bishops, abbots, earls, and greater barons," as well as those who hold of the king in chief below the rank of the greater barons—all this on forty days' notice—and the action of those who obey the summons is to be taken to represent the action of the whole. Here we have a rough attempt, albeit in rudimentary form, to define what will become the national assembly for purposes of taxation. In it is at least the seed of the basic principle that no financial burden may be imposed upon the people without the consent of Parliament, as well as that of Parliamentary representation. If men had not yet grasped these principles in their full modern sense, and especially the essential interconnection between taxation and representation, they had at least made a start in that direction.

The role of Chapter 39 has been even more consequential in the evolution of constitutional liberty. This is true although it was probably intended merely as a written confirmation of the baronial right, recognized by feudal custom, not to be tried by inferiors, but only by men of baronial rank. The breadth of the language used has made it serve a far wider purpose. Coke, in his seventeenth-century commentary on Magna Charta, could read it as a guaranty of trial by jury to all men; as absolutely prohibiting arbitrary arrest; and as solemnly undertaking to dispense to all full, free, and speedy justice—equal to all. Even more suggestive for an American, in Coke's commentary, the crucial phrase at the end of the chapter, "by the law of the land," is read as equivalent to "due process of law" (a connotation that it had begun to acquire as early as the time of Edward III)—thus providing the link between the Great Charter and the most important clause of modern American Constitutions.

Of course, we read our own conceptions into the document sealed at Runnymede when we make of it an organic instrument designed, in Henry Hallam's phrase, to "protect the personal liberty and property of all freemen by giving security from arbitrary imprisonment and arbitrary spoliation." Yet, intended so broadly or not by its framers, it can scarcely be doubted that the ultimate effect of Magna Charta, in Edward Creasy's words, "was to give and to guarantee full protection for person and property to every human being that breathes English air."

More important to the constitutional historian than the literal intent of the men of Runnymede is the meaning that future generations were able to read into their words. If, as Maitland has strikingly put it, it was possible for later men to worship such words only because it was possible to misunderstand them, the significant thing, after all, is that the words were written in a way that could be "misunderstood" so as to serve the needs of later ages. Because of this, to quote Maitland again, the "document becomes and rightly becomes a sacred text, the nearest thing to a 'fundamental statute' that England has ever had." In age after age, men will turn to the Charter as a continuing source of inspiration and authority in their struggles to bridle the "Johns" of their day.

For the truly great thing about the Magna Charta has been what J. C. Holt terms its adaptability—the ability to mean all things to all men—to project itself into the dreams and necessities of ages that the men of 1215 could, at best, not even dimly foresee. Thus it was that a document that may itself have been only a product of feudal class selfishness was able to serve as the basis for molding the foundations of a Parliamentary monarchy in the next two centuries, as the vehicle to enable the Parliamentary leaders to resist the misdeeds of Stuart kings four centuries later, and even as the core of the rights of Englishmen asserted by American colonists against the England of the eighteenth century. "What Magna Carta has become," says Justice Frankfurter, "is very different indeed from the immediate objects of the barons at Runnymede." Those who look at Magna Charta with only the pedantic rigor of the thirteenth-century specialist are bound to miss the mark so far as its ultimate significance in the history of freedom is concerned.

Indeed, the vital thing about the Great Charter is, not any specific provision contained in it, but its very coming into being —which alone has justified its continuing renown and significance. The mere existence of such a document, extorted from the king as it was, has been a standing condemnation of governmental absolutism. Instead, the Charter itself tells us that, in Winston Churchill's phrase, "here is a law which is above the King and which even he must not break. This reaffirmation of a supreme law and its expression in a general charter is the great work of Magna Carta; and this alone justifies the respect in which men have held it."

Magna Charta means that the king himself is and shall be bound by the law. This was the root principle laid down at Runnymede. With it, the bridling of power by law, which is the essential theme of English constitutional history, may be said to have begun its development. What follows is intended to ensure that such principle will survive and ultimately rise paramount as the *rule of law* that Anglo-Americans traditionally cherish as the central and most characteristic feature of their constitutional system.

2

PARLIAMENTARY SEEDTIME

LOOKING BACK over the centuries, we tend too often to think of the growth of the English system of representative government as an all but inevitable development. This deterministic approach is, however, far from historical reality. On the contrary, English constitutional history, more often than not, illustrates the truth of Tolstoy's characterization of history as a tissue of disconnected accidents. This is particularly true of the period immediately following Magna Charta. That vital period was dominated by two fortuitous accidents: the death of King John the year after the grant of the Great Charter and the character of his son, Henry III.

Had John himself not died when he did, just before his fiftieth birthday, it is very possible that the course of constitutional evolution would have been drastically different. John had given his consent to Magna Charta unwillingly and insincerely. With Runnymede behind him, he exerted all his efforts toward obtaining the abrogation of the document that had been forced from him. Armed with a papal declaration that the Charter was "null and void of all validity for ever," as well as substantial armed forces, he was far from the tyrant at bay that the historians traditionally picture when he suddenly died at Newark in October, 1216.

John's passing drastically altered the situation. Even though the reforms contained in Magna Charta had been extorted from John, the advisers of his infant son, Henry, accepted them in all sincerity. The first act of the nine-year-old king was to reissue the Great Charter (though in slightly altered form). Subsequent reissues were granted in 1217 and 1225, and these were followed by numerous confirmations in this and succeeding reigns. The reissued Charter was intended as a program to rally the nation round the throne of the young king. It was both a statement of the new government's policy and a bid for the support of the barons who, in opposition to John, had called in Prince Louis of France to aid them overthrow that monarch. But, whatever the motivation, the important fact is that the essential principles of the document that had been forced from the unwilling John were now voluntarily accepted as the rule of government by his son.

The acceptance by John's successor of the basic terms of the Great Charter converted it from a document that furnished the standard of opposition to government to one consented to, by and large, by the entire nation. "It is . . . ," says Bishop Stubbs, "by no means the least curious feature of the history, that so few changes were needed to transform a treaty won at the point of the sword into a manifesto of peace and sound government." Thenceforth, the Great Charter was to serve as the basis of the English Constitution.

From Magna Charta to the principles of Parliamentary government involved a development that took the better part of five centuries. Yet, if John's Charter itself contains no mention of any Parliament, it is still accurate to say of the period following his reign that it may, in Winston Churchill's words, "be called the seed-time of our Parliamentary system, though few participants in the sowing could have foreseen the results that were eventually to be achieved." It was in Henry III's reign that the very term *Parliament* was coming into use, supplanting older terms such as *colloquium*. In the next reign—that of Edward I—the great outlines of the Parliamentary institution have already been drawn.

Magna Charta itself, it will be recalled, confirmed the customary principle that the king could not unilaterally alter the traditional feudal reliefs and aids. But it did so in terms that contained within themselves the basis upon which the future government by representative assembly could be built. Chapter 12 of the Charter (we saw in the last chapter) barred the imposition of any scutage or aid "unless by common counsel of our Kingdom." And Chapter 14 defined, at least in elementary outlines, the composition of the assembly by which such "common counsel" could be given and provided the manner in which it could be summoned. From these sections of the Charter granted at Runnymede, the essentials of the Parliamentary structure were to develop during the reigns of John's son and grandson.

From a constitutional point of view, it was fortunate, not only that John died when he did, but that he left as his undisputed heir a boy only nine years old. For the first time since the days of Ethelred, the throne had fallen to a child; that circumstance made it impossible for the Crown to attempt any reversion to the tyranny of John. Instead the balance, for the time being at least, reverted to that baronial interpretation of the polity that had prevailed in the movement for the Charter itself. In addition, the new king could scarcely be expected for years to take an active role in governing the nation. In his place, there was established a council of regency endowed with the actual powers of government.

The experience during the minority of Henry III made men aware of the fact that the power to reign and the power to govern could feasibly be placed in different hands. Without such experience, it might have been impossible to attempt the constitutional experiments that dominated the latter part of the reign.

Henry himself, even though he was weaker personally than his father, resembled his predecessor in his inability to obtain the support of the nation during much of his reign. In fact, it was this support that had enabled him to accede to the throne and prevail over the claim of Louis of France upon John's death. But Henry did not see it that way. "At a time," he is reported to have said in later years, "when we were orphan and minor, when our subjects were not only alienated from us, but were organized against us, it was our mother, the Roman Church, which brought this realm once more under our authority, which consecrated us King, crowned us and placed us on the throne."

Feeling as he did, Henry remained throughout his reign under the constant influence of the Papacy. In particular, he did not resist the increasing financial demands that the Pope—beset in his desperate struggle with the Holy Roman Emperor—made upon England. The king's liberality with English money for papal projects and his subservience to Rome in other respects were copious sources of discontent among the barons and the nation.

Particularly galling to the people were the swarms of legates and nuncios that proliferated during much of Henry's reign. To them must be added the constant stream of foreign favorites with which the king was wont to surround himself, especially after his marriage to Eleanor of Provence—men ever grasping for the rich perquisites of office, as well as the profitable wardships, marriages, escheats, and benefices (which the barons had been accustomed to regard as their own)—and all for the sake of profit in a country to whose national interests they were callously indifferent. The situation was strikingly expressed by a contemporary chronicler:

> Through the queen were so many French folk brought,
> That of Englishmen one counted right nought;
> The king gave them their will as each were king.
> They took the poor men's goods, but paid nothing.

Well might the English clergy, led by the sainted Bishop of Lincoln, Robert Grosseteste, join with the barons in the rallying cry of "England for the English."

The troubles of Henry's reign (brought on though they were, in the main, by that shiftless monarch himself) were complicated by the continuing inflation that had magnified the problems facing King John. The expense of government continued to increase, but, once again, there was no corresponding increase in royal revenues. The barons, as was true of the rest of Henry's contemporaries, could scarcely understand, much less sympathize with, the embarrassments that the rising scale of prices forced upon government. Not unnaturally, they attributed the king's constant demands for money to his extravagance, especially his spending of money on his foreign favorites. Not that Henry did not give them reason for their belief, but his profligacy was not the sole source of his financial and political troubles.

To what has been said must be added the king's unwise Continental commitments and the military disasters to which they led. Foremost among these was what Thomas B. Costain has well termed "The Sicilian Absurdity," which arose out of Henry's acceptance of the Sicilian crown for his younger son Edmund. "This," says Winston Churchill, "was a foolish step, and the conditions attached to the gift raised it to the very height of folly." The whole affair was part of a papal scheme to rid southern Italy of

German power and ultimately to unite the Sicilian kingdom to the papal dominions. To aid the Roman design, the English king was to furnish an army and, in addition, to assume papal debts amounting to 135,000 marks—an enormous sum in those days.

When the obligations assumed by the king were made known to the assembled magnates of the realm in 1257, they gave rise to a storm of indignation. Henry had presented the young Edmund to the barons and clergy, declaring with pride, "How comely and well worthy he is of all your favor! How cruel and tyrannical must be they who would deny him effectual and seasonal help, both with money and advice!" Both the barons and the clergy, in Costain's phrase, "proceeded to show how cruel and tyrannical they could be by refusing all financial aid and advice." The Sicilian burden, compounded by new failures in Wales and Scotland, brought the opposition to the royal ineffectiveness to a head. "Despised, discredited, and frightened"—to quote Churchill again—"without money or men, the king faced an angered and powerful opposition."

What makes the culmination of dissatisfaction with Henry's government somewhat paradoxical is the fact that the monarch was never popularly considered a bad king in the sense that his father was. Certainly no chronicler could depict Henry as the tyrant that tradition has left us as the accepted picture of King John. Henry, without a doubt, intended to be a good king and, what is more, fully believed that he was. Like most such men, he never realized that he was weak, both in intellect and will, always subject to the influence of someone stronger than himself without even knowing it.

Yet it remains true that the weak character of King Henry was actually what George B. Adams calls "one of the happy accidents of monarchical succession," since, "During this long period the character of the king was what determined the fate of the germ of constitutional liberty unconsciously given existence in 1215." A strong, effective ruler might well have restored the monarchy to the position it had under Henry II—thus reducing the great concessions obtained from John to a mere historical aberration. What was needed was a king like Henry—vacillating, weak, wrongheaded—to drive the nation into opposition and so continue the constitutional progress that had begun at Runnymede.

The opposition to King Henry was, however, faced with a

fundamental dilemma that flowed from the very nature of the constitutional gain that had been extorted from King John. As already pointed out, with John's death, the Great Charter was accepted by all as the essential rule of sound government. If only its terms were adhered to, so the national consensus went as the misgovernment under Henry continued, all would be well. But Magna Charta itself—fundamental advance though it doubtless was in the constitutional progress of the nation—contained one basic lacuna: a failure to provide adequate machinery for its effective enforcement.

The question of enforcement is, of course, one that has plagued statesmen and jurists throughout political history. It is easy enough to lay down constitutional principles in accord with the theoretical conceptions of the would-be constitution-maker. The provision of adequate enforcement machinery is quite a different matter. All the constitutional principles in the world, "though they were written in letters of gold upon the most imperishable tablets," will be but empty words if they are treated as self-executing. Without some independent means of enforcement as rules of law, the provisions of a constitution are no more than mere maxims of political morality.

From a practical point of view, the great gap in the Charter secured at Runnymede was the lack of effective machinery to ensure that its principles would be enforced. The substance of subsequent constitutional progress has consisted in the filling in of such gap. Not that the men who wrote the Great Charter were themselves unaware of the importance of enforcement machinery. Knowing John's character, they realized that, regardless of the solemnity of the promises obtained from that monarch, he might well, once the compulsion of force had diminished, act as though the event at Runnymede had never taken place. They therefore sought to deal with the problem of enforcement toward the end of the document drawn up by them.

Chapter 61 of Magna Charta provides for the choice by the barons of twenty-five of their number, "to observe and hold, and cause to be observed, the peace and liberties we have granted and confirmed to them by this our present Charter." If those liberties were broken and the king refused to correct the situation, the twenty-five were to rouse the community of the whole realm and make war against the king "until redress has been obtained as they deem fit." The enforcement of the Great Charter was thus to be committed to a council, to be chosen by the whole baronage. In substance, the king was conferring upon a committee a legal right to organize rebellion, whenever they deemed that he had broken any provision of Magna Charta.

As a working sanction, Chapter 61 was both crude and impracticable. In the words of McKechnie's leading study of Magna Charta, "The only expedient for compelling the king to keep his promises was clumsy and revolutionary; quite worthless as a working scheme of government." This was realized soon after the Charter itself was sealed, and much of the effort during the reign of John's successor consisted of attempts to secure new "sanctions" against governmental misbehavior.

The national consensus, we have seen, had quickly come to accept John's Charter as the basis of sound government. In face of the abuses that developed under John's son, the first attempts at correction sought to get the king to observe Magna Charta's provisions. The obvious way to accomplish this was to secure from Henry his solemn oath in the matter. Over and over again, Henry was made to swear to observe the Charter granted by his father. Twice, in 1237 and 1253, he issued formal confirmations of the *"libertates Magnae Cartae."* The second act of confirmation, we are told, was performed with particular solemnity, including the passing of a sentence of excommunication against all violators. The king himself was made to affirm, "So help me God, all these will I faithfully keep inviolate as I am a man, a Christian, a knight, a crowned and anointed king."

But Henry was not the man to be bound by his confirmations and promises to observe the Great Charter. To quote McKechnie again, "Henry's attitude towards the charters was a settled one: he confirmed them with a light heart when he could obtain money in return, and then acted as though they did not exist." If such behavior be thought singular in a man whose devoutness was remarked by all, we should remember that to Henry and his adherents the Great Charter was a document extorted by force, a usurpation that stripped the king of his God-given prerogatives and had, as such, been declared invalid soon after its issue by Pope Innocent III.

Henry regarded the charters issued by his father and himself, not as landmarks of liberty and justice, but as disgraceful infringements of his inherent rights as a ruler, worthy only of being evaded to the fullest extent possible. We can observe something of the king's true feeling from the royal exultation expressed when it was learned that the original copy of Magna Charta had been destroyed by fire. It was mistakenly believed in the royal household that the Charter itself ceased to exist and its restrictions on the Crown were consequently no longer legally binding.

By 1253, when still another confirmation was secured from Henry, the opposition had come to see that it was useless to attempt to bind the king by mere writings or promises. Henry had repeatedly shown that formal confirmations of rights alone were not enough to bind men determined to disregard them. A king like Henry, surrounded by officials whose constant purpose was to evade Magna Charta's limitations, had to be bound by something more than his word. The opposition party, which had by the continuing misgovernment gained the adherence of most of the articulate elements of the nation, saw that a more drastic scheme of constitutional reform was now necessary.

It was in 1258 that the reformers were able to fix upon a program to curb the royal misgovernment. Conditions at that time were summed up by a monastic chronicler: "So many foreigners of divers tongues had multiplied in England for many years and had been enriched with so many revenues from lands and towns. . . . The ancient laws and customs were decayed and rendered of none effect; the only law was what seemed good to the strong man, and justice could only be bought with money. At length in this year, the earls and barons, the archbishops and bishops, and the other great men of England, seeing the low estate of the land and as if divinely awakened from sleep, banded together and displayed a lion-like courage."

The plan of what may be called the national party (in contrast to those who still adhered to the king) was revealed during the 1258 meeting of the Great Council of the Magnates—or "Parliament," as it was coming to be called. Henry, in serious trouble because of his need for money to satisfy the papal envoy and to repel the Welsh, asked for a tax of a third of all property in the kingdom—a demand so "burdensome, unheard-of, terrible" that it united the barons in their determination to make the day of unenforceable promises alone a thing of the past.

When the day came for the Council session to be resumed,

says an eyewitness, "the noble and brave men, the earls, barons, and knights came to Court, that is to Westminster, in great array, their swords by their sides. . . . At the threatening aspect of the barons in their complete suits of mail, the king was seized with sudden terror. 'What is this, sirs?' he said. 'Am I your prisoner?' " The baronial answer, though disclaiming violent intent, insisted that the hated aliens must be banished and the counsel of the barons followed. " 'And how see you that I shall follow your counsels?' The barons replied: 'Swear, with hand on holy gospels, you and your son and heir Edward, that you will do nought without the advice of the twenty-four good men, the elected bishops, earls, and barons; . . . that you will without delay hand the Great Seal to a loyal person selected by the twenty-four." Reluctantly, the king yielded, the magnates chose the committee of twenty-four, and the Great Council adjourned for five weeks, to meet at Oxford to work out the details of governmental reform.

The scheme of reform drawn up by the twenty-four and adopted in a spirit of unwilling resignation by the king came to be known as the Provisions of Oxford. They amounted to nothing less than a fundamental reorganization of the machinery of state. The committee of twenty-four was to be replaced by a council of fifteen, chosen by four electors, themselves to be named by the committee of twenty-four. The council of fifteen "shall have the power to give honest counsel to the king in the government of the realm . . . and to amend and redress all that they see to need amendment and redress, even in matters concerning the Justiciar and all other officials." In effect, the fifteen were to constitute the permanent government of the kingdom, sitting continuously with the king and advising him on all points of policy; moreover, they would have a constraining power over all the king's public acts (i.e., more or less a power of veto).

It is not expressly stated in the Provisions, but it has generally been assumed that the appointment of the great officers of the realm was to be in the hands of the council of fifteen. Every year these officers were to render to the council a strict account of their doings. The whole of the royal revenue was to be paid into the Exchequer, which was also to be subject to annual audit. In addition, the Chancellor was to seal no grants without the assent of the fifteen.

According to Edward Jenks, the scheme of government laid down in the Provisions of Oxford was "so thorough and so startling, that nothing but a complete conviction of his own helplessness could have induced the king to accept it." Without a doubt, the Provisions made for a drastic shift in the governmental center of gravity—with the actual power to govern transferred from the king to what was, more or less, an oligarchic council selected from the barons. The new scheme removed from power (though not from the throne) a king who could not be trusted and set up a government chosen by and responsible to a wider constituency.

To the present-day observer, looking back at what the Provisions of Oxford and later attempts at constitutional reform during the reign of Henry III sought to accomplish, it seems almost incredible that men of the thirteenth century could have drawn up a governmental framework which, as we shall see, anticipated so strikingly that evolved during later centuries by the English Constitution. Yet, if we cannot really explain the existence of this visionary program, so far in advance of its time, part of the explanation, at least, is to be found in the character of the head of the opposition to the king, Simon de Montfort.

We need not subscribe unreservedly to the hero theory of history to realize that great men do make a difference. Certainly the emergence of Simon de Montfort to supply the leader that the national and baronial opposition had lacked was the stimulus that made possible the tremendous constitutional progress that occurred both in the reign of Henry III and that of his son, Edward I.

What makes the historic role of Simon de Montfort somewhat paradoxical is the fact that, in the beginning at least, he seemed to be only one of the alien adventurers who made his fortune from the king's favor. Born a Norman, Simon had come to England and secured the Earldom of Leicester (to which his family had a claim) as well as marriage to the king's sister. As time went on, however, Simon fell out with the king and Henry could say, during a public quarrel, "Never have I repented anything so much as that I allowed you to enter England and take over lands and honors here!"

As Henry's credit steadily declined, the elements hostile to his misgovernment turned to Simon, who soon became the dominant figure—the "brain and driving force," in Churchill's words—among the opposition. There can be little doubt that popular trust in the Earl of Leicester had been growing. He was one person who had been able to stand up boldly to the king, in the face of royal wrongs. But Simon was more than a man who felt resentment for Henry's acts of injustice against him. His acquaintance with Robert Grosseteste and Adam Marsh, two of the greatest of medieval philosophical scholars, had given him broad ideas about morality and politics. Intensely religious, he was one to sacrifice himself, if need be, for a cause that was to outstrip the mere desire to replace the royal rule with that of an oligarchy.

Of one thing we can be sure: the nation itself was coming to feel increasing trust in Earl Simon and his abilities. Public feeling, in particular, was on his side, as the people came to recognize his sympathy with their difficulties and his resolve to right their wrongs. To the chroniclers of the day, Simon was a hero who had earned the nation's gratitude. "As of old Simon Maccabaeus had risen in arms for his father Judah," wrote one of them, "so Simon rose to defend to the death the liberties and rights of England." And the gleeman sang of him as one,

> Who hates the wrong and loves the right,
> Who shall obtain the upper hand;
> For he is strong and has great might.

Earl Simon it was, too, who led the opposition in arms when, after the king had repudiated the Provisions of Oxford, civil war became inevitable. It was his generalship that defeated the numerically superior royal army at Lewes in 1264. The victory there delivered the king, his heir, and his principal supporters into de Montfort's hands and made him the virtual master of the kingdom. The year or so that followed—characterized as "Simon's Protectorate" by the leading biography of the great Earl—was pregnant in constitutional implications.

The first important act of the victorious Earl was to reconstitute the essential frame of the government set up by the Provisions of Oxford (though with important modifications). This was done in what the chroniclers called the *Mise of Lewes,* containing the terms dictated by Simon soon after his victory, as well as in an act of the Parliament that met a month later. "For the reform of the kingdom," provides the new scheme of government, three "discreet and faithful" persons, called electors, are to receive from the king the power to select nine councillors, to act on their behalf. The king must act according to the advice of the nine in disposing of all governmental business, and in naming the Justiciar, Chancellor, Treasurer, and all other officials. The nine were thus to guide the king in all his official acts, and three of them were always to be present in court. The formal plan seems to have been that any three of the nine could serve at the king's side; but, in practice, the select trio were Simon de Montfort and two of his principal supporters—with Simon having the dominant voice. To his contemporaries, at least, de Montfort was the real ruler—in every respect, as Churchill terms him, master of England.

The scheme of government instituted after the victory at Lewes was a refinement of that provided for under the Provisions of Oxford. The cumbersome committees of twenty-four and fifteen were replaced by the more workable single council of nine—with its practical functions performed by the three-man executive which Earl Simon dominated. In its essentials, nevertheless, the system imposed upon the defeated king was a revised version of that set up in the 1258 Provisions.

What de Montfort and his colleagues were providing for in their attempted governmental revisions strikes the twentieth-century observer, armed with the perspective of seven hundred years' hindsight, as an amazing anticipation of later constitutional development. Winston Churchill, with his gift for phrase that cuts to the heart of the matter, has said that the system set up after Lewes was one "whereby the rights of the Crown were in theory respected, though in practice the king and his son were to be subjected to strict controls. . . . [Simon] saw himself, with the King in his hands, able to use the authority of the Crown to control the baronage, and create the far broader and better political system which, whether he aimed at it or not, must have automatically followed from his success."

In modern terms, what de Montfort and those of his party were seeking to accomplish was to set up a polity in which the king reigned, but did not govern, and an Executive which governed but did not reign. Certainly, we now know, such was to be the governmental structure ultimately evolved in later centuries. Yet, sound though it was to prove as a goal for English constitutional development, it was too drastic a change to be attained during the thirteenth century. Men of that day, almost primitive in their political conceptions, could hardly be expected to be prepared for, much less understand, what has proved to be perhaps the most subtle of governmental systems.

Nor should we (despite our more refined views on political science) be too quick to condemn the rejection of Earl Simon's governmental scheme. It may well be that after Henry III's maladministration what the nation needed most of all was a strong yet able ruler, such as Henry's son Edward was to prove to be. Conciliar government could scarcely provide such rule, unless it was completely dominated by a man like Simon himself. But the whole point about such government is that it contains within itself checks that make such one-man dictatorship unworkable. Simon as virtual ruler of the realm was bound to provoke a split within his own party which, combined with the royalist opposition, would lead to his eventual overthrow. The country may have needed a stern but just ruler, of the type of Henry II, but it was not yet ready to yield to this kind of ruler in the person of one who was not himself a monarch of the royal blood.

The one way that Earl Simon might avoid the frustration of his statesmanship was to broaden the base of his support. As it turned out, however, his efforts in this direction only increased his dangers. The barons resented his attempts to rely upon the lower ranks in the social hierarchy. They rightly realized that such reliance would confront them with an even greater menace than that from which the victory at Lewes had so recently delivered them.

There is little doubt that Simon succeeded, at least in large part, in his efforts to achieve a broader support for his government than that of the baronial party alone. The people themselves (so far as one can tell so long before there was anything like a popular voice in public affairs) supported the new government more fervently than it did any of its predecessors. "Now England breathes again," declared the famous "Song of Lewes," written after Simon's victory. So strong an impression, in truth, did Earl Simon make upon the mass of the people that, soon after his death people were making pilgrimages to commemorate his "martyrdom." Throughout the land, the name of the dead leader came to be placed just below that of St. Thomas à Becket.

Yet, as Thomas B. Costain points out, the acclaim of the people, while gratifying, was nowhere near as important as it might seem today. Popular support was not what mattered then in the practical working of government. What did count was the support of the men who controlled the land that was at that time the source of political, economic, and military power—the barons.

From a historical point of view, the most consequential step taken by de Montfort, in his effort to broaden the base of his support, was his summoning of a Parliament to meet in London early in 1265. The primary purpose of this Parliament was, Charles Bémont puts it in his leading biography of Earl Simon, "to crown the victorious work so well begun at Lewes." The assembly was intended to place the stamp of legality upon the new governmental system. This was done at formal ceremonies in which both the king and his son, Prince Edward, solemnly swore to observe the terms laid down in 1264, as well as the Great Charter and the Provisions of Oxford. If either failed to keep his oath, "it should be permitted to all members of [the] kingdom to rise in revolt without running the risk of forfeiture."

The Parliament of 1265 is, however, much less celebrated for its work than for its composition. It is called the Great Parliament, not because of what it did, but because it has gone down in history as the first Parliament that was representative of the entire nation. The writs of summons to the 1265 assembly had, of course, gone, in the king's name, to the great prelates of the realm, as well as to the earls and barons (though those among the peers who were avowedly hostile to Simon's cause were not included in the summons). But the summons was not limited to the nobility of the realm. In addition, in each county, the sheriff was "to cause to come" two of the most loyal, honorable, and discreet knights. And a similar summons was dispatched to every city and borough directing each of them to send two to four "good and loyal men."

The key feature of the 1265 Parliament was the representation of the shires, cities, and boroughs. For the first time, the country gentry and the burgesses sat with the great magnates when they met to discuss the business of the realm. Such a Parliament—in which mere knights and commoners participated with bishops and barons—had never been seen before. But the Great Parliament's real innovation was the inclusion of representatives from the cities and boroughs. Representation from the shires had already been incorporated in the Parliamentary structure; the session summoned a month after Lewes had, indeed, included two knights from each county. The novelty lay in assembling representatives of the towns in conjunction with those of the counties—representatives who could make no pretense to the status of nobility.

It was his inclusion of ordinary knights and commoners in the Parliamentary membership that led men in later years to call Simon de Montfort the Founder of the House of Commons. But more recently, historians have called this characterization an exaggeration. Certainly Earl Simon, in causing the writs of summons for the 1265 Parliament to go out as they did, could scarcely have imagined that out of the summons to commoners would grow a House of Commons, which would some day assume the primacy, not only in the national assembly, but in the very government structure itself.

In the middle of the thirteenth century, the Parliament itself was no more than an instrument of the royal power. Its purpose was to serve the Crown, whether by advice or, more likely, by the swords and purses of the men who mattered in the realm. If de Montfort broadened its composition, it was primarily to broaden the base of his own support. The whole Parliament itself, it should be noted, was chosen primarily from among Earl Simon's partisans. Thus, only the earls who were Simon's allies were summoned. It was natural then for Simon to do the same for the towns in which he had received much of his support. By permitting their representatives to sit in the session, he might create a national coalition behind his policies, as well as ensure a warmer response to his program in the national assembly itself.

Yet, if it was the need to strengthen more closely the bond uniting the lesser gentry and the urban bourgeoisie to his cause that was the primary motive behind Earl Simon's action in expanding the composition of his Parliament, it is unlikely that he was totally unaware that there were broader implications in his move. At any rate, it cannot be doubted that the Great Parliament was to serve as a vital precedent in the centuries-long struggle that followed to enable all the people to secure a voice in shaping their own destiny.

Nor can anyone deny that it was Earl Simon who, whatever his immediate motives, established the precedent which, in the end, came to be followed regularly and, as such, led to the development of the Parliamentary system. True, it was Edward I who gave the precedent lasting acceptance by relying upon it in his reign, but it was his uncle's example that Edward followed when he summoned commoners to sit in all his Parliaments. That alone justifies the fact that Simon de Montfort's statue was centuries later to be placed in front of the entrance to the House of Commons.

His future place in history must, however, have been the furthest thing from Earl Simon's mind at Evesham, on August 4, 1265, when—little more than a year after his victory at Lewes— he and his principal followers were slaughtered by a vastly superior royalist army led by Prince Edward. On the field at Evesham, after the royalist triumph, the whole of Simon's policy must have appeared a miserable failure. Looking back over the centuries, we can see that this appearance was deceptive. The great Earl's age may not have been ready for the governmental revolution he sought to institute. But we know, to paraphrase Edward Jenks, that the wheel of time was to bring about this ideal of his also, in the centuries to come. And his attempt to broaden the political base was to bear fruit in the reign of his nephew, Edward I. Though it was Edward who was fated to restore the royal power and, in the process, to destroy de Montfort, when he became king he put into practice some of the most important ideas of the uncle he had slain.

"It was from me that he learned it!" Simon de Montfort is said to have cried when he led his outmaneuvered army out of Evesham to meet the converging forces of Prince Edward. Had he lived to see the reign of England's greatest monarch, Simon could have made that comment as much about his nephew's political tactics as about his military ones.

3

EDWARD I AND PARLIAMENT

HENRY HALLAM begins his now-classic *Constitutional History of England* (the first work to bear the title itself of constitutional history) by listing the essential checks upon the royal authority that had developed by the accession of Henry Tudor in 1485. The two most important of these, according to him, were: "1. The king could levy no sort of new tax upon his people, except by the grant of his parliament, consisting as well of bishops and mitred abbots or lords spiritual, and of hereditary peers or temporal lords, who sat and voted promiscuously in the same chamber, as of representatives from the freeholders of each county, and from the burgesses of many towns and less considerable places, forming the lower or commons' house. 2. The previous assent and authority of the same assembly was necessary for every new law, whether of a general or temporary nature."

By the time of Henry VII, England had evolved much of the foundation of Parliamentary government. The basic principles of taxation and legislation only with the consent of the representative assembly were natural developments in the two and a half centuries that followed the grant of Magna Charta. This is not to say that they were necessarily inevitable developments, but only that one can trace their logical growth in the years following the events at Runnymede.

So far, we have carried the course of constitutional evolution to the end of the reign of Henry III (1272). Though, as pointed out, it must have seemed that the thrust of forward progress instituted under the leadership of Simon de Montfort came to an end with his defeat and death at Evesham, this judgment was premature. The restoration of the royal power did not turn back the constitutional clock to the days of Norman absolutism. Henry's son, Edward I, we have said, was to bring to fruition much of de Montfort's program. By the end of Edward's reign, indeed, some of the most important moves had been made in the direction of the essential checks mentioned by Hallam.

But the first vital step was taken during the reigns of Edward's two predecessors, when the baronial opposition transformed the vague feudal conception of limitation of power to almost a constitutional principle. In Magna Charta, the notion of limited governmental authority is reduced to written form, subscribed by the king himself. Yet the Great Charter itself would have accomplished next to nothing if John had been succeeded by a king like Henry II or Edward I. Such a strong ruler could readily have relegated the Charter itself to constitutional limbo. Instead, the happy accident of Henry III's accession enabled the seed planted at Runnymede to grow into a flourishing plant.

It was during Henry III's reign that men began to accept as settled the idea of a king whose authority was limited by law. Listen to Bracton, the great legal commentator of the day: "Just as Jesus and the Virgin submitted to the Law, so the king must be submissive to it also. His power cannot be entirely without check." The king may be first in the realm; still, his authority must not be arbitrary: "since he is the minister of God upon earth, he may only do what is just, and the Roman maxim *quod principi placet legis habet vigorem* [what pleases the prince has the force of law] cannot be applied here."

The constitutional struggles of Henry III's reign—and particularly the victories won under de Montfort's leadership—gave new perspective to the concept of limited governmental power. Bracton, influenced by his reading of Roman law, felt impelled to cite the famous words of Justinian's *Institutes* on princely power, but he did so in a way that gave them a new meaning. The law, says Bracton, has made the king ruler; it is by virtue of the law that he reigns; hence, this law sets limits to the *placita principis.* Then follows his most famous passage:*"Rex non debet esse sub homine, sed sub Deo et lege* [the king should not be under man, but under God and law]."

The emphasis in Bracton (himself both a participant in and a student of the government of his day) is more upon responsibility than upon power. There is even one passage in his work that declares that the king is not only subject to God and the law, but also to his court, made up of the earls and barons—"for the earls are so called because they are the king's companions or fellows, and he who has a fellow has a master." It is generally felt that this passage is an interpolation by an annotator, written during the revolt that culminated in the battles of Lewes and Evesham.

That such a passage could be written, however, shows both the kind of constitutional thinking that was in the air and how far the notion of limited power had progressed during the thirteenth century. Never again, at any rate, could an English king pretend to the position of absolute master of the realm. More and more, the controlling conception was to be that of partnership in government as between the king and the council of the realm—a partnership that was to fluctuate and even, at times, all but break down. Still, in the end, it was as a partnership between King, Lords, and Commons that the modern English polity was to evolve.

That the days of royal pretensions to absolutism were not to revive with the defeat of the opposition party at Evesham was shown by what happened when Edward I came to the throne. Edward was in many ways the strongest of English kings— personally attractive and popular, lofty in stature and character, already an experienced leader and administrator, at one and the same time a great warrior and legislator. Winston Churchill neatly sums him up: "[Edward] presents us with qualities which are a mixture of the administrative capacity of Henry II and the personal prowess and magnanimity of Coeur de Lion."

Certainly a man as personally strong as Edward, who came so grandly out of the Baron's War, could have attempted a revival of Norman absolutism or the tyranny of his grandfather. But he had learned too much from both his uncle and the unhappy experiences of his father to try wholly to undo the constitutional progress that had been made. Instead, he sought to use the lessons taught his predecessors to place both the monarchy and the realm upon a wider footing of national support.

In history's pages, Edward I has usually been characterized as the "English Justinian." This description is nevertheless both too broad and too narrow. Edward did not give his leadership and name to a fully developed corpus of law that was to dominate the jurisprudence of half the world for untold centuries after his death. English law itself was scarcely developed enough to allow men to conceive of, much less achieve, the kind of codification that was possible in sixth-century Byzantium.

Even more important is the fact that the comparison between the great English king and the Byzantine lawgiver ignores the key difference in the nature of their jurisprudential achievements. In Maitland's famous words, "it is something like a comparison between childhood and second childhood. Justinian, we may say, did his best to give final and immutable form to a system which had already seen its best days, which had already become too elaborate for those who lived under it. Edward, taking the whole nation into his counsels, legislated for a nation which was only just beginning to have a legal system of its own."

The difference between the work of Edward and that of Justinian is the difference between legislation and codification. The codifier works best in an age of revival and renaissance; his is the task of preservation and classification, not of creative origination. The great codifier is, by definition, anything but a radical innovator; transforming action makes for too much discontinuity, too great a break with the past, whose experience is to be reduced to systematized form.

How different the task of a great legislator like Edward I! His role is that of transforming innovation—his task to establish new principles and methods in the formative period of a legal system. From this point of view, Edward's reign has been accurately called a unique period in the history of English law. Lord Hale, writing toward the end of the seventeenth century, could say that "the very scheme and model of the administration of common justice between man and man was entirely settled by this sovereign." In truth, affirms Hale, more was done in Edward's reign to settle and establish the distributive justice of the kingdom than in all the ages since that time put together.

To settle the system of justice between man and man, Edward I and his advisers (particularly his Chancellor, the great lawyer Robert Burnell) produced a whole mass of legislation. There was in fact, no parallel until almost our own day to the spate of legislative activity that characterized the first eighteen years of the reign. The first statute of consequence, the Statute of Westminster I (1275), has been called almost a code by itself; containing fifty-one sections, it covers the whole ground of legislation. It made many changes in procedure and administration, the most significant of them designed to protect the citizen against the officers of the Crown itself. Then came the Statute of Gloucester (1278), which made important changes in the land law, and the Statute of Mortmain (1279), intended to check the feudal losses that resulted when land was given to the Church. The Statute of Winchester (1285) revived and strengthened the institutions of local government that were to play so important a part in the development of the English character.

In the same year as the Statute of Winchester came the great Statute of Westminster II, which like its predecessor of the same name of a decade earlier, covered the entire range of substantive law and procedure. Its famous first chapter, *De Donis Conditionalibus,* strengthened the system of entailed estates and lies at the foundation of the whole notion of legal estates in land upon which the Anglo-American law of property is based. To this law was added, in 1290, the equally noted Statute of Westminster III, *Quia Emptores,* which was likewise a landmark of the land law. It permitted free alienation and, at the same time, forbade subinfeudation of the type that had made such a crazy quilt of the feudal structure.

Not only did Edward I's legislation form the foundation of English law for centuries; his two most famous statutes—*De Donis* and *Quia Emptores*—are still rightly considered pillars of our real-property law. Well might the contemporary annalist say: "Certain statutes the king published, very necessary for the whole realm by which he stirred up the ancient laws that had slumbered through the disturbance of the realm; some which had been corrupted by abuse he recalled to their due form; some which were less evident and clear of interpretation he declared; some new ones useful and honorable he added."

So far as we know, Edward I played a prominent personal part in the framing and execution of the legislative program accomplished during the first half of his reign. We are told, indeed, that Edward himself had much the mind of a lawyer. He was, according to Stubbs, by instinct a lawgiver; and he lived in an age that saw men like Louis IX, Frederick II, and Alphonso the Wise— monarchs who were also celebrated as framers of laws and constitutions. Certainly, as we shall see in the next chapter, the age of the common law and the lawyers was coming in. In virtually every branch of law and administration, the process of definition went forward.

The legislative measures adopted during the first part of Edward's reign dealt with the distributive justice of the kingdom —i.e., with the decision of cases between man and man, or what we would now term private law. This is what has made them of such consequence in English legal history, for they helped provide a firm foundation to the nascent common law that was then becoming established. To the constitutional historian, on the other hand, Edward's great contribution lay in the field of public rather than private law. He it was who first gave the developing Constitution a solid base upon which progressive history could erect a structure that has been at once the admiration and the goal of so many peoples.

It is particularly the progress made in public law during his reign that makes the characterization of Edward I as only a latter-day Justinian entirely inadequate. Justinian's codifiers took the rules of Roman public law more or less as they found them and stated the constitutional principles of their day in terms that justified even the most extreme excesses of Byzantine autocracy. Such was emphatically not the case with those who, under Edward's aegis, were the makers of the English polity at the end of the thirteenth century. The system they established rejected the autocratic concept of plenary princely power. Instead, there began in Edward's day that self-limitation of governmental authority that is really the essential characteristic of all constitutionalism.

It would, certainly, be wrong to assume that Edward and his advisers had anything like the constitutional development that subsequently occurred in mind when they brought to fruition the progress that had been made earlier in the century—or even that they intended their work to serve as a precedent for the limitation of royal power that was the eventual outcome. When Edward gave permanent form and status to the institution of Parliament that was evolving, he did it as a matter of royal convenience—so that he could secure more effective financial support for his policies—not to divide up the sovereign power between the Crown and the representatives of the people. And yet it was in this division of authority that Edward's work would result. The Parliamentary institution may well have been intended by the great monarch as an instrument of more efficient royal government. But here, as in so many other cases (to paraphrase a remark once made by Maitland), what started as the prerogative of the king was eventually to become the right of the people.

It was in the reign of Edward I that perhaps the most important moves were made in the direction of establishing the essential checks on royal power mentioned by Hallam in the passage which began this chapter. More specifically, it was under Edward that the Parliament took definite shape as a working institution in which were vested the vital functions of taxation and legislation.

The word "parliament" itself is, of course, derived from the French verb *parler*. As originally used, it meant a talk. In its Latin form, it appears first to have been applied to the talk held by monks in their cloisters after dinner. As time went on, it came to be applied to solemn conferences, such as those held between popes and kings. When Henry III summoned a conference of the great men of the realm in 1246 to discuss grievances, he was said by the chronicler Matthew Paris to hold a Parliament. The word, we are told, struck root in England and was soon applied regularly to the national assemblies that were summoned under Edward I. From a word that first signified the talk itself, it came to mean the body of persons assembled for talk—a meaning it has ever since retained.

The word "Parliament" as thus derived is peculiarly appropriate to describe what is still essentially an instrument of discussion; Parliamentary government, in Macaulay's phrase, is government by speaking. "When I was in the Army," says Quintin Hogg, a leading M.P., "critics sometimes said to me that they could not understand what Members of Parliament were about. 'They seem to do nothing but talk,' was the complaint. My reply was, 'That is why they are called a Parliament.' The right to talk . . . is the foundation on which the whole of Parliamentary Government is built."

Parliament is the instrument for that government by discussion which is the great English contribution to the theory and practice of government. It has, in truth, always been the practice in England that in serious and important matters the king ought not to act without counsel and consent. In Saxon times, the kings sought such counsel and consent from the Witenagemot, or Assembly of Wise Men—the closest thing to a national assembly before the Conquest. Thus, Alfred issued his famous code "by the counsel of my witan." Kemble, in his work on *The Saxons in England,* lists 147 Witenagemots during the years 698 to 1066. Nevertheless, the Saxon assembly seems to have been a very unstable and indefinite body, with its composition and powers both vaguely defined.

The tradition of counsel and consent continued after the Conquest, despite the fact that in other respects the Norman kings were far closer to despotic rulers than their Saxon predecessors had been. "Thrice a year," says the *Saxon Chronicle* of the Conqueror, "King William wore his crown every year he was in England; at Easter he wore it at Winchester, at Pentecost at Westminster, and at Christmas at Gloucester; and at these times all the men of England were with him—archbishops, bishops and abbots, earls, thegns and knights."

When the Saxon chronicler spoke of "all the men of England," he probably meant the wise and great men who might have been expected to attend a Witenagemot. To the modern observer, on the other hand, William's assembly appears more feudal in nature, composed in all probability of the king's tenants in chief. What is important, all the same, is the notion of a body, ill-defined though it doubtless was, whose counsel and consent were customary before important governmental action. It was such a body that, over the next two and a half centuries, was to develop into the Parliament of Edward I's day. "What we find," according to Sir Courtenay Ilbert's sprightly little book on Parliament, "is the transformation of the body whose counsel and consent is required from a merely feudal body, a body of great vassals or tenants in chief, to a body more representative of the nation at large."

More than anything else, what brought about the transformation from feudal council to Parliament as the representative assembly of the nation was the financial weakness of the medieval monarchy. The revenues of the king were largely derived from the income accruing from Crown lands, and the limited extent to which feudal custom enabled him to impose financial imposts. We have already seen that one of the basic concepts of the feudalism established after the Norman Conquest was that of fixed obligations, both from vassal to lord and from subject to king. The king himself could not hold his tenants in chief and their vassals to more than feudal custom permitted, without their consent.

This feudal principle was, we have seen, given what we would today term statutory form in Chapter 12 of Magna Charta, under which "No scutage or aid shall be imposed in our kingdom, unless by common counsel of our kingdom." In addition, we saw in our discussion of the Great Charter, that document also stated in rudimentary form the assembly through which the common counsel of the nation could be given.

We have already emphasized the constantly increasing need of the king for revenue—a need brought on by the natural growth of the kingdom and of its central government and magnified by the continuing inflation which plagued the governments of the period, particularly those of John and Henry III. The royal attempts to secure additional revenue were restricted by the feudal principle that barred unilateral attempts by the Crown to increase the traditional imposts that might be levied. John had sought (successfully for a time) to increase the customary feudal obligations without consent, only to provoke the united resistance which led to Runnymede. On the other hand, such resistance could be avoided if the approval of the national assembly could be obtained.

Edward's great-grandfather, Henry II, had shown how revenue could be combined with consent when he imposed the famous Saladin Tithe of 1188, a tax on movables that was assessed by a jury of neighbors—a jury representative of the taxpayer and his local parish. "This," says Ilbert, "brought into connexion the ideas of taxation and representation." What was needed next was development of the notion that the necessary consent was to be given by the national assembly, itself composed of representatives of the estates that made up the realm. For that to happen, the assembly itself had to be more than a feudal council made up of the great magnates alone.

It was during the reign of Edward's father, Henry III, that the necessary transition was begun. The financial difficulties that constantly beset Henry led him frequently to call the barons and prelates to lend him pecuniary aid. In 1242, the proceedings of the assembly were formally recorded for the first time—the first authorized account of a Parliamentary debate. In 1246, the word "Parliament" was first used by the chroniclers to characterize the national assembly called by the king. On March 18 of that year, says Matthew Paris, "a most general Parliament of the whole magnates of the kingdom assembled at London, according to the king's summons."

The assemblies summoned by Henry served the vital function of making available the financial assistance that he so urgently needed. Sitting in state with the barons in 1244, we are told, the king "with his own mouth asked a pecuniary aid from them." The same scene was repeated with increasing frequency prior to the baron's rebellion under Simon de Montfort. Henry's misgovernment led to refusals by the barons unless the king promised to redress the grievances of the realm, and that, in turn, as we shall see, was to lead to a Parliamentary right to withhold financial aid until the measures desired by the representatives of the nation were enacted.

In the thirteenth century, however, the crown conceived of the national assembly only as the machinery through which it could readily secure the necessary financial support of the nation. From the governmental point of view, this machinery could be improved by a broadening of the representative base, for that would enable the assembly to pledge the direct assistance of a wider proportion of the nation—a broadening made desirable by the diffusion of wealth (particularly among a slowly rising commercial class) which was putting an end to the monopoly that had theretofore been possessed by the great landed magnates.

In 1254, when the Crown was in particularly great need of money, each sheriff was required to send two knights from his county to consider, with the barons of the realm, what aid they would give the king in his great necessity. This, says Stubbs, is an important landmark in Parliamentary history. As a surviving copy of the writ of summons shows, the knights were to represent, not the tenants in chief, but the counties themselves and the free men who resided in them. The aid asked for has become a national, more than a feudal, grant, and the assembly summoned to grant it has begun to lose much of its feudal character.

Then, in 1265, as we saw in the last chapter, Simon de Montfort summoned to his famous Parliament representatives, not only of the counties, but also of the cities and boroughs. For the first time, knights and burgesses sat with the great magnates, and the assembly could be said to be representative of the whole realm, albeit in rudimentary form. Earl Simon's purpose in thus broadening the composition of Parliament, it was emphasized in our previous discussion, was to widen the base of his own support in the nation by uniting the lesser gentry and the urban bourgeoisie to his cause.

When Edward came to the throne, he took advantage of the developing national assembly to resolve what should have appeared to those who thought about it as the critical dilemma of the government of the day. To carry on the task of governing a growing nation in an age of change and expansion—described by Thomas Costain as "the magnificent century"—the Crown had an ever-increasing need of revenue. But existing feudal law and custom sharply restricted the amount of money that the king could raise on his own authority alone. The experience of Edward's grandfather and father, when they sought to avoid the feudal limitations upon their financial positions, was bound to serve as a warning to a prince who was to prove himself a master of statecraft. Those monarchs had only succeeded in uniting the entire nation against their rule in their attempts to circumvent the customary restrictions upon the royal power.

On the other hand, the effort of Edward's uncle, Earl Simon, to secure the support of the national assembly, at the same time broadening its base to make it representative of all the estates of the realm, must have been most suggestive to a ruler who wished to meet the Crown's necessities without running the risk of alienating the nation. As an instrument to obtain the consent of the people whom it could be said to represent, the developing Parliament could serve as the means of acquiring needed revenue without any violation of feudal law or the Great Charter.

In Edward's reign, there is a constant development of the Parliament as the representative assembly of the nation. More than that, one can discern a steady evolution in the composition of the assembly until, by the Model Parliament of 1295, the great outlines of the representative institution have been established.

Soon after Edward became king in 1273, a great convocation of the entire realm was held to take the oath of fealty to the new monarch: to Westminster, we are told, "came archbishops and bishops, earls and barons, abbots and priors, and from each county four knights, and from each city four citizens." This assembly, Stubbs tells us, was in its essence if not in its form a Parliament. The first formal Parliament summoned by Edward was that which met in 1275. The Statute of Westminster I, the principal product of that assembly, states that that body contained not only the prelates and barons, but also "the community of the land thereto summoned."

Later in 1275, a second Parliament was summoned for the express purpose of raising money. To that assembly we know that elected knights of the shire (and perhaps even burgesses as well) were summoned. Thus the first Parliament summoned by Edward at which a general contribution was asked was a representative body. When the king sought the financial aid of the realm he sought it from an assembly with a composition broader than that of the great magnates alone.

In succeeding years of the reign, the representative principle continued to grow. In 1278, to the Parliament that produced the Statute of Gloucester, the king called the most discreet of his realm, "ausi bien des greindres cum les meindres." In 1283, the Parliament of Shrewsbury included two knights from each shire, as well as representatives of twenty-one selected towns. In 1290, two knights from each shire participated in the Westminster Parliament, and, in 1294, four.

Then, in 1295, came what has ever since been called the Model Parliament, which settled the general form of the representative institution for all times. In calling this assembly, Edward took the formal step that placed the representation of the Commons upon an established basis, one that was never thereafter to be challenged. The model for all future Parliaments was composed of representatives of all the estates of the realm. To the 1295 meeting, the king summoned separately the two archbishops, eighteen bishops, sixty-nine abbots and heads of religious orders, seven earls, and forty-one barons. In addition, writs were directed to the sheriffs to cause to be elected two knights from each county, two citizens from each city, and two burgesses from each borough. Sixty-three knights of the shire and one hundred and seventy-two citizens and burgesses who were thus chosen came to the session at Westminster. It is one of the fascinating footnotes of history that we know the actual names, not only of the great prelates and nobles, but even of the humble burgesses who came in November, 1295, in response to the royal summons.

The summons itself was couched in language worthy of the historic occasion. The form of the summons, which Stubbs calls remarkable, may be regarded as virtually the very inauguration of the representative system. It begins with the basic principle of self-government—that what concerns all should be considered by all: "As the most righteous law, established by the provident circumspection of the sacred princes, exhorts and ordains that that which concerns all shall be approved by all, it is very evident that common dangers must be met by measures concerted in common." This, Edward Jenks tells us in his biography of Edward I, "may have been intended as a mere rhetorical flourish, [but] it is to us the keynote of the drama." The notion of representative government is, for the first time, stated as a great constitutional principle. The great representative assembly had come into being —to serve as the center and focus of national political life until our own day.

"Many things," says Samuel R. Gardiner in his *History of England,* "have changed, but in all main points the Parliament of England, as it exists at this day, is the same as that which gathered round the great Plantagenet. It is especially the same in that which forms its chief glory, that it is the representative, not of one class, or of any portion of society alone, but of every class and every portion, which at any given time is capable of representation." The Commons, who will now sit as a matter of course in all future Parliaments, are already conceived of as representing those from whom they are chosen and, through them, the large bulk of the nation. The summons states expressly that they are to bring full power from their constituents to execute (*ad faciendum*) what should be decided upon by the general assembly.

From the time of Edward I, the Parliament is a body framed on the model of 1295. All that is necessary now is for the assembly to divide into the two Houses, which separate the Commons from the nobility of the realm. The notion of three separate estates, which underlay comparable Continental assemblies (like the Estates General then coming into existence in France), was fortunately never dominant in England. Edward may have intended his Parliament to represent the three great classes into which medieval society was divided: clergy, barons, and commons—those who pray, those who fight, and those who work, in Maitland's characterization. But the clergy *qua* clergy soon split off from the national assembly, preferring to meet in their own clerical convocations. The great prelates continued to attend, but rather as feudal lords and great holders of land than as merely clerics.

The next necessary step was for the knights of the shires to throw in their lot with the representatives of the cities and boroughs. Originally, they were drawn from the same class as the barons; but, as time went on, the title of baron (which at the beginning meant only "man") came to be confined to the greater men who were summoned separately, as contrasted to the lesser freemen who were left to be represented by the elected knights of the shire. The knights who came to Westminster mingled themselves with the citizens and burgesses. Thus, Parliament became an assembly of two Houses: the one composed of the great men, spiritual and temporal, who were summoned in their own right as lords of the realm; the other of men neither noble nor clerical, who represented what Stubbs calls "the organised bodies of freemen of the shires and towns; and the estate of the commons is the 'communitas communitatum,' the general body into which for the purposes of parliament those communities are combined."

Not only was the essential form of the national assembly established under Edward I, but also the Parliament in his reign was coming to exercise the two basic functions that were to become the fundamental prerogatives of the English legislature: those of taxation and legislation.

The power of taxation is, of course, the organic birthright of any legislature worthy of the name. Even in feudal times, we have seen, the notion persisted that the king might not impose more than the customary feudal obligations without the consent of his vassals—a principle that was given constitutional form in Chapter 12 of Magna Charta. We must also remember that the experience of his predecessors led Edward to realize the convenience to the Crown of summoning representatives of the country to grant financial aid in the name of the entire nation. It was to improve and broaden the base of the representative institution so as to make it a more effective source of financial support that led Edward to experiment with the changes in the composition of the assembly that led ultimately to the Model Parliament itself.

There is no doubt, as already indicated, that Edward and his advisers looked upon the national assembly as essentially an instrument of the Crown—as the organ through which the king could secure the ready financial support of the nation, at a time when the tremendous expenses of the Welsh and Scottish wars and the utterly inadequate amount of the ordinary feudal revenue made such support necessary. But here, as in so many other instances, men and institutions, once established, proved to have a will of their own; what began as the chosen instrument of the king was ultimately to develop into the great machinery for vindicating the rights of the nation. Edward may not have intended to create more than the tool of an orderly despotism; instead, his great work was the formation of the basis of constitutional monarchy.

What from the Crown's point of view started out as a duty in the assembled Lords and Commons to grant the money that had caused them to be summoned soon grew into an exclusive power to approve new taxes and a resulting control of the purse that was to prove the almost irresistible instrument for the development of Parliamentary government itself. It is indeed almost amazing how soon the principle that no new tax could be levied without the approval of Parliament became established. The consistent royal practice of summoning Parliament whenever there was need of money, so that the necessary sums might be granted, quickly developed into the rule that no financial levies might be imposed without prior Parliamentary grant.

Only two years after the Model Parliament itself met, in 1297, the Parliament, just established as it was in its definite form, was able to assert its right to power over the purse. Edward was then more in need of money than ever, in order to carry out his attempt to subjugate Scotland, which darkened the last years of the great king's reign, as well as to meet the expenses of a Continental expedition against Philip the Fair. The Parliament called to grant the needed funds imposed as its price an express royal Confirmation of the Charters, which included in its provisions specific limitations upon the royal power to impose taxes.

The key provision of the 1297 Confirmation, in fact, was a

virtual recognition by the king of the exclusive right of the Parliament to authorize taxation: "for no occasion from henceforth will we take such manner of aids, tasks, or prises, but by the common assent of the realm, and for the common profit thereof, saving the ancient aids and prises due and accustomed." This passage is from the officially accepted French text of the 1297 Confirmation. There is, however, also extant a Latin version, which came in later times also to be accepted as authoritative under the name *De Tallagio non Concedendo*. Its language goes even further than the official text, saying flatly that, "No tallage or aid shall be taken without the will and consent of the archbishops, bishops, and other prelates, earls, barons, knights, burgesses, and other free men of our realm." This language, extending even to the imposts levied upon the Crown's demesne lands, was even more restrictive upon the royal right of taxation than what is now considered the authentic version. In one sense it may be said that Edward's Confirmation of the Charters was only a restatement of Chapter 12 of Magna Charta. But there are two essential differences. In the first place, there is the fact that almost a century of post-Magna Charta acute controversy and fruitful experience was part of the English constitutional heritage when Edward put his seal to his 1297 Confirmation. After the opposition to the unilateral exactions of John, the barons' rebellion against Henry III, the organic experiments of Simon de Montfort, and Edward's own efforts at associating the community of the realm with the grant of funds, the principle first articulated in Chapter 12 of Magna Charta had acquired a constitutional force of its own that made it ripe for incorporation into positive law.

Even more important was the fact that, by 1297, the great lacuna in Chapter 12 of Magna Charta—the lack of enforcement machinery—had been at least partially filled. When John's Charter declared that no scutage or aid should be imposed "but by common counsel of our kingdom," it was stating a hortatory principle that might serve as a theoretical limit on the royal power but could scarcely function as a working rule of constitutional law in the absence of a national council more clearly defined than the assembly of feudal days. Under Edward I, the Commune Concilium of the Angevin kings grew into a true Parliament. Now, when the principle of taxation only through the national assembly was restated, there was a power behind it with due machinery for its enforcement.

What stands out, at any rate, is that since the 1297 Confirmation of the Charters the great principle that no taxes ought to be levied without the consent of the nation expressed through the national assembly has been recognized as a fundamental rule of positive public law. After 1297, in Maitland's phrase, "we may fairly say that . . . the imposition of any direct tax without the common consent of the realm was against the very letter of the law." This is not, to be sure, to say that the great principle was thenceforth always followed in practice. For nearly a century, the king did not always concede the lack of unilateral royal power; in many instances, the Crown sought to raise money in ways that clearly violated the spirit, if not the letter, of the prohibition. Thus Edward I himself, in 1304, tallaged his demesne lands and never regarded himself as precluded from imposing the custom on wool.

More and more, however, the principle of Parliamentary control of taxation came to be the governing rule, in practice as well as theory. The difficulties of the weak Edward II, the necessities of the strong Edward III that obliged him continually to apply for large supplies of money to carry on his foreign wars—these led by the end of the fourteenth century to the nearly uniform acceptance of the taxing power of Parliament, at least so far as the imposition of direct taxes was concerned. The exclusive right of the Parliament to levy taxes had become a fundamental constitutional axiom.

From the field of finance we must turn to that of legislation, for the power of the Parliament soon widened from that of taxation to include that of legislation as well. Indeed, it may be said that the power of legislation grew naturally, and almost inevitably, from that of taxation. The power of the purse is the crucial power in any polity; the possessor of that power will normally be able to "call the tune" throughout the governmental system. In our own day, it is the power of the purse that enables the legislature to control every aspect of the governmental machine. In the fourteenth century, it was this power that permitted the Parliament to exact, as a *quid pro quo,* a vital share in the power to legislate.

The king summoned a Parliament when he needed money. On

the other hand, the king's subjects always had grievances for which they desired redress. What was more natural than for the two to be tied together, with the representatives of the nation voting the necessary funds on condition that the grievances complained of be redressed? The national assembly bought with hard cash a long series of statutes confirming or conferring rights, concessions, and privileges that had been sought by petitions presented in Parliament.

In addition, the king would frequently use Parliament for the purpose of giving added authority to his own decrees, for much the same reasons that had led to the submission of financial requests to that body. The result was that throughout the fourteenth century, Parliamentary legislation became more and more common—both through the enactment into law of the redress of grievances required as a condition for the grant of funds and the Parliamentary ratification of royal decrees.

The constant participation by Parliament in the legislative process led to the principle (analogous to that developed with regard to the power of taxation) that no statute might properly be enacted without such participation. As early as 1322, it was enacted that "the matters which are to be established for the estate of our lord the king and of his heirs, and for the estate of the realm and of the people, shall be treated, accorded and established in parliaments by our lord the king, and by the consent of the prelates, earls and barons, and the commonalty of the realm, according as hath been heretofore accustomed."

This was more or less a statement of the principle that legislation requires the consent of the prelates, peers, and commonalty of the realm. The writ of Edward I summoning the Model Parliament had stated the elementary principle that that which concerns all should be approved by all; now, in 1322, the fundamental formula of English constitutional law can be stated. From that time onwards, to quote Maitland again, "it seems an admitted principle that the consent of both houses was necessary for a statute."

4

THE COMMON LAW

IN HIS *Canterbury Tales,* Chaucer says of his Serjeant of the Lawe,

> In termes hadde he caas and doomes alle,
> That from the tyme of kyng William were falle . . .
> And every statut coude he pleyn by rote.

By the latter part of the fourteenth century, then, a knowledge of statutes and decided cases was the mark of a learned lawyer. This indicates, at the least, that by Chaucer's day, there was already a developed system of English law. If this were a constitutional history of some other country, such fact would be of interest, but scarcely of crucial significance. It is, however, of crucial significance in the constitutional history of England, for the development of the English Constitution is intimately related to the growth of what, as early as the time of Edward I, was coming to be called the *Common Law.*

An outstanding feature of the English polity has always been that it is preeminently a legal polity. If it is customary to think of English government as virutally synonymous with free government, that is true only because Englishmen are the heirs of a successful struggle to bridle governmental power by the law of the land. From the beginning, the growth of English constitutional institutions and of the rights and liberties of Englishmen has been influenced and controlled by legal forms and methods. By the time of Edward I, the dominant interest in the Parliament was already that of the common lawyers and it was they who, in Theodore F. T. Plucknett's phrase, "were mainly instrumental in making parliamentary supremacy a fact."

It was the common lawyers who were largely responsible for developing and preserving that rule of law which was to become the central and most characteristic feature of the English system. It was the diffusion of the common law throughout the realm that led men to realize the role that law could play even in controlling governmental power. Hence, Macaulay could say that "The principle that the King of England was bound to conduct the administration according to law, and that, if he did anything against law, his advisers and agents were answerable, was established at a very early period."

Above all, it was the almost inexorable unfolding of the common law, by pervasive process of accretion rather than abrupt avulsion, that placed the rights of Englishmen upon a firm case-by-case basis, enforceable in the courts of the land. There was never need in England to write on a revolutionary *tabula rasa* without regard to existing traditions and experience. "Even the framers of Magna Carta," Winston Churchill tells us, "did not attempt to lay down new law or proclaim any broad general principles. This was because both sovereign and subject were in practice bound by the Common Law, and the liberties of Englishmen rested not on any enactment of the State, but on immemorial slow-growing custom." Thus, the common law itself was in its origins based upon the custom of the realm. "The Common Law," writes Sir Frederick Pollock, himself a leading common lawyer, "is a customary law if, in the course of about six centuries, the undoubting belief and uniform language of everybody who had occasion to consider the matter were able to make it so. To this day 'coutume' is the nearest equivalent that learned Frenchmen can find for its English name."

Bracton's great fourteenth-century work—still the landmark treatise on early English law—was entitled *De Legibus et Consuetudinibus Angliae,* plainly showing the close connection between law and custom when the common law was first becoming a developed system. And, two centuries later, Christopher St. Germain could still say, in his classic *Doctor and Student:* "And because the said customs be neither against the law of God, nor the law of reason, and have always been taken to be good and necessary for the commonwealth of all the realm; therefore they have obtained the strength of a law, insomuch that he that doth against them doth against justice: and these be the customs that properly be called the *common law*."

The term "common law" itself first came into use during, or shortly after, the reign of Edward I. The word "common," Maitland informs us, is not, in this respect, opposed to "uncommon"; rather, it means *general,* and the contrast to common law is "special law." Before the coming of the Normans, law was essentially a local and particular phenomenon; there was no national law applicable to the entire country. It was the growth of the royal power under the Norman and Angevin kings that made it possible for there to be a "common law"—a law common to the whole land administered by the royal judges of the king's courts. By the time of Henry II (1154–1189), it was already clear that such common law was going to prevail throughout England.

The growth of the common law is closely connected with the growth of the common-law courts. At the time of the Norman Conquest, there was no central court that administered a law common to the whole country. Instead, England was covered with a network of different kinds of local courts, and the law that they administered was the customary law of the district, often varying drastically from place to place. As Sir William Holdsworth puts it in his monumental *History of English Law,* "The political dissension which enabled the Normans to conquer the country was reflected in the diversity of the laws and the courts by which it was governed."

The Norman Conquest did not put an end to the legal confusion; in some respects, indeed, it increased it by adding the distinction between Norman and Saxon as a basis for even greater diversity in application of the law. But the Normans gave to England the strong central government that she sorely lacked. Whatever his defects, the early Norman king was a strong ruler with the power to make his will felt in the entire land. Above the local and manorial courts there now towered a royal court, staffed by the ablest men of the day, whose law was everywhere and at all times the same.

During the early part of the twelfth century, the royal court was already starting to make its influence felt. The *Leges Henrici*

Primi, written during the reign of that king, recognized the law of that court as superior to all other law. It is, however, not yet accurate to think of the jurisprudence of the king's court during the reign of the Norman kings as the dominant element in the law of England that it was soon to become. In the main, before Henry II, that court was only a court for great men and great causes. The task of centering the whole work of justice in one small body of learned men had begun but was scarcely yet accomplished.

To understand the development of the common-law courts, we must bear in mind the position of the Crown as the fountainhead of justice—a position that, in theory, it still occupies in the British system. Even in Saxon times, the king, to some extent, was considered to possess a residual power of justice, with his Witan sitting as a court of last resort in great and exceptional cases. But the Witan was far from a central national court, for it acted rarely and only then in grave default of justice in the regular local courts.

After the Conquest, the Norman kings governed through the Curia Regis, which in form was but a continuation of the Witan. Like its Saxon predecessor, the Curia Regis was a repository of both legislative and judicial power. It should be realized that the doctrine of separation of powers (which is so important to the modern constitutionalist) would have seemed completely strange to the men of Norman England. On the contrary, it was eminently natural to them that whatever powers of central government the king had should be exercised through one and the same body—his royal court. In this connection, the word "curia" or "court" itself had not yet acquired its preeminently judicial connotation. Instead, it was usually applied to assemblies gathered for the purpose of transacting important public business, as well as to the household and personal attendants of the king. The medieval court might, as Plucknett tells us, "be at the same time legislative, judicial, deliberative, and even festive."

The present-day observer must, therefore, look at the Curia Regis of the Norman kings, not as a court in the modern sense, but as the governmental organ in which were concentrated the three great governmental powers—in which legislative, executive, and judicial powers (traditionally kept separate since Montesquieu) are telescoped into a single central body.

As a judicial body, the Curia Regis had three principal functions: (1) it was a court of last resort in cases of default of justice in other courts; (2) it was a feudal court for the tenants in chief; and (3) it tried causes in which the king had a special interest—primarily criminal cases, which came to be called pleas of the Crown.

As the judicial work of the Curia Regis increased, it was most natural for those engaged in this work to become differentiated from those performing other tasks. Ultimately the differentiation led to the splitting off from the Curia of three separate law courts. The mass of judicial work became too great for one undifferentiated body and the result was the creation of the common-law courts.

The first offshoot from the Curia Regis was the Exchequer, which developed as both a fiscal bureau and a court for all cases relating to the royal revenue. The Exchequer, we are told by R. L. Poole, a leading historian of that institution, "first came into existence when the chequered table was arranged for working the accounts about the middle of the reign of Henry I." The name was derived from the chequered cloth on which the accounts were figured. In the Exchequer, according to the 1179 *Dialogus de Scaccario,* "as in a game of chess the battle is joined between the kings, so here the battle is joined and the main contest is between the treasurer and the sheriff who is accounting, in the presence of the other judges who are there to see and judge."

At first, the Exchequer was purely an administrative body, with the job of collecting and paying out the royal revenue. It came to be seen, however, that many questions relating to the revenue raised issues of law that could best be dealt with separately. Thus the Exchequer developed into a court to hear such issues, under a chief baron and other *barones Scaccarii.* But the Exchequer Barons, limited in their jurisdiction as they were, were scarcely sufficient to serve as the sole separate dispensers of royal justice. Other tribunals had to develop as well if the growth of a national system of justice was to go forward.

Under the Norman kings, the practice was established of sending itinerant judges, the so-called Justices in Eyre, to hear cases throughout the country. At first they were sent intermittently, but by the reign of Henry II they traveled regularly around the country. By Henry II's reign, too, it was seen that this

ambulatory justice was not enough. In 1178, the chronicler
Benedictus Abbas says, the king learned that the people were
much aggrieved by the number of itinerant justices. The chronicler goes on to tell us that, "by the counsel of the wise men of the
realm, he selected five only, two clergymen and three laymen, all
of his private household. And he decreed that these five should
hear all the complaints of the realm and do right and should not
depart from the Curia Regis but should remain there to hear
men's complaints; and if any question arose among them which
they could not resolve, it should be presented to the king for
hearing, to be decided by him with the advice of the wise men of
the realm."

It is probable that, in this 1178 act, Henry II deliberately
established a new court—a permanent and central tribunal,
which came to be known as the Court of Common Pleas. From
Henry's act in setting it apart, there commenced the sittings of
the Curia Regis "in Banco"; in the older books, indeed, the
Common Pleas was known as "The Bench." Its job, as time went
on, became hearing what we should call private-law cases—i.e.,
suits between subject and subject.

To the justices of the Bench, the king had delegated the power
to dispense justice between private individuals. Yet, though they
could and did deliberate outside the royal presence, they still
tended to follow his person. This practice must have been most
burdensome to ordinary suitors, particularly when the king was
absent from the realm, as was more often true than not during
the last years of the reign of Henry II and that of Richard I, who
was essentially an absentee monarch.

The obvious solution—to have the Bench sit in one permanent
location—was adopted in the reign of John. By then, the tribunal
had ceased to follow the king habitually and instead normally sat
at Westminster. In fact, by the time of Magna Charta, it was
considered an abuse for John to try an ordinary private-law case
elsewhere. It was in recognition of this that Chapter 17 of the
Great Charter provided expressly that "Common pleas shall not
follow our court, but shall be held in some fixed place." Magna
Charta confirmed the common understanding that common pleas
(as suits between subject and subject had come to be called)
should not have to follow the king as he went, often on the
impulse of the moment, from one part of his realm to another;

thenceforth they would be heard by a bench of judges at Westminster—a place ever since considered the natural home of the common law.

The fixing of the Common Pleas at Westminster broke up the unity of the Curia Regis. But it also emphasized the great dividing line that had developed in nonrevenue litigation. This litigation had come to be divided into two broad classes, with the line between them based upon the existence or nonexistence of a direct royal interest in the particular case. Cases in which the royal interests were specially affected by the issue were known as "pleas of the Crown"; those in which only the interests of ordinary individuals were involved were, as we have seen, known as "common pleas." The setting up of a permanent judicial home for common pleas led naturally to a comparable development for pleas of the Crown. One group of judges had been set apart for the hearing of common pleas; the next step was to set apart a second group to deal with pleas of the Crown. It was more than a century after the Court of Common Pleas had become a distinct court, with its own judges and records, that the same position was attained by the newer tribunal.

There thus grew up a third royal court, which came to be known as the Court of King's Bench. That was true because it was theoretically held before the king himself (*coram rege*); its full medieval title was "The Justices assigned for the holding of pleas before the King himself." The newer court was not fixed like the Common Pleas in one settled place, but, being held *coram rege,* followed the king in his travels throughout the realm. The practice of journeying about with the king continued for some time. In truth, though it was actually abandoned in the fourteenth century, till the end of its career in 1875 the King's Bench was said to be a court held *coram ipso domino rege.* Since the pleas of the Crown were assigned to the King's Bench, this meant that it was vested with a general jurisdiction of criminal cases. In addition, it could handle civil cases in which the Crown had an interest—notably those, such as trespass, in which the defendant was charged with a breach of the king's peace. In later years, not content with this, it sought by means of fictions to usurp business from the Common Pleas.

Even more important was the fact that, as a tribunal theoretically held in the presence of the king, King's Bench could assert a superior status over other tribunals and officers. As such, it could correct "errors" of other courts and could exercise superintendence over the due observance of law by all royal officers, sheriffs, and other officials. The exercise of this supervisory power by the King's Bench is intimately related to the development of the rule of law itself; in Holdsworth's phrase, "The fact that the court of King's Bench has always exercised this jurisdiction was not the least of the causes which ensured the supremacy of the common law in the state."

Our picture of the developing English system of justice must thus be one of a splitting off of three separate courts from the Curia Regis—the one undifferentiated central organ through which the Norman and Angevin kings governed. The three courts had parceled out between them the entire field of justice, at least so far as it had developed by the fourteenth century: to the Exchequer went all litigation affecting the revenue; to the Common Pleas went private-law cases; to the King's Bench went all nonrevenue cases (particularly criminal cases) in which the Crown had an interest.

The development of the English common-law courts may seem somewhat strange to today's observer, who lives in an age in which governmental institutions, and especially courts, do not just "grow," like Topsy. Our courts today are all the results of definite legislative acts, not the products of gradual growth.

Yet, even in modern times, the type of development that resulted in the common-law courts has not been unknown. An outstanding example (which, in recent years, has become of increasing interest to Anglo-American jurists) is the development of the *Conseil d'Etat* as the supreme administrative court in France. Its evolution from a purely executive tribunal to a court is roughly similar to that of the courts at Westminster from the Curia Regis. Both histories show the submission of petitions to the advisory council of the chief executive; specialization within the council to dispose of such petitions; and a judicialization of the specialists, accompanied by their separation from the other, purely executive, parts of the council.

The development of the common-law courts made it possible for the royal justice virtually to take over the field. But, reciprocally, it was also the success of the royal justice in superseding that dispensed by the feudal courts and other local tribunals that made the growth of the central courts necessary. It was under Henry II that the first great steps were taken to ensure that the justice dispensed by the king's courts would ultimately be the only justice dispensed in the kingdom; and, correlatively, it was then too that the common-law courts first began to split off from the Curia Regis. As far as the growth of English law is concerned, indeed, there is no doubt that the reign of Henry II marks a crucial turning point.

It is a well known doctrine of English law that legal memory begins with the accession of Richard I in 1189. The origin of this doctrine is to be found in certain statutes of Edward I's time, because a man living then could have been told by his father of what the latter had seen in 1189. Yet, as Winston Churchill tells us, a more appropriate date could scarcely have been chosen, "for with the close of the reign of Henry II we are on the threshold of a new epoch in the history of English law. . . . A modern lawyer, transported to the England of Henry's predecessor, would find himself in strange surroundings; with the system that Henry bequeathed to his son he would feel almost at home."

During the reign of Henry II, the justice dispensed by the king's judges began to be the common justice of the realm. The reason was that in the royal court the litigant could, in Maitland's words, "obtain a stronger and better commodity than any that was to be had elsewhere, a justice which as men reckoned in those days was swift and masterful; he could there force his adversary to submit to a verdict instead of finding that his claim was met by some antique oath with oath helpers." The result was that, more and more, men bypassed the feudal and other local courts and brought their judicial business to the king's judges.

To understand the rapid growth of the royal justice, which was soon to become the only justice of importance in the kingdom, we must realize the primitive nature of legal procedure before the great reforms instituted by Henry II. To us today, the primary purpose of a trial at law is the ascertainment of the true facts in the case, to which the law of the land can be applied, so that a just decision may be made disposing of the particular litigation. The facts are to be determined on the basis of the evidence submitted before an impartial trier of fact, whose sole concern is to arrive at the truth in the light of the evidence and arguments presented to him. However imperfect our rules of procedure and evidence may be in practice, their goal is clearly that of providing a rational method by which the actual facts may be found in any contested case.

The modern conception of trial procedure, however, would have been completely foreign to those who lived during the century following the Norman Conquest. The notion of proof of facts through evidence had not yet developed. Instead, more primitive methods were used. Thus, the Assize of Clarendon (1166) provides that "if anyone is captured with stolen goods, and is of bad repute and can produce no testimony of public purchase . . . he shall not make his law. And if the goods were not gotten publicly . . . he shall go to the water."

The passage quoted mentions two methods of arriving at truth: "making his law" and "going to the water." The first was the so-called wager of law—the most common method of proof in civil cases. Under it, the party who had to prove his case had to find the required number of "oath helpers" (compurgators) to swear that in their opinion his oath was trustworthy. If he could produce the requisite number and they took their oaths in the proper form without any slips, then his case was deemed proved. The other method, "going to the water," was a form of the so-called ordeal, which was employed in serious criminal cases. The two most common forms of the ordeal were that of the hot iron and that by water. To us today, both compurgation and the ordeal appear almost ridiculous as methods of arriving at the truth. And the same is true of the method of trial by battle introduced after the Norman Conquest. All three methods could have an element of rationality only in an age of unquestioned religious faith, when the sanctity of oaths and appeals to the supernatural were parts of the divine doctrine proclaimed under the aegis of a universal Church.

When the unquestioned faith of an earlier day began to give way, what rational basis there had been for the traditional modes of proof disappeared: what had been conceived of as an appeal to Heaven was seen to be but an appeal to mere chance or brute force. Men would scarcely be willing to submit their property or persons to the outcome of this kind of appeal as soon as a better method of litigating rights and obligations became available.

During the reign of Henry II, just such a better method was

coming to be provided by the king's court. The legal reforms with which that monarch's name is associated involved, in large part, so improving the justice dispensed by the Crown that men came to the developing royal courts as a matter of course, in preference to the local tribunals, which acted in accordance with the far less effective traditional methods of deciding disputes.

For the primitive methods by which issues were tried in the local courts, the king's court during Henry's reign began to substitute trial by inquest—an inquiry into the truth through the sworn testimony of a group of neighbors. Such inquest was to evolve into the institution of the jury. Its use was not original with Henry II. It was, on the contrary, derived from the Frankish and Norman law and had been employed in England from the time of the Norman Conquest. The great *Domesday Book* (in some ways the outstanding administrative achievement of the Conqueror's reign) was essentially an inquisition into the details of property ownership made, in the words of a contemporary chronicler "by the oath of the sheriff, and all the Barons and their Frankish men, and of the whole hundred, and of the priest, reeve, and six villeins from each township." In addition, the inquest procedure was sometimes used to decide private litigation. Thus, in 1080, in a suit about some land at Ely, a writ was issued ordering a number of Englishmen who knew the state of the land in question before the Conquest to be chosen and to swear to what they knew.

Yet, though there are instances of similar writs, they were most rare before the days of Henry II. It was that monarch who converted the inquest procedure into a normal part of the governmental machinery, both in the field of administration and that of justice. In administration, it was used by the Crown to obtain information about royal rights, local customs, the conduct of officials, and any other matters in which the king had an interest. The 1170 Inquest of Sheriffs required interrogatories to be answered with regard to the sheriffs' conduct; and the 1188 Ordinance of the Saladin Tithe required those summoned in each locality to answer questions as to the property of their neighbors, so that the tax might be assessed fairly.

It was, however, in the field of justice that the new procedure made its most significant contribution. By the Assizes of Clarendon (1166) and Northampton (1176), the inquest became an essential part of the criminal law. Under them, questions were to be addressed to twelve men chosen in each locality who were to answer upon oath "whether . . . there be any man who is accused or believed to be a robber, murderer, thief, or a receiver of robbers, murderers, or thieves." From the procedure thus laid down grew both the grand and petty juries that were to become the fundamental institutions of Anglo-American criminal law.

Even more significant to one interested in the growth of royal justice was the use of the inquest procedure in the field of civil litigation. Under Henry II, it became a part of the ordinary procedure open to almost every litigant in the royal courts. The Grand Assize and the so-called possessory assizes applied the inquest procedure to determine the most important type of civil case—that involving questions regarding the ownership and possession of land.

By the Grand Assize (about 1179) the defendant, in an action to recover possession of land, might, instead of submitting to trial by battle, put himself upon the Grand Assize. Four knights were then chosen by the parties; they chose twelve others, who came before the royal judges to testify who had the greater right to the land. Glanville, the classic legal treatise written during Henry II's reign, tells us what a boon the king granted by such procedure— "a certain royal boon . . . by which wholesome provision is made for the lives of men and integrity of their fortunes, so that, in maintaining their right to the freeholds which they possess, suitors may avoid the dubious issue of trial by battle."

Under the possessory assizes, the most important of which was the assize of novel disseisin (1166), a person who was dispossessed (disseised) of his land could obtain a writ directing the sheriff to summon twelve men to testify before the king's justices with regard to whether there had been a wrongful ejectment of plaintiff.

Maitland has called the ordinance that instituted novel disseisin one "which was in the long run to prove itself one of the most important laws ever issued in England." Bracton himself tells us that many sleepless nights were spent over its issue. Certainly, it has been said, the principle it introduced was both novel and far-reaching. The possession of property is henceforth to be protected by royal writ and inquest of neighbors. No longer will private right be at the mercy of those who could control the local courts. Under Henry II's reforms, starting with the novel disseisin and culminating in the Grand Assize, no man need answer for his property without royal writ and an inquest that provides the most rational method of determining the truth of the claim against him that had yet been developed.

It is hard to overestimate the importance of the extensions of the inquest procedure under Henry II. By the series of enactments, or assizes, summarized in the preceding paragraphs, a rational method of trial was thrown open to the entire community. This method was now available to settle questions involving the ownership and possession of land, which meant, of course, at a time when land was virtually the only property of consequence, that it could be used in most areas of civil litigation.

We can readily imagine the beneficial effect of the principle of royal protection of possession and ownership in an age in which the rights of property themselves had too frequently been at the mercy of the stronger members of the society. For the first time, perhaps, men were given that security of ownership which is the *sine qua non* of economic progress.

At the moment, however, we are concerned primarily with the impact of the reforms instituted by Henry II upon the growth of royal justice. That such impact was very great can hardly be gainsaid. To quote Maitland again, "There can be no doubt that one result of these various measures was to increase at a rapidly accelerating rate the amount of judicial business that was transacted in the king's name." It is scarcely surprising that litigants preferred to have their cases tried in tribunals which gave assurance of decisions that bore more than fortuitous connection with the true rights of the parties.

It is not difficult, in the light of what has been said, to understand the reasons for the popularity of the king's court or to see why the volume of its business became so great that, as already seen, it developed into three separate tribunals, with the most important step in that direction being the creation in 1178 of the bench that became the Court of Common Pleas. The result was that what before Henry II was essentially only a court for great men and great causes became a tribunal to which the entire nation could resort. By the time of Edward I, indeed, the king's courts had become virtually the only judicial tribunals of importance in the land. From an extraordinary tribunal, they had developed into the ordinary courts for the whole realm.

The method by which the royal justice displaced that dispensed by the different local tribunals was as statesmanlike as it was effective. Direct assault upon the plethora of feudal and other nonroyal courts would only have provoked resistance which, tied in as it would have been with the national struggle against the Crown under John and Henry III, might well have rendered the development of a centralized system of justice impossible. Even as things turned out, it should be noted, the opposition to the royal justice was able to include in Magna Charta a provision (Chapter 34) that protested the drawing away of land-title cases from the feudal to the royal courts.

The opposition could, all the same, scarcely succeed in preventing either the Crown from furnishing a more effective justice or the mass of the community from taking advantage of it. To be sure, the motives of the king in fostering the development of a superior system were far from disinterested. The extension of the royal justice meant the extension of the Crown authority and it also meant an increase in the royal revenue. The king's writ could be obtained by the ordinary litigant, but only for a price. A great part of English legal history is to be explained by the fact that the king's courts and their judges were paid by fees; therefore, as Maitland puts it, "more business . . . meant more money, and they had a keen interest in attracting cases to their courts."

In expanding the jurisdiction and increasing the effectiveness of the royal courts, the Crown may have been interested primarily in the fees to be collected from litigants. But here, once again, what started from the self-interest of the Crown was to develop into a basic right of the subject. What had originally been a mere purchasable favor became an ordinary right of the individual to resort to the common law to vindicate his rights of person and property.

For a fee that soon came to be fixed by custom, the litigant could obtain the appropriate royal writ necessary for the institution of an action in the royal courts. Thus, the English system of justice began to develop the procedure by way of original writ that long remained its most salient feature. "As yet," says Maitland, in an oft-quoted passage, "the king is no mere vendor, he is a manufacturer and can make goods to order. The day has not yet come when the invention of new writs will be hampered by the claims of a parliament. But still in Glanville's day the *officina iustitiae* has already a considerable store of ready-made wares and English law is already taking the form of a commentary upon writs."

By Edward I's day, the royal writ-making power had come to be limited. The Provisions of Oxford (1258), discussed in Chapter 2, laid it down that the Chancellor should seal no writs other than the existing writs, without the sanction of the king and Parliament. In 1285, it required a statute (the famous *in consimili casu* provision of the Statute of Westminster II) to permit the Chancery to vary the old writs slightly to fit new cases as they arose. Thenceforth the growth of the common law was restricted to the remedies contained in the existing writ system. For more than two centuries litigants had to fit their cases into the framework of the existing remedies.

An important consequence of the development of the king's courts and the growth of the common law administered by them was the rise of a separate legal profession. As the royal justice expanded its domain, the knowledge of the law became more and more the sphere of a learned profession, made up of the judges—the small compact body of justices of the king's courts, professionally learned in the law—and the attorneys who appeared before them. As the common law grew in bulk, going to law required the help of specialists who had devoted their lives to the subject. By the end of the thirteenth century, there existed the beginnings of an organized legal profession. Gradually, the tradition was established that the royal judges were to be drawn from the most eminent practitioners at the bar.

An outstanding characteristic of the English legal profession and the system of law developed by it has always been that of extreme insularity. This feature has been dominant from at least the time of Edward I—the time when, we saw, it was first accurate to speak of the existence of a "common law" throughout the realm. At that time, too, the law began to be taken over by the practitioner of the type of Chaucer's Serjeant of the Lawe, who devoted his life to the study and mastery of English cases and statutes exclusively.

From the beginning, the English legal profession has been characterized by inbreeding. As already mentioned, the royal judges soon came to be chosen exclusively from those who practiced at the bar of the king's courts. But it was the judges also—and through them the established profession—who were given the control of legal education. By a writ of 1292, "the lord King enjoined [the royal judges] to provide and ordain at their discretion a certain number . . . of the better, worthier and more promising students . . . , and that those so chosen should follow the court and take part in its business; and no others." The 1292 writ provided for perpetuating the legal profession by placing aspirants under the control of the judges. Legal education itself came to mean study of English law exclusively, through observation of the living law in the courts themselves and attendance at the Inns of Court, formed for the purpose and controlled by those established in the profession.

The consequence of all of this, Maitland tells us, "is that from the beginning of Edward's reign, English law becomes always more insular, and English lawyers become more and more utterly ignorant of any law but their own." In practice, this meant that Roman law and Roman institutions did not become dominant in England, as they were to become dominant during the movement known as "the Reception" on the Continent. From the time of Edward I, English law developed in its own parochial pattern, largely free of Roman-law influence.

That English law was thus saved from Romanism has had enormous consequences—both from a juristic and a constitutional point of view. Juristically speaking, it has led to the division of the Western world into the two great legal systems of the civil law and the common law. Nor, if we speak only of juristic methods and techniques, was the English system entirely the gainer. To quote Maitland again, "if our lawyers had known more of Roman law, our law—in particular our land law—would never have become the unprincipled labyrinth that it became."

From a constitutional point of view, on the other hand, the development in isolation of English law, freed from Romanizing influences, had the most beneficial effects. The Roman law, particularly as it had been codified under Justinian, had become a fundamental instrument of imperial absolutism. Its essential principle was that the will of the Prince has the force of law. The dominion of Roman law, in England as in other countries, would inevitably have brought absolutism in its train.

Instead, from almost the beginning, the English system was

based upon the principle that the king himself is subject to law. The law itself, as developed and administered by the common-law courts, was regarded as being above and beyond the men who exercised governmental authority for the time being. If the judges are still merely the king's servants—they hold their offices for centuries to come at the royal pleasure—still, from the time of Edward I, there is a separate body of judges, drawn from men who devote their lives to the law, who are expected to be non-political. Their function, from the beginning, is seen to be that of holding the balance evenly, not only as between subject and subject, but even when the interests of the Crown itself are at stake.

From the fourteenth century, then, English constitutional development is profoundly affected by the existence of an established system of law, upon which the rights of Englishmen could be firmly based, and an elite professional corps ever ready to preserve the common law and the rights derived from it from any and all encroachment. The common lawyers over the centuries well fulfilled the truth of de Tocqueville's dictum that, "In all free governments, of whatever form they may be, members of the legal profession will be found in the front ranks." It was the common lawyers, more than any other class, who molded and preserved both Parliamentary government and the rule of law as the essential elements of the English Constitution.

Above all, the self-contained system developed by the common lawyers was, as Maitland has commented, tough law. Its toughness enabled it to survive as the bulwark of English liberty over the centuries and to resist the Romanizing elements that sought, particularly under the Stuarts, to shape it into an instrument of royal absolutism. The common law was by then too strong to be overthrown even in favor of the system that had become dominant in the rest of western Europe.

The Stuart attempt to subvert the common law was, however, still centuries away from the time of which we have been speaking in this chapter—when the common law was being formed as a fundamental feature of the English system. Thenceforth the law and the lawyers were to play primary parts in English constitutional development, culminating (as we shall see in Chapters 7 to 10) in the preservation of both representative institutions and the rule of law, during the seventeenth-century effort to convert the English polity into a Continental-type monarchy.

5

STREAM OF PARLIAMENTARY
PROGRESS

> Not all the water in the rough rude sea
> Can wash the balm off from an anointed king;
> The breath of worldly men cannot depose
> The deputy elected by the Lord.

THUS SPEAKS Shakespeare's Richard II upon his return from Ireland to face Bolingbroke's rebellion. Yet the crucial fact about Richard's reign is that, in the end, the king was deposed: an anointed monarch was rendered "bankrupt of his majesty" by mere worldly men.

The deposition of Richard II (1399) was a capital event in English constitutional development. It demonstrated that, as John Selden put it in his *Table Talk* more than two centuries later, "A King is a thing men have made for their own sakes, for quietness' sake. Just as in a Family one man is appointed to buy the meat." When the king is guilty of such misgovernance that he subverts the very fundamental law of the realm, the nation that made him may also unmake him. When Richard was read the instrument of deposition and was told the reasons assigned for his removal, he is reported to have said, "not so, but because my governance pleased them not."

It is true that there had been, in 1327, another deposition—that of Edward II—but the ouster of that worthless king was scarcely the pregnant precedent that the removal of Richard II became. From a constitutional point of view, one may say that Edward II resigned the kingdom in favor of his rightful heir, who at once succeeded as Edward III. The same cannot truly be said of the replacement of Richard II by Henry IV. The rightful monarch, whose legitimate title is never disputed, is deposed in favor of one who is legally a mere usurper, not endowed with any color of hereditary right. With Richard's deposition, Winston Churchill tells us, "The last of all English kings whose hereditary title was indisputable disappeared."

Most important was the fact that Richard II was deposed by the assent of Parliament and for alleged reasons that, in the main, consisted of violations of the fundamental law of the land. Edward II had been forced to abdicate for personal, rather than constitutional reasons. The Articles of Accusation against him were based upon his utter incompetence; he had completely neglected his royal work, "giving himself up to unseemly works and occupations, neglecting to satisfy the needs of his realm." The same was not true when Richard II was removed from the throne. The Parliament voted to depose him after a series of formal charges which, in Maitland's words, "are not vague complaints of badness and uselessness, but accuse him of having broken the law." The majority of the charges were based upon Richard's infractions of the Constitution as it had by then developed—above all by his acts setting himself up as an absolute monarch.

From a constitutional point of view, the overthrow of Richard II was a revolution against extreme absolutism. Richard had proclaimed and acted upon a theory of absolute monarchy so far-reaching that it would never again be asserted by an English ruler—not even by the most immoderate advocates of Tudor and Stuart tyranny. Richard, the Articles of Accusation against him declared, had said that the laws were in his mouth and often in his own breast, and that he alone could change and frame the laws of the kingdom; and that the life of every liegeman, his lands, goods, and chattels lay at the royal will; and he had acted upon the saying.

Richard II's policy, as Stubbs summarizes it, "was a resolute attempt not to evade but to destroy the limitations which for nearly two centuries the nation, first through the baronage alone and latterly through the united parliament, had been labouring to impose upon the king." Under Richard, the theory that the law is only the will of the Prince is, for the first and only time, given brief effect in the English system. The Parliament is packed with the king's supporters; he obtains from them a revenue for life and a solemn recognition of the power of his prerogative. In addition, he secures the delegation of the powers of Parliament to a committee of eighteen, all of whom are submissively devoted to the king.

Not content with this, Richard maintains the most extreme theory of prerogative, illustrated by the condemning charge brought against him in 1399, under which he is declared to have affirmed that the laws were in the mouth and breast of the king, who by himself could change and frame the laws of the kingdom. By this, he meant that the king alone had a legislative power at least as extensive as that possessed by Parliament.

Richard pressed the power to legislate by royal ordinance beyond all bounds. The chronicles complain that the acts of the Parliament are consistently overridden by the king. "What is the use," they ask, "of statutes made in Parliament? They have no effect. The king and his privy council habitually alter and efface what has previously been established in Parliament."

Richard's deposition put an end, not merely to the practice, but also to the theory of extreme absolute royal power, based upon the limitless prerogative of the Crown. As Maitland put it, "it is as representatives of a different theory—that of a king below the law—that the House of Lancaster is to reign." Thenceforth English constitutional development could proceed along the lines of limited monarchy and Parliamentary government toward which it had been tending during the period prior to Richard II's reign.

In Chapter 3, it was seen how during the reign of Edward I the Parliament took shape as a working institution in which were coming to be vested the vital functions of taxation and legislation. Under the great king's son and grandson, the development of Parliamentary power continued. Indeed, it is only by understanding the extent of progress in this respect under Edward II and III that we can appreciate the drastic change that Richard II sought to institute by his concept of absolute royal authority. Let us summarize some of the essential steps in the development of Parliamentary power between the reign of Edward I and that of Richard II.

By the end of Edward I's reign (as we saw in Chapter 3), the Parliament had already taken the shape familiar to us, as an assembly consisting of two Houses—the one consisting of the Lords spiritual and temporal, the other of the representatives of the Commons, of the realm. It is probably true that, as Stubbs claims, from the very beginning the Lords and Commons sat apart. By the later Middle Ages, they clearly sat in separate buildings—the Lords in the Parliament Chamber of the royal palace, the Commons in the Chapter House or Refectory of Westminster Abbey. From the beginning, too, Westminster was the usual seat of Parliament, though sessions were also held in other towns.

It was during the reign of Edward I also that the great principle was recognized as a rule of positive law that no taxes ought to be levied without the consent of the nation expressed through the national assembly. The 1297 Confirmation of the Charters, we saw, contained a clear recognition by the Crown of the exclusive right of the Parliament to authorize taxation.

In addition, soon after the death of Edward I, the power of the Parliament to participate in legislation was acknowledged. In 1322, the Parliament enacted the fundamental doctrine of English constitutional law that legislation requires "the consent of the prelates, earls and barons, and the commonalty of the realm, according as hath been heretofore accustomed."

Certainly, by the time of Edward III (1327–1377), it was the established principle that nothing was to be entered on the statute rolls that had not received what Lord Coke was to term the "threefold assent" of King, Lords, and Commons. Already, during the course of the century, the legislative formula of a statute was coming to be what it has ever since remained: "The king our sovereign Lord . . . at his Parliament holden at Westminster . . . by the assent of the Lords spiritual and temporal and the commons in the said parliament assembled [and by the authority of the same parliament] hath done to be made certain statutes and ordinances in manner and form following." The bracketed portion was added during the fifteenth century, to indicate that it is from the whole Parliament that statutes derive their force.

During the period between the reigns of Edward I and Richard II the Parliament was able substantially to confirm its position with regard to taxation and legislation, as well as to strengthen itself as an effective governmental institution. We should be cautious, however, about speaking too cavalierly about the period, for our information about its constitutional details is, at best, all too sketchy. Nothing like the complete records of the time have survived; even the Parliament rolls for part of the period have been lost.

Even more important is the fact that matters of interest to the constitutional historian were not necessarily those which attracted the notice of the contemporary chroniclers. Edward III was a great warrior and conqueror. The glitter and extravagance of his court, the glory of the victories at Crécy and Poitiers, the chivalry of the Garter, the exploits of the Black Prince—this is the stuff of which the chronicles, especially that of Froissart, speak. In the perspective of a nation's development, nevertheless, these are but the things that glitter for a moment—the surface, as it were, of the stream of English history.

> Below the surface stream, shallow and light,
> . . . there flows
> With noiseless current, strong, obscure and deep,
> The central stream.

During the fourteenth century, the central stream of Parliamentary progress flowed on with undiminished force. It was that progress, indeed, which made it impossible for success to crown a scheme of absolutism such as that which Richard II sought to institute.

Paradoxically perhaps, it was the very magnificence of Edward III's reign that was the chief contributing cause of the constitutional gains made under that monarch. The extravagance of the king and the ever-mounting costs of the war with France made it necessary for the Crown constantly to seek financial support from the Parliament. The royal revenues and customary feudal dues were scarcely sufficient for more than a fraction of the king's needs and he was compelled to ask for numerous Parliamentary grants.

But, as is often true of men who embark upon grandiose projects, Edward, seeking to make good his claim to the French throne, was not interested in the details of governmental power. "Like Richard I," Stubbs tells us, Edward III "valued England primarily as a source of supplies, and he saw no risk in parting

with prerogatives which his grandfather would never have resigned." Provided the financial exigencies of the moment might
be met, the king was scarcely concerned that the cost was con·
stitutional concession to the rising national assembly—and particularly to the Commons who were coming to be recognized as
the true representatives of the nation.

It was during the reign of Edward III that the separation of the
two Houses, which gave its essental shape to the Parliamentary
institution, achieved its definitive form. In the very first Parliament of Edward III, the knights of the shire, who had previously
acted with the barons, joined the citizens and burgesses and sat
together with them as "the Commons." This union—never thereafter broken—of the country gentry with the burgesses, to form
the estate of the realm destined ultimately to prevail over all
other powers, has been well characterized as a turning point in
the constitutional history of England.

During the reign of Edward III, too, the Commons began to
elect a Speaker to preside over their sessions. By the end of the
reign, the position and title had become settled; the man elected
by the knights and burgesses was said "avoir les paroles" for the
Commons. After his election, the custom was to present him to
the king as the Commons' chosen "parlour et procuratour." The
Speakership became an essential institution in the development of
the position and powers of the House of Commons. Not only was
it the Speaker's job as presiding officer to ensure free and orderly
debates; he was also the principal spokesman of the House, ever
vigilant to maintain its dignity and assert its prerogatives as they
were being developed. As early as Henry IV, we are told, the
freedom of language used by Speakers roused the ire of the
Crown.

Just as important in the evolution of the Parliamentary institution was the development of the principle of frequent and regular
Parliamentary sessions. As soon as the national assembly received its basic form in the Model Parliament of 1295 itself, the
holding of Parliamentary sessions became quite frequent. We
must not, to be sure, make the mistake of assuming that the
entire nation (as is true of its present-day descendants) looked
upon the legislative assembly as the great protective institution,
which should be constantly in session to safeguard the interests of
the people. To the nation at large, the Parliamentary session may

well have seemed more of a burden than a privilege: frequent Parliaments were all too often synonymous with frequent taxation.

Yet there were many who mattered who realized that the regular session of the estates was the only effective check upon the arbitrary power of the king. Thus, in 1258, the Provisions of Oxford went so far as to direct the calling of three Parliaments every year. The Lords Ordainers, who controlled the government during part of Edward II's reign, directed that Parliaments be held once or twice every year.

Then, in 1330, near the beginning of the new reign of Edward III, a statute provides that Parliaments should be held once a year and oftener if necessary. In 1362, toward the end of the reign, the provision for annual sessions is repeated: "a parliament shall be holden every year, as another time was ordained by statute." The principle thus laid down was kept during most of the fourteenth century: annual Parliaments were the rule under the last Plantagenets. When the nation found Richard II attempting to dispense altogether with Parliament and reduce the national assembly to a committee controlled by the Crown, they were roused to action to prevent the overthrow of their rights.

Maitland tells us that, during this period, "The frequency of parliaments, if theoretically secured by the statutes just mentioned, was practically secured by the king's need of money." Hallam has gone even further and said that, though the English have never been slow to shed their blood in defense of liberty, most of the limitations by which at different times they have succeeded in binding the royal power have been purchased with money.

There is profound truth in the Hallam observation. Many of the most important documents in the development of English liberty admit expressly, indeed, that they are granted in return for stipulated sums. The 1225 Confirmation of the Charters (which contains the version of Magna Charta that took its place at the beginning of the English statute book) states specifically that, "for this concession and for the gift of these liberties . . . the archbishops, bishops, abbots, priors, earls, barons, knights, freeholders and all men of the realm granted us a fifteenth part of all their moveable goods." The 1297 Confirmation of the Charters contains a comparable express recognition of the price paid to the Crown—"a fifth part of all their moveable goods"—for the rights recognized in the nation. Later documents of both Edward I and his son include similar statements.

It was, however, during the reign of Edward III that these examples were converted into the common practice. It was soon realized that the redress of grievances could be obtained as the *quid pro quo* for the granting of monetary aid. The financial needs of Edward III led him readily to grant the *quid pro quo;* the immediate financial relief outweighed the possible ultimate diminution of the prerogative.

As early as 1339, the Parliament showed clearly its disposition to impose conditions before consenting to a grant. The king, himself, to induce them to be liberal, had told the Commons that the Chancellor was empowered to grant some favors to the nation "as grantz et as petitz de la commune." To which the Commons answered that, if their conditions were not met, they would not be bound to grant the aid.

From 1340 on, the statute book customarily contains the conditions on which the money grants of the different years are bestowed. It soon became the regular practice under Edward III for the Chancellor at the opening of Parliament to declare the king's willingness to hear the petitions of his people, with regard to grievances or amendment. By the later years of Edward III, it had become common to attach conditions to money grants. To obtain the one, the Crown had to grant the other. Here, it has been rightly said, was the beginning of the modern system of Parliamentary appropriations.

It was in the reign of Edward III as well that some of the most important uncertainties with regard to the Parliamentary power of the purse were resolved. We have seen that in his 1297 Confirmation of the Charters, Edward I had accepted the great principle that no taxes ought to be levied without the authorization of Parliament. Yet, it was also pointed out that that principle was not always observed by the Crown. Edward I himself, we noted, tallaged his demesne lands and considered it within his power to impose the custom on wool.

Under Edward III, the Parliament sought to check these assertions of direct taxing power by the king. In 1332, when Edward III levied imposts upon the Crown's demesne lands, the estates remonstrated and the king desisted. Then, in 1340, a statute was enacted prohibiting every species of tax not authorized by Parliament; it had the effect of abolishing the royal prerogative of tallaging demesne. Shortly thereafter, the prerogative over the custom was similarly restricted. In 1362 and 1371, it was enacted by statute that thenceforth no subsidy or charge upon wool should be set without the consent of the Parliament. After these laws, no attempt at unauthorized taxation of merchandise was made, at least till after the accession of the Stuarts.

But the growth of Parliamentary power during the fourteenth century did not stop with the establishment of the principle that no direct taxes may be imposed without the consent of the national assembly. The power of the purse (as any present-day student of the legislative process—whether on Capitol Hill or at Westminster—well knows) is the instrument through which the legislature is able to control nearly every aspect of the governmental machine. Under the later Plantagenets, too, the Parliament sought to use its newly acquired financial power to control the manner in which the administration of government itself was carried on.

In the first place, the Parliament attempted to take into its own hands control over the expenditure of the grants that it had made. The most obvious method of accomplishing this was by providing in the grant itself that the funds appropriated should be spent only for certain specified purposes, and no others. Edward III appears to have readily yielded to the Parliamentary desires in this respect. As early as 1346, the subsidy for the year was given for a stated purpose—the defense against the Scots. By 1390, control over appropriations had become more elaborate: of the forty shillings on the sack of wool appropriated, the king was to have ten for his present needs and thirty for the continuance of the war.

It is, nevertheless, scarcely enough merely to assert a power to grant funds only for specified purposes; it is one thing to say that money shall be spent only in a stated manner and quite another to prevent it from being spent in entirely different ways. In the Parliament of 1376, for example, a member of the Commons declared that "all we have given to the war for a long time we have lost because it has been badly wasted and falsely expended."

To ensure that funds were being spent for the purposes for which they were appropriated, Parliament began to demand the production of the royal accounts. Such demand was clearly made in 1340 and 1341. In 1341, the Lords and Commons jointly demanded that commissioners be appointed to audit the accounts of officers who had received money on the king's behalf. Similar demands were made in 1376. Then, in 1377, two treasurers were appointed in Parliament to supervise expenditure of granted funds. In 1379, the king, without being asked, presented his accounts, and, from that time, treasurers of the subsidies were regularly appointed to account to the next Parliament for both receipts and expenditures.

The development just discussed was of crucial constitutional significance. The Parliament, by securing the power to supervise expenditures, had made much of the progress necessary toward obtaining the authority to control administration that is now one of its essential powers. More than that, the steps taken amount to a recognition that it is to the Parliament, as representatives of the nation, as well as to the king, that the government is responsible. As Stubbs summarizes it, "The regular audit, in parliament, of ministerial work and official accounts, which was now demanded, was an assertion that it is to the nation, not to the king only, that the ministers are accountable."

Though we should be careful not to regard the events of six centuries ago through the distorting perspective of our modern conceptions, we cannot help but note the growth under Edward III, albeit in a most primitive form, of that doctrine of ministerial responsibility that has become an outstanding feature of the British Constitution. In the Parliament of 1376, known to the chroniclers as the Good Parliament, the weapon of impeachment was used for the first time as a remedy to secure the removal and punishment of ministers who had abused their public trust. Among those impeached were the chamberlain and steward, who held two of the principal offices of the royal household.

Impeachment as a Parliamentary weapon has become all but obsolete in modern times, when it has been replaced by ministerial responsibility in a system of Parliamentary government. Before the development of this system in its modern sense, however, impeachment was the effective legal device by which the king's ministers could be held directly responsible to Parliament for their official acts. Later history was to show that even the proudest of ministers would walk warily in the face of the ancient weapon—accusation by the Commons of the realm at the bar of the House of Lords.

It is in the light of the constitutional progress that has just been summarized that the attempt of Richard II to institute a system of absolute monarchy must be judged. A reader of the Shakespeare play on that monarch is struck by the abandonment of his supporters as soon as Henry of Lancaster landed in England. When Richard returns from Ireland, he is all but deserted and the extent of his aloneness is made poignantly clear:

> All souls that will be safe, fly from my side;
> For time hath set a blot upon my pride.

That Richard was abandoned by virtually the entire nation is, in large part at least, to be explained by what the system of government he sought to impose meant to the constitutional progress that had been made. "During 1398," Winston Churchill tells us, "there were many in the nation who awoke to the fact that a servile Parliament had in a few weeks suspended many of the fundamental rights and liberties of the realm." When Bolingbroke returned the following year (ostensibly only to claim his lawful rights as heir to "time-honoured Lancaster"), the whole nation turned from the king who stood revealed as would-be destroyer of the Constitution as it had till then developed.

Richard II's deposition put an end both to the practice and theory of absolute royal power. Henry IV came to the throne under an entirely different theory—that of the king below the law. Indeed, the very inauguration of the Lancastrian dynasty gave positive force to Bracton's celebrated dictum that the king has above him the law which makes him king.

Henry IV owed his throne, not to hallowed hereditary right, but to the assent of the nation, embodied in an act of the estates of the realm. A king who thus owed his royal position to the Parliament could scarcely seek to dispense with that institution when he exercised the powers that had been conferred upon him. And the same was true of his dynastic successors, who suffered from the same taint of title, in the absence of the Parliamentary prop that supported their assertion of royal authority. In Stubbs's words, "the house of Lancaster had arisen by advocating constitutional principles, and on constitutional principles they governed." If the deposition of Richard II ended the theory of supreme prerogative, so did the accession of Henry IV make the validity of a Parliamentary title indispensable thenceforth to royalty.

In light of what has just been said, we may speak of Henry IV as beginning the "New Monarchy" (though it is more usual to reserve that term for the accession of Henry Tudor). It is true that Henry IV's first Parliament formally declared that the new monarch "should be in as great royal liberty as his progenitors were before him." But practical considerations, stemming from the need for Parliamentary support as the very source of his power, made Henry's "royal liberty" less great than that of his predecessors. To the Parliamentary declaration, Henry replied "that it was not his intent or will to change the laws, statutes, or good usages, or to take any other advantage by the said grant, but to guard the ancient laws and statutes ordained and used in the time of his noble progenitors."

The theme so sounded by Henry IV was the basic principle that governed the reigns of the three Lancastrian kings. This principle is best stated in the writings of the greatest jurist of the fifteenth century, Sir John Fortescue, himself a firm supporter of the House of Lancaster through all its turns of fortune. His writings, Stubbs tells us, "represent the view of the English constitution which was adopted as the Lancastrian programme and on which the Lancastrian kings had ruled."

In all of Fortescue's works—particularly in his classic *De Laudibus Legum Angliae* (about 1469)—the dominant note is that of the absence of absolute royal power in England. He sharply contrasts the absolute governments of the Continent, notably that of France. The contrast is emphasized in an oft-quoted passage: "There be two kinds of kingdoms of the which that one is a lordship called in Latin *dominium regale* and that other is called *dominium politicum et regale*. And they differ in that the first king may rule his people by such laws as he maketh himself. . . . The second king may not rule his people by other laws than such as they assent to. And therefore he may set upon them no taxes without their own consent."

The kingdom of England, according to Fortescue, was emphatically of the second kind: "The king makes not the laws, nor imposes subsidies without the consent of the three estates of the realm." Above all, the king exists for the sake of the kingdom, not the kingdom for the sake of the king: "for the preservation of the laws of his subjects, of their persons and goods, he is set up, and for this purpose he has power derived from the people, so that he may not govern his people by any other power."

Fortescue's writings demonstrate that the constitutional progress, which was the outstanding feature of English history before Richard II, was resumed after that monarch's deposition under his Lancastrian successors. It is not too much, in truth, to say that when the Wars of the Roses began the English polity had, in fact, become virtually the limited monarchy that Fortescue described.

The outstanding constitutional feature of the Lancastrian reigns was the continuation of the growth of Parliamentary power that had been interrupted during the reign of Richard II. As emphasized, the Lancastrian title to the throne itself was in nature Parliamentary, rather than hereditary (in other than a factitious sense). This made it wholly natural for the king to look upon the Parliament more and more as a partner in the governmental process. This was particularly the case because of the constant Lancastrian need for money. Neither Henry IV nor his son or grandson was strong enough to raise money by extra-Parliamentary methods.

The consequence was the continued growth of Parliamentary power, especially in the field of finance. Noteworthy in this respect was the development of the basic constitutional notion that it is the Commons of the realm that is to have the primary role in matters of taxation and expenditure. In the beginning, the practice apparently was that each estate should tax itself. By the end of the fourteenth century, separate taxation of each estate by its own representatives came to an end, except perhaps for the clergy. The Lords and Commons joined in a grant and the formula developed that put the Commons (upon whom the bulk of taxation fell) into the foreground. The ordinary form of the grant became: "by the commons with advice and assent of the lords spiritual and temporal." This formula, first employed in the grants made in 1395, was used in 1401 and 1402 and thenceforth became the constitutional form.

The superior position of the House of Commons, which the formula so developed implies, was dramatically confirmed by Henry IV himself early in his reign. In 1407, the king put the question of what amount of aid was needed for the public defense directly to the House of Lords. The Lords replied with a statement of the sums they deemed necessary. The king then summoned several of the Commons to hear and report to their House the opinion of the Lords. The lower House at once objected to this: "the commons were thereupon greatly disturbed," asserting and affirming that this was "a great prejudice and derogation of their liberties." Henry then yielded the point and expressly assented to the principle that money grants are to be initiated in the House of Commons. In addition, the king stated that, after the grant originated in the Commons had received the assent of the Lords, it was for the Commons to announce the grant (generally on the last day of the session) "by the mouth of the Speaker of the Commons."

Thus was settled the primacy of the House of Commons in matters of finance and the practice ever since followed for money grants to be originated in the lower House, to be reported to the king only after both Houses are agreed, and to be reported by the Speaker of the Commons. The basic step has been taken toward that exclusive control over taxation which the House of Commons was successfully to claim in later ages.

Also in the reign of Henry IV, the practice that had developed for Parliament to exercise control over the manner in which funds granted had actually been spent was continued and even expanded. In 1406, the Commons had objected to making a grant until the accounts of the last grant were audited. Henry IV dismissed their claim with the brusque statement that "kings do not render accounts." But the king's boast proved a vain one: in the following year, the accounts were laid before the Commons without even being requested. And this practice continued throughout the Lancastrian period. In 1433, Lord Cromwell, the treasurer of the kingdom, laid before the Parliament an elaborate statement of the national accounts, which shows how thorough the audits rendered had become.

In addition, the Parliamentary power of legislation was strengthened in important respects. The power to legislate, we have seen, grew out of the tie-in between the grant of supplies and the redress of grievances. In the reign of Edward III, the statute-book began to contain the conditions upon which money grants were bestowed. In 1401, the Commons prayed that, before they made any grant, they might be informed of the answers to their petitions for the redress of grievances. King Henry's answer was a flat refusal: "that this mode of proceeding had not been seen or used in the time of his progenitors or predecessors." In practice, however, the Commons' demand was soon secured by the procedure, adopted during the reign, of delaying the grant to the last day of the session, by which time the bulk of the petitions had already received their answer.

There was, however, still an important gap in the Parliamentary power to demand the redress of particular grievances as the *quid pro quo* for the grant of supplies. There was always the danger that, though the king granted the petition of the Commons, the statute giving effect to the petition (drawn up after the Parliament is dissolved) would differ in important details from what the Commons had demanded. For many years, there were complaints about the tampering with petitions before they were turned into statutes.

Then, in the second year of Henry V (1414), a royal guaranty was obtained. The Commons prayed "that there never be no law made and engrossed as statute and law, neither by addition nor by diminution, by no manner of term or terms, the which should change the sentence and the intent asked." The king, in reply, granted that "from henceforth nothing be enacted to the petitions of his commons that be contrary to their asking, whereby they should be bound without their assent."

In the next reign, the practice (ever since followed) was adopted of initiating legislation by bill rather than petition; the bill contained the statute asked for in exactly the terms in which it was to be approved. The role of the king became solely that of assenting to or negativing the bills passed by the two Houses.

It was under the Lancastrian kings, too, that the fundamental principle (first established, by the time of Edward III) that no enactment may be considered a statute that has not received the assent of King, Lords, and Commons, was fully confirmed. In the 1414 Parliament, the Commons went so far as to assert that "it hath ever been of their liberty and freedom that there should no statute . . . be made unless they gave thereto their assent."

This claim by the Commons—that no statute had ever been made without their assent—was, of course, contrary to historical fact. But it does show how settled the place of the lower House in the legislative process had become. Later in the century, it was ruled expressly by the judges that no enactment could be called a statute unless the Commons had agreed to it.

Just as important to one concerned with the working of Parliament as the Parliamentary powers of taxation and legislation is how the Houses are constituted and the privileges that enable them to fulfill their high functions. In this respect, it is the developing House of Commons that is of particular interest to the constitutional historian, for significant steps were taken in the fifteenth century to ensure proper application of the representative principle.

The fourteenth- and fifteenth-century House of Commons usually consisted of about two hundred burgesses and seventy-five knights for the shires. We know relatively little about the actual mode of election during the fourteenth century. But we do know that Richard II had been able to pack the session that voted him absolute power; his interference in the elections of 1397 was specifically stated as one of the grounds of his deposition. It is not surprising, therefore, that one of the concerns of Richard's Lancastrian successors was to regulate elections to the Commons. In 1406, a procedure was provided for election returns to be made by sworn indentures of the sheriffs, mayors, and bailiffs, certified by some of the voters. The purpose was to prevent the sheriffs and other officials from making false returns, and, in 1410, a heavy penalty was imposed for the making of such returns.

Other statutes governed the qualifications of voters. A 1413 law restricted the franchise to residents within the county, city, or borough concerned. Then, in 1430, came the statute of Henry VI which, because elections had lately been made by "very great, outrageous, and excessive number of people of small substance and no value, whereof every one of them pretended a voice equivalent, as to such elections, with the most worthy knights and squires," provided that only those could be electors who were resident persons "whereof every one of them shall have free tenement to the value of forty shillings by the year at the least above all charges." The 1430 statute laid down the rule that governed electoral qualifications for four centuries. Until the great reform legislation that broadened the franchise in the nineteenth century, only the "forty-shilling freeholder" class could be electors in the English counties.

Among the matters that greatly concerned the developing Parliaments of the fourteenth and fifteenth centuries was the securing of the basic privileges that are the *sine qua non* of the effective functioning of a legislative assembly. Much of Parliamentary history, indeed, is an account of the legislative struggle to obtain these privileges for its members. In the words of the United States Supreme Court in 1951, "The privilege of legislators to be free from arrest or civil process for what they do or say in legislative proceedings has taproots in the Parliamentary struggles of the Sixteenth and Seventeenth Centuries."

But the history of Parliamentary privilege starts at an even earlier date. It is usually said to begin with the case of Thomas Haxey in 1397. He had brought into the House of Commons a petition complaining of extravagance in the king's household. The king took offense and the House gave up the name of the offender with a humble apology. He was then condemned by the Parliament to die as a traitor. But the sentence was not carried out; the Archbishop of Canterbury saved him by claiming him as a clergyman, and he was pardoned shortly afterwards.

After Richard II was overthrown, the sentence against Haxey was reversed on the petition of the Commons that it was contrary to right and the usage of Parliament. The annulment shows that as early as 1399 the privilege of freedom of debate was already recognized as fundamental to the proper functioning of the legislative assembly. Referring to Haxey's case, Maitland affirms that, "Such an interference with the freedom of debate seems to stand almost alone in our medieval history." Yet there are other aberrational cases as well, notably, the imprisonment of the Speaker in 1376 and 1453.

Such calling of members to account for their Parliamentary behavior was plainly contrary to the general practice as it developed during the fourteenth and fifteenth centuries. The rule normally recognized was that stated in a petition to the Commons of 1455, that all members "ought to have their freedom to speak and say in the house of their assembly as to them is thought reasonable without any manner, challenge, charge, or punition therefore to be laid to them in anywise."

Under the Lancastrian kings, the freedom of Parliamentary debate was fully recognized. In 1400, Henry IV acknowledged the right of the Commons to debate freely and promised not to interfere in their deliberations or to listen to unauthorized accounts of their activities. In 1407, Henry again specifically recognized the Parliamentary freedom of deliberation, declaring that the two Houses might "commune among themselves . . . of the estate of the realm and of the remedy necessary for the same." The freedom of Parliamentary discussion under the Lancastrians is amply shown by the scope of the matters actually discussed by the assemblies called during the reigns of Henry IV and his successors: the full range of domestic administration and foreign policy is covered in the Parliamentary debates of the period.

To what has been said of Parliamentary development in Lancastrian England must be added what appears to the present-day observer a precocious attempt to anticipate that control of administration by the legislature which is an outstanding feature of the modern British Constitution. The effort was made by the Parliament to impose its control over the royal council, which may be compared (bearing in mind the distortion inevitable in the use of modern analogies) to the Cabinet which is now at the head of the executive branch in Britain.

In the first place, Parliament succeeded in having members of the council nominated in Parliament and attempted to regulate their conduct by imposing prescribed oaths for them to take. Not content with this, the Houses several times sought to fix the wages paid to councillors. There are also indications of an effort to have the Parliament exercise something like a veto over the naming of council members; in addition, we know of instances in which royal officials were dismissed at the instance of the Commons.

According to Stubbs, "the council thus nominated, regulated, and watched by the parliament was a substantive and most valuable feature of the Lancastrian system of government." At the same time, it seems plain that, though (like the system of government briefly instituted by the barons' rebellion under Simon de Montfort against Henry III) it constitutes one of the precursors of the modern system of Parliamentary government, it was premature, coming as it did so soon after the Parliamentary institution itself had begun to develop.

We may, in fact, make a similar statement with regard to the whole course of Lancastrian political development. George B.

Adams could call the whole system of government in fifteenth-century England "startlingly and prematurely modern." The twentieth-century observer, who looks at the constantly expanding activity of the Lancastrian Parliaments, setting precedents that were to prove pregnant in later centuries' struggles to curb royal power, is bound to feel that the country is practically on the verge of the modern Constitution.

This view is erroneous. The liveliness of the Lancastrian Parliament should not lead us to assume that the representative assembly had already solidified its place as the dominant institution in the polity. On the contrary, to quote Stubbs's conclusion in his summary at the end of his discussion of England under Lancaster and York, "the constitution had in its growth outrun the capacity of the nation; the nation needed rest and renewal, discipline and reformation, before it could enter into the enjoyment of its birthright."

The required constitutional pause was provided by the Wars of the Roses and the system of strong royal government instituted by the Tudor dynasty.

6

CONSTITUTIONAL CONSOLIDATION

ONE CALLED ON to discuss the influence of the Wars of the Roses on English constitutional progress cannot help recalling a famous passage from *The Memoirs of Sherlock Holmes*. In a case involving the disappearance of a champion race horse, Holmes was asked by the horse's owner: " 'Is there any point to which you would wish to draw my attention?' "

"To the curious incident of the dog in the night-time."
"The dog did nothing in the night-time."
"That was the curious incident," remarked Sherlock Holmes.

The historian who is asked about the influence of the Wars of the Roses on English constitutional progress will answer, as Holmes did, that those wars had no influence—that they constituted merely a hiatus in English constitutional history. "So far as I can understand it," says Maitland, "the confusing struggle which we call the Wars of the Roses is not . . . a contest between opposite principles—it is a great faction fight in which the whole nation takes sides."

Certainly, the bloody conflict between Lancaster and York well illustrates Edmund Burke's observation that "Laws are commanded to hold their tongues amidst arms." The Wars of the Roses brought the rapid progress of the English Constitution discussed in the last chapter to an almost complete halt. The reign of Edward IV, which was the immediate outcome of the triumph of the White Rose, was the first in centuries that saw no legislation enacted to further the rights and liberties of the subject.

Yet, paradoxical though it may appear at first glance, the significant point is the very fact that the violent termination of the Lancastrian dynasty put a temporary end to the constitutional progress. Without that pause, it is most unlikely that the English Constitution would have actually evolved along the lines it ultimately took. Precocity in political development all too often bears out the truth of Margaret Fuller's observation that "For precocity some great price is always demanded sooner or later in life." But for the Wars of the Roses and the Tudor dynasty to which it led, the English Parliament might have met the fate of the Castilian Cortes and the French States-General, which had two centuries earlier been assemblies at least as proud and powerful as those which were then coming to sit at Westminster.

The Wars of the Roses and the reigns of the Yorkist kings which briefly followed them constitute a particularly unattractive period of English history. "Historians," Winston Churchill tells us, "have shrunk from the Wars of the Roses, and most of those who have catalogued their events have left us only a melancholy and disjointed picture. We are however in the presence of the most ferocious and implacable quarrel of which there is factual record."

Nor did the cruelties of the period cease with the downfall of the House of Lancaster. As Stubbs put it, in describing the reign of Edward IV after the Yorkist triumph at Tewkesbury (1471), "The cruelties and extortions which followed Edward's victory need not detain us, although they fill up the records of the following years." The situation under Edward IV was neatly stated by a contemporary chronicler: "The rich were hanged by the purse and the poor by the neck." It is in Edward's reign, in 1468, that we find the first recorded instance of the use of torture in England—an iniquity that became an evil precedent for Edward's successors.

Edward IV was followed by his brother Richard III. The last of the Yorkist kings has gone down in history as the very epitome of "naked villainy" and evil incarnate, to whom (in Churchill's characterization) not only is every possible crime, and some impossible ones, attributed, but who is also presented as a physical monster, crookbacked and withered of arm. Recent attempts to whiten Richard's reputation have scarcely sufficed to alter the general verdict—made familiar to us through Shakespeare's play—under which "every tale condemns [him] for a villain."

But despite their evils it was the Wars of the Roses and their outcome—resulting first in the excesses of the House of York and finally in the dominance of the House of Tudor—which molded directly the shape which English constitutional development ultimately took. In addition to the pause in constitutional progress, the Wars of the Roses had an important immediate effect, which shifted the Parliamentary center of gravity to the House of Commons. That Chamber, which had been growing in authority and prestige throughout the fourteenth and fifteenth centuries, was thenceforth to be the fulcrum upon which the development of the legislative institution was to turn.

When the Commons were first called upon to play a part in the national assembly, there is no doubt that their House was looked upon as a very junior part of the Parliament, sitting in the shadow of the great magnates of the realm. Nor is it likely that the representatives of the yeoman and the tradesman would have been able easily to wrest the position of superiority from a House of Lords made up of men whose pedigree went back to knights who had broken the Saxon ranks at Hastings and scaled the walls of Acre and Jerusalem. But the old nobility was no more; its ranks had been virtually decimated by the bloody conflict between Lancaster and York.

Winston Churchill has graphically summarized this effect of the Wars of the Roses: "The Plantagenets and the proud, exclusive nobility which their system evolved had torn themselves to pieces. The heads of most of the noble houses had been cut off, and their branches extirpated to the second and third generation." In 1451, Henry VI had summoned fifty-three lay peers to Parliament; only twenty-nine peers were summoned by Henry VII to his first Parliament in 1485, and of those a substantial number had been recently elevated to the peerage. During the century that followed, the ranks of the nobility were filled by new elevations, largely from among the gentry. By the end of the Tudor period, it was only the rare member of the House of Lords who could trace his escutcheon back before Bosworth Field.

The significant consequence was that the Parliamentary primacy was now to be transferred to the House of Commons, which was to become more and more the vital center of English constitutional development. When the great struggle was to be resumed against royal pretensions to absolute prerogative, the leadership against the Crown claims would be found almost entirely among the representatives of the commonalty.

The virtual elimination of the old nobility of the realm also tended to remove from the Crown the aristocratic prop that was a basic support of the royal prerogative in Continental countries. Instead, Macaulay tells us, "After the wars of York and Lancaster, the links which connected the nobility and the commonalty became closer and more numerous than ever." The heirs of the nobility sat alongside the gentry and burgesses in the House of Commons; the Lords' membership was made up largely of men who had, not long before, been among the ranks of the third estate. With no line sharply dividing the patrician from the plebeian, the Lords and Commons were able to cooperate in defense of Parliamentary power and privilege to an extent scarcely possible in neighboring countries.

Just as important to the ultimate development of the English Constitution was the fact that (tenuous though his claim may have actually been) Henry Tudor purported to come to the throne as the heir of the House of Lancaster. The Yorkist kings, who obtained the Crown through the violent defeat of the House of Lancaster and its supporters, had felt far freer to rule without adhering to the constitutional limitations that had developed under their Plantagenet and Lancastrian predecessors. Edward IV, in particular, when once the victory of the White Rose had been secured, was able to rule in virtual disregard of such limitations. In the phrase of Stubbs, "generally, the Lancastrian rule was a direct continuity, and the Yorkist rule was a break in the continuity, of constitutional development."

The consequence of Henry VII's claiming the throne as the heir of the House of Lancaster—as Earl of Richmond, he had, indeed, been characterized as the nearest thing to royalty that the Lancastrian party possessed—was that he and his Tudor successors observed all the constitutional forms that had been developed before the Wars of the Roses. The Tudor monarchs, arbitrary though their actual powers may have been, never asserted any claim to be above the law. Instead, they scrupulously governed through the form of partnership with Parliament, which had evolved as the dominant feature of the Constitution. Consequently, even when the royal power was, as under Henry

VIII, at its zenith, the legal limits of such power remained, in theory, where they had been in previous centuries.

In truth, we may say (paraphrasing a passage from Stubbs) that the Tudors, with Lancaster, observed the forms of the Constitution, while, with York, they manipulated them to their own ends. The expanded royal authority, which is the outstanding feature of the Tudor period, flows from the fact that the Crown is able to get what it wants through submissive and subservient Parliaments. "In the changed circumstances," as Maitland states, "the king is beginning to find out that parliamentary institutions can be made the engine of his will."

The form of government with and through the Parliament was, as stated, maintained even throughout what historians have come to term the Tudor dictatorship—when the reality was one of well-nigh complete royal control of the governmental machine. In fact, it is in the Tudor period that we find the most extreme assertions of Parliamentary power that exist in the English statute book. Perhaps the most striking illustration of this assertion was a statute enacted during the reign of Henry VIII that provided for the boiling of the Bishop of Rochester's cook to death.

Even when the Tudors extended their powers to the extent of constitutional innovation, they followed the form of legalizing their action by Parliamentary statute. This was the case even with regard to Henry VIII's famous Statute of Proclamations enacted in 1539. That law—described by Maitland as "the most extraordinary act in the Statute Book"—provided that proclamations issued by the king "shall be obeyed observed and kept as though they were made by Act of Parliament." Yet even this English "Lex Regia"—far-reaching though it may have been in giving to royal proclamations the full force of law—was not as absolutist as it appeared.

In the first place, the Statute of Proclamations contained, by its very terms, substantial limitations upon the power conferred. Thus, it was expressly provided that neither the common law nor statute might be infringed by a proclamation, nor might the breach of a proclamation (unlike that of most criminal statutes at the time) be made a capital offense.

Most important, however, was the fact that the 1539 Lex Regia did not really involve any surrender of the commanding position that had been won by statute law in the legal order. On the contrary, as Sir David Lindsay Keir puts it, "the whole tenor of the statute bears witness to its acceptance of the legislative supremacy of Parliament." And it was so considered by succeeding generations. "Henry the Eighth," said a member of Parliament in the time of Charles I, "would not have prayed the aid of an act of Parliament if by law he could have done it of himself." Hence, we may say, even that Tudor monarch whose very name has become synonymous with royal absolutism recognized the need to place the Parliamentary imprimatur upon his exercises of prerogative power.

What has just been said was true as well of that exercise of governmental authority which was most extreme both in its extent and implications—namely, the institution of the English Reformation. The break with Rome and the setting up of an independent Church, with all the consequences flowing therefrom, involved all but unprecedented assertions of public power. The form in which the power was exercised was that of legislation enacted by the estates of the realm.

The Reformation Parliament, which sat from 1529 until 1536, the longest duration till then recorded, passed the various statutes by which the English Reformation was accomplished: from the first Act of Annates (1531), doing away with payments by newly appointed prelates to the Pope, to the Act in Restraint of Appeals (1533), abolishing all appeals to Rome from ecclesiastical courts, to the second Act of Annates (1534), taking away the papal power to nominate to bishoprics, to the Act of Supremacy (1534), which finally acknowledged the ecclesiastical supremacy of the Crown, declaring expressly that the king is the "only supreme head in earth of the Church of England." The English Reformation was capped by statutes of 1536 and 1539 authorizing the destruction and spoliation of the monasteries, which, Henry Hallam tells us, "poured in an instant such a torrent of wealth upon the crown, as has seldom been equalled in any country by the confiscations following a subdued rebellion."

The Reformation legislation effected a complete transformation of the spiritual foundation upon which the society of the early sixteenth century was built. Today, indeed, it appears as extreme in its impact upon the community as anything decreed by modern totalitarian fiat, intruding as it did so drastically into the realm of religious belief and doctrine and involving confiscation of the largest property owner in the kingdom. At the same time, it can scarcely be doubted that such statutes (which would, beyond any question, lie far outside the constitutional pale if enacted by any American legislature) strikingly demonstrate the doctrine of Parliamentary supremacy and the fact that it had already become the dominant feature of the English Constitution.

The doctrine of Parliamentary supremacy was summed up a century ago by J. L. De Lolme in an aphorism which has become almost proverbial: "It is a fundamental principle with English lawyers, that Parliament can do everything but make a woman a man, and a man a woman"—(and legally speaking, we may add parenthetically that Parliament can even do these things). From a legal point of view, Parliamentary supremacy means that a statute, enacted by the estates of the realm and assented to by the sovereign, is at the apex of the hierarchy of legal commands that have positive effect within the British legal order. A statute, until amended or repealed, constitutes the supreme law of the land—unrestrained by the constitutional limitations by which American legislative power is confined.

All this is self-evident to the modern student of the British Constitution. But it was also plain in Tudor times, particularly after the legislation of the Reformation Parliament. Not all men, it is true, accepted the implications inherent in the doctrine of unlimited sovereignty in the legislative assembly. Sir Thomas More, charged with denying the royal supremacy enacted in the Supremacy Act, asserted that the statute was repugnant to the law of God. Such appeal to a fundamental law limiting the legislative capacity of the Parliament was, however, more appropriate to an earlier age (or perhaps a later one, during which comparable American constitutional doctrines were to flourish).

G. M. Trevelyan has characterized the anticlerical revolution instituted by Henry VIII, through the instrumentality of the Parliament, as that which, "more than any other single event may be held to mark the end of mediaeval society in England." Throughout the Middle Ages, there had been a basic limitation fixed upon temporal sovereignty: it had no power in spiritual matters; instead, these were vested in a Church which stood apart from, if not above, the State. "But now," Maitland tells us, "statutes have gone to the very root of religion; the orthodox creed is a statutory creed and that creed has been changed more than once. Thus statute has given the most conclusive proof of its power."

Having eliminated her only rival for legal supremacy, the Parliament stood unchallenged as the sole possessor of legislative sovereignty in the realm. And its supremacy in this respect was recognized by contemporary observers. For example, according to *The Commonwealth of England*—a book published by Sir Thomas Smith, himself Secretary of State to Queen Elizabeth— "The most high and absolute power of the realm of England consisteth in the Parliament. . . . And to be short, all that ever the people of Rome might do either in *centuriatis comitiis* or *tributis,* the same may be done by the parliament of England, which representeth and hath the power of the whole realm, both the head and body."

The discussion thus far should not, all the same, lead us to an erroneous impression of where the primacy in the polity really lay in Tudor England. In legal theory, no doubt, legislative supremacy was vested in the Parliament, which enacted statutes, like those instituting the English Reformation, which can only be characterized as revolutionary in nature. Certainly the Tudor Parliaments constantly intervened in matters that, to the modern political scientist at least, are far beyond the legitimate scope of legislative power—conscience and belief, sanctity of private property, the liberty (and even the life) of the citizen—as well as regulating most aspects of the economy in such detail that it appeared quaintly out of line with more recent notions of the proper role of the State in economic affairs (at least before the renaissance of paternal government in our own day).

But if the Tudor Parliament was, in legal theory, vested with legislative sovereignty, it should not be forgotten that, in practice, that body's authority was used primarily as the instrument for giving effect to the royal will. If the main theme of English constitutional history has been that of a constant increase in Parliamentary power and a corresponding diminution of royal authority, it must not be thought that this development has unfolded in a strictly consistent fashion—with each step in Parliamentary progress leading inexorably to its successor in the growth of representative government.

A picture of English constitutional history developing in terms of a completely consistent evolution is bound to be somewhat distorted. A more accurate record would be one of ebbs and flows. While the basic tide is that of the development of Parliamentary power, there are inevitably periods when the Parliamentary flood recedes and the dominant theme, although temporary, is one of resurgent royal authority.

The most important period of royal resurgence in English history was that during the reign of the Tudor dynasty. It is, in truth, not too much to say that, in most respects, the Tudor monarchs were more successful in giving effect to royal power and policies than any other British reigning house. Paradoxically perhaps, it was the very Tudor success that ultimately helped save and strengthen the Parliamentary institution. Monarchs who could secure what they desired from submissive assemblies were quite content to govern through the form of Parliamentary legislation. As Maitland aptly put it, "parliament is so tractable that the king is very willing that king in parliament should be recognized as supreme—it strengthens his hands that what he does should be the act of the whole nation." Hence, Henry VIII could, without intending any diminution in the practical authority of the Crown, declare, in a famous 1543 speech to Parliament: "We be informed by our judges that at no time do we stand so highly in our Estate royal as in the time of Parliament, wherein we as Head and you as Members are conjoined and knit together in one body political."

The consequence was that a period of royal domination, which might have resulted in the English Parliament meeting the fate of comparable Continental assemblies, had no such dire outcome. Instead, the reigns of the Tudors was a period of consolidation and apprenticeship for the Parliament. In the House of Commons particularly, men were acquiring mastery over Parliamentary procedure and principles, as well as a knowledge of legislative strategy and tactics that was to serve their successors well in the next century.

During the early part of the Tudor period, the nation was quite content to have the constitutional locus of power shift unmistakably to the Crown. The primary need, after the internal disorders that were the inevitable byproduct of the Wars of the Roses, was the mastery of the prevailing lawlessness of the period. In the words of a contemporary, "The hed agreth not to the fete, nor fete to the handys, no one parte agreth to other; the temporalty grugyth agayn the spiritualty, the commyns agayn the nobellys, and subjectys agayn ther rularys."

In England, as on the Continent, at the time, it was realized that only a strong king could curb the lawlessness from which all classes of society had been suffering. Under Henry VII, the crying need for order was masterfully met. From the beginning of his reign, Henry set himself the tasks of eliminating the lawless practices of overmighty nobles, of maintaining order, and of seeing that justice was properly administered. And he succeeded to an extent that can only be explained by the fact that his policies coincided with the felt necessities of the times.

"What he minded he compassed," wrote Francis Bacon, in a famous passage in his *History of Henry VII.* In the reign of that monarch, the prevailing lawlessness of the previous century was done away with; rival sovereignties were wiped out; the governmental authority, previously so diffused, was concentrated in the royal hands; the poverty of the Crown (which Fortescue had pointed to as the prime cause of the Lancastrian weakness) gave way to a system of finance that made the Crown independently wealthy. When Henry VIII succeeded to the throne, his position and power were virtually unquestioned.

To accomplish the change from the lack of governance, which had too frequently characterized the fifteenth century, to the effective monarchy of the Tudors, Henry VII and his successors made ever-increasing use of that prerogative power which English constitutional theory had always recognized in the Crown. Henry VII, said Nathaniel Bacon, "taught the people to dance more often and better to the tune of prerogative than all his predecessors had done."

The institution through which the expanded prerogative of the Tudors was exercised was the King's Council—the sixteenth-century derivative of that earlier body from which the three royal courts had evolved. It was the Council that, under the Tudors, exercised the authority needed to reform the medieval machinery of government and to create the new machinery needed by the emerging modern State.

Like its medieval predecessor—the Curia Regis—the Tudor Council was characterized by a concentration of the different governmental functions. Though primarily an executive and administrative body, the Council also possessed wide legislative and judicial powers. It was the Council that was responsible for drafting the royal proclamations by which the Tudor government sought to carry on the regulation of the life of the community that changing conditions had made necessary—proclamations that were vested with the full force of statute. This force was recognized even after the repeal of the Statute of Proclamations in the first year after Henry VIII's death. "When the common state or wealth of the people require it," it was said in the Star Chamber, "the king's proclamation bindes as a lawe."

Just as important as the executive and legislative authority of the Tudor Council was its judicial power. Indeed, its possession of the residual judicial authority of the Crown was what enabled the Council to serve as the principal tool for bringing order to a country ravaged by the pre-Tudor dynastic conflicts. In particular, it was the judicial role of the Council, exercised in the main through the Court of Star Chamber, that enabled the Crown to deal with the mass of disorder cases arising from the disturbed state of the country.

Hallam, near the beginning of his *Constitutional History,* goes so far as to assert that the submission of the country to the Tudor rulers is to be explained by what he terms "that illegal and arbitrary jurisdiction exercised by the council," which operated "to deprive the subject, in many criminal charges, of that sacred privilege, trial by his peers." According to Hallam, "the forced submission of our forefathers was chiefly owing to the terrors of a tribunal, which left them secure from no infliction but public executions, or actual dispossession of their freeholds."

To the present-day historian, Hallam's assertion of the Conciliar jurisdiction as the principal cause of Tudor power appears extreme. At the same time, it can scarcely be denied that, in the Star Chamber and the other prerogative courts that they employed, the Tudors had an unusually effective judicial instrument at their disposal.

The Star Chamber itself developed, much as the common-law courts had at an earlier date, as more or less a judicial committee of the Council, to which most of the judicial work of that body came to be delegated. As time went on, the Star Chamber gradually acquired the characteristics of a separate court of law, with the Chief Justices and other judges always present, its own staff of officials, and rules of pleading and procedure that were gradually being established. And, interestingly enough—though in our day the very term Star Chamber has come to be synonymous with a tribunal that condemns in secret, without hearing the accused—in actuality, the Star Chamber itself, like other courts, heard cases in public. In Bacon's phrase, "it is a supreme court of Judicature ordinary; it is an open council."

It used to be thought that the Court of Star Chamber was created by a famous statute of Henry VII, the Act of 1487—later misleadingly entitled *Pro Camera Stellata*. That statute recites that certain offenses had become very common, "to the increase of murders, robberies, perjuries, and unsureties of all men living, and losses of their lands and goods, to the great displeasure of Almighty God." It then empowered certain members of the Council to call specified types of offenders (those guilty of riots, unlawful assemblies, and the like) before them for examination, "and such as they find therein defective, to punish them after the form of their demerits, . . . in like manner and form as they should and ought to be punished, as if they were thereof convict after the due order of the law."

The Act of 1487 did not even mention the Star Chamber by name; but, for a long time past, a room bearing that name had been used for the judicial work of the Council. A century and a half later, when the Parliamentary opponents of the Stuarts sought to do away with the Star Chamber as an instrument of royal absolutism, they asserted that it had usurped powers beyond those conferred by the 1487 Act by which it had been created. The 1641 statute abolishing Star Chamber was based expressly upon this view, its preamble asserting that the judges of that tribunal "have not kept themselves to the points limited by the said statute."

The view that now prevails looks upon the 1487 Act as all but irrelevant to the actual history of Star Chamber. The jurisdiction of the Court of Star Chamber was but the derivative of the jurisdiction which the King's Council had exercised from an earlier time, and the tribunal itself was a judicial offshoot from the Council, to which the latter had delegated most of its judicial authority. The Act of 1487 set up a temporary committee of the Council to deal with certain offenses; but that did not affect the jurisdiction in other cases possessed by the Council and exercised by the Star Chamber.

Largely because of the way it was later misused as a tool of Stuart tyranny, the Star Chamber itself was to become an object of obloquy and its name the very definition of all that a judicial tribunal should not be. Yet the Star Chamber under the Tudors was far from the institution of abuse that it was to become under the succeeding dynasty.

On the contrary, to its contemporaries, the Star Chamber in the Tudor period was both a beneficent and necessary institution. It was the only tribunal in the land that could hope to deal with powerful offenders and prevent them from trampling upon the rights of both Crown and subjects. The purpose of Star Chamber, said Sir Thomas Smith, was "to bridle such noblemen or gentlemen who would offer wrong by force to any manner of men." According to Bacon, the Star Chamber was "one of the sagest and noblest institutions of this Kingdom." And, in this instance, Bacon's view was also that of his arch-rival Coke, for, in his *Institutes,* the latter said of Star Chamber, "It is the most honourable court . . . that is in the Christian world. . . . This court . . . doth keep all England quiet."

Yet, though we must acknowledge that the jurisdiction exercised by the Star Chamber was, in the main, a most beneficial one during Tudor times, we must also recognize that, even at that time, it contained within itself the seeds of the instrument of Stuart absolutism that it was later to become. It must not be forgotten that, from the Crown's point of view, perhaps the main purpose of the Star Chamber was to protect the public interest, rather than merely to serve as a dispenser of justice in the cases brought before it. As such, that tribunal was considered particularly bound to inquire into matters that might affect the safety of the realm. The Star Chamber, said William Hudson (whose classic treatise on that institution was written just before the Star Chamber began to be regarded as a tool of royal tyranny), was "the curious eye of the State and the King's Council prying into the inconveniences and mischiefs which abound in the Commonwealth."

As such, the Star Chamber was as much a political body as it was a judicial one. "By the arm of sovereignty," affirms Hudson, "it punisheth errors creeping into the Commonwealth, which otherwise might prove dangerous and infectious diseases, or it giveth life to the execution of laws, or the performance of such things as are necessary in the Commonwealth, yea, although no positive law or continued custom of common law giveth warrant to it."

To enable the Star Chamber to perform its role as a judicial watchdog of the State, it was permitted to develop its own procedure, which, where the case was deemed to demand it, might dispense with the vital procedural safeguards that had already become established in the ordinary courts. Star Chamber was based instead upon the inquisitorial methods of the Roman law; the common-law rules of evidence were disregarded and the accused was examined on his oath—in contrast to the common law, in which it was already recognized that no one might be compelled to accuse himself—from which our privilege against self-incrimination is derived.

Even worse was the fact that, since the basic principle governing Star Chamber was that it was an extraordinary tribunal whose main function was to preserve the safety of the State, it was governed by the rule stated by it in 1606: "Exorbitant offenses are not subject to an ordinary course of law." This meant that even torture might be used, and constantly was used, in cases that Coke termed *in causa criminis laesae Majestatis*. This led Selden to say in his *Table Talk* that, while torture was unknown in the courts, "they take a man and rack him I do not know why or when; not in time of judicature but when somebody bids."

A tribunal like Star Chamber—vested with extraordinary powers exercised for primarily political purposes—could easily be used for improper ends, as it was in fact used during the first part of the seventeenth century. As Maitland summed it up, "that [Star Chamber] was a tyrannical court, that it became more and more tyrannical, and under Charles I was guilty of great infamies is . . . indubitable. It was a court of politicians enforcing a policy, not a court of judges administering the law."

The Tudor monarchs, it can scarcely be doubted, had broad notions of their own prerogative and, acting through the Council and Star Chamber, they frequently exercised authority that was arbitrary in nature. Macaulay was, indeed, able to assert that "The government of Henry the Seventh, of his son, and of his grandchildren was, on the whole, more arbitrary than that of the Plantagenets." And the nation, as a whole, without question, acquiesced in the strong Executive that was thought necessary. If the prerogative seemed at times overweening, still it was recognized that it was that prerogative as wielded by the Tudors that had brought order and prosperity and, under Elizabeth I, preserved the very independence of the nation.

A casual observer might readily conclude that the Tudor monarchs were far more absolute than they actually were. Certainly until the latter part of Elizabeth's reign, one might well ask, with Hallam, "what had become of that English spirit which had not only controlled such injudicious princes as John and Richard II, but withstood the first and third Edward, in the fulness of their pride and glory." At the end of the Tudor period, Sir Walter Raleigh could say, in the Preface to his *History of the World,* that Philip II "attempted to make himself . . . an absolute monarch over the Netherlands, like unto the kings and sovereigns of England and France." And Shakespeare could write his *King John* without even mentioning the Magna Charta.

To one familiar with the reality of the Tudor polity, however, it is practically absurd to compare the English sovereign of the period to Philip II or Francis I or to find a parallel (as Hume did in a famous passage) between the Tudor government and that of the Grand Turk. In reality, the Tudor prince was far from an absolute monarch; his arbitrary acts were trifling compared to those of his Continental counterparts. And the government, even in the days of Henry VIII, was more a monarchy bounded by law than any other kingdom of the time.

That the reality of Tudor power was less absolute and oppressive than it may at first glance appear may be attributed to several factors. In the first place, there is the vital fact that, even during the heyday of the Tudor power, the constitutional forms of Parliamentary government, as they had developed to that time, continued to be observed. Thus, constitutional theory never swerved from the fundamental principle of Parliamentary supremacy—with the sovereign power vested in the king in Parliament, rather than in the monarch alone.

Even in an age characterized by the submissiveness of the realm to the Crown, men never forgot the basic constitutional truth. In 1566, the Speaker of the Commons, while addressing a queen noted for the jealousy with which she guarded her regality, could still say, "By our common law, although there be for the prince provided many princely prerogatives and royalties, yet it is not such as the prince can take money or other things, or do as he will at his own pleasure . . . , but quietly to suffer his subjects to enjoy their own, without wrongful oppression; wherein other princes by their liberty do take as pleaseth them."

It is important to recognize that the Tudor ability to establish a despotism comparable to that of Continental countries was limited by their lack of the engine through which such despotism is normally established—namely, military force. This was the vital point emphasized by Macaulay in the introductory pages of his *History of England:* "It was . . . impossible for the Tudors to carry oppression beyond a certain point; for they had no armed force, and they were surrounded by an armed people."

The lack of a standing army effectually prevented the Tudor polity from degenerating into a despotism. The Tudors might, to paraphrase Macaulay, safely be tyrants within the precincts of the court; but their authority really rested upon the support and consent of the people, who they well knew could not be pushed too far. When Henry VIII, without Parliamentary consent, sought an illegal contribution amounting to one-sixth of his subjects' goods, the people rose in arms, saying that if the king could do this "then were it worse than the taxes of France, and England should be bond, not free." That imperious monarch himself quickly yielded before an opposition that might otherwise speedily have ripened into a general rebellion.

Here, in fact, was the true basis of Tudor power: that it was exercised with the willing consent of the people, who recognized the necessity for strong government—first, to curb the lawlessness that was the rampant result of the previous lack of effective rule, and then to save the State from foreign aggression. Elizabeth spoke truly when, in her famous 1588 speech at Tilbury, on the approach of the Spanish Armada, she affirmed, "I have placed my chiefest strength and safeguard in the loyal hearts and goodwill of my subjects."

In many ways, indeed, the relationship between the greatest of Tudor monarchs and her subjects was, as Winston Churchill has termed it, one long flirtation. Certainly no other British sovereign has ever inspired greater devotion from those living under his rule. Both men living then and their descendants have concurred in thinking of the days of Elizabeth as a Golden Age. In Elizabeth's so-called Golden Speech to her last Parliament in 1603, she declared, "Though God hath raised me high, yet this I count the glory of my crown, that I have reigned with your loves."

The love and respect that all felt for the great queen were what made the people and their elected representatives willing to submit to the continued royal primacy, even after the danger of foreign invasion had passed. But the period of popular tutelage was almost at an end. The rule of the Tudors had brought unparalleled strength and prosperity to the nation. More than that, the age was one of adventure and discovery, when the English became aware of their island destiny and began to build the commercial and colonial empire that was soon to cover the globe. It was in Tudor days that, in G. M. Trevelyan's neat phrase, England ceased to be the anvil and became the hammer.

The Elizabethan age saw the growth of all but unbounded confidence and even exultation in the English nation. In 1589 Hakluyt could declaim, with pride, in the dedication to his *Voyages,* "Which of the Kings of this land before her Majesty, had their banners ever seen in the Caspian Sea? . . . What English ship did heretofore ever anchor in the mighty river of Plate? Pass and repass the unpassable . . . strait of Magellan, range along the coast of Chili, Peru and all the backside of Nova Hispania, further than any Christian ever passed . . . ?"

Men who had carried the English banner to the farthest corners of the globe, who had stood undaunted against the mightiest power of the day, who had brought unheard of wealth to their country and themselves, who had produced the towering masterpieces of the world's literature, men who, in a word, had made and were made by "The spacious times of great Elizabeth" —such men could not long be kept in political apprenticeship.

Already during the reign of Elizabeth herself the people's representatives had begun to chafe at the bit of the royal tutelage. As the reign went on, there came to be a growing opposition in the House of Commons, which claimed that Parliament could discuss freely any of the "griefs of the commonwealth." In particular, the Commons made constant efforts to discuss the question of the queen's marriage and that of the succession to the throne, despite express attempts by the Crown to prohibit such debates.

Then, in 1601, the opposition that had been gathering for a generation came to a head in the Parliamentary battle against monopolies. The queen had taken it upon herself to grant patents of monopoly over most important articles of ordinary commerce. In the House of Commons, an angry Member read out a list extending from iron manufacture to vinegar, starch, and glass. "Is not bread there?" exclaimed another Member. Scarcely a family in the realm did not deem itself aggrieved by the exorbitant prices that were the inevitable results of the royal grants. When the Commons took up the question in 1601, it was found impossible to suppress the debate. So strong was the popular feeling that Cecil, the chief minister of the Crown, himself told how his coach was surrounded, with exclamations of "God prosper those that further the overthrow of these monopolies, God send the prerogative touch not our liberty."

Elizabeth had the good sense to avoid the direct challenge to her prerogative, in which the Parliamentary opposition had behind it the unified sense of the nation. Instead she yielded gracefully, promising the Parliament "that some [monopolies] should be presently repealed, some suspended, and none put in execution, but such as should first have a tryal according to the law for the good of the people." Then, after having herself thus redressed the grievance, the queen, in Macaulay's words, "thanked the Commons, in touching and dignified language, for their tender care of the general weal, . . . and left to her successors a memorable example of the way in which it behooves a ruler to deal with public movements which he has not the means of resisting."

But the crucial point is that her successors did not at all have the great queen's ability of dealing with the forces of a growing nation. The achievements of the Tudors and the substance of royal power wielded by them had all been based upon the willing consent of their subjects. Neither the achievements nor the all but unquestioned authority could be continued by the alien dynasty to which the scepter descended. Ignorant of both the institutions and temper of the people they were called upon to reign over, the Stuart kings soon found themselves at odds with much of the nation. The result was that constitutional conflict which, more than anything else, has shaped the form of the modern British polity.

7

"THE COOK AND THE BACON"

WE HAVE NOW ARRIVED at that period of English history which was the most fruitful for the development of the English Constitution. This period—which S. B. Chrimes terms "the Heroic Age in English Constitutional History"—begins with the accession of James I in 1603 and ends with the expulsion of his grandson, James II, in 1688. It was during the Stuart reigns that the main outlines of the modern British system were definitely established, with the constitutional focus shifting irrevocably to the people's representatives in Parliament.

It was then, too, that the English met and mastered the doctrine of royal absolutism, newly established across the Channel and in much of the Continent, which was proclaimed by its proponents as the irresistible wave of the future. Thenceforth there was to be no doubt that the British polity was to be, in practice as well as theory, one of limited monarchy. The Stuart concept of government, which was to cost one king his life and another his throne, was rejected as heresy repugnant to the basic principles of the Constitution.

Of particular significance to the American observer, it was the principles established by the successful struggle against the Stuarts which Americans of the eighteenth century would rely upon in their resistance to the Britain of their day. When the colonists rallied round assertion of the "rights of Englishmen," they considered themselves the direct heirs of those Englishmen who had contended against the Stuart pretensions to absolute prerogative. In many ways, indeed, the men of the American Revolution were still Englishmen of the seventeenth century, continuing the traditions of the Long Parliament against the Charles I's of their day.

The death of Elizabeth I was recognized by all as the end of an era. With the establishment of the Stuart dynasty, there began a period of constitutional conflict such as had not theretofore been experienced in English history. Above all, the Stuart era was one of transition, during which changing circumstances constantly altered the constitutional balance, as now one side and then the other gained ascendance in the political structure.

"Upon Thursday," wrote Thomas Dekker of the day in 1603 when the last Tudor monarch died, "it was treason to cry God save king James of England, and upon Friday, high treason not to cry so." And the same was to be true of the end of rule by Stuart kings in 1688, when before the Glorious Revolution, it was treason to be against King James II and after that monarch's ouster it was treason to be for him.

When James I came to the throne, the English Constitution was a peculiar mixture of medieval and more modern elements. "We live in what virtually amounts to a museum," Prince Philip is reported to have told the British in 1964, "which does not happen to a lot of people." But it is something which has happened to the English during most of their history. Certainly it was no less true of Stuart times than it is of the present day. If anything, in fact, it was the survival and ultimately the dominance during the seventeenth century of medieval institutions and ideas that made the English constitutional development of the period so different from that of Continental countries.

Along with the medieval institutions of Parliament and the common law, which served as checks upon executive power, there existed the newer institutions, such as the Council and Star Chamber, which made for the strengthening of the authority of the Crown. Throughout western Europe, the sixteenth and seventeenth centuries saw a conflict between the more modern and medieval institutions and ideas. But, whereas on the Continent, by the end of the sixteenth century, the victory was with the former and the doctrine of absolute monarchy which they served, the same was not true in Britain. There, as Sir William Holdsworth tells us, the "new institutions . . . were at most supplementary to and co-ordinate with the older institutions, and with the mediaeval common law, which still remained, as in the Middle Ages, 'the highest inheritance of the king by which he and all his subjects are ruled.' "

In the England of the seventeenth century, it was precisely the medieval institutions of Parliament and the common law that proved to be the insurmountable obstacle to the ambition of the Stuart kings to establish an absolute monarchy upon the pattern of those on the Continent. The resistance of the Parliamentary leaders and the common lawyers made it impossible for the Stuarts to bring the government and law of England into line with the new theory of absolutism that had swept all before it across the Channel. "On the contrary," says Holdsworth, "the mediaeval institutions and ideas proved to be stronger than the modern, and, by the end of the century, they had mastered and assimilated them."

The conflict in England during the first part of the seventeenth century between the older and newer notions of law and government can perhaps best be illustrated through the conflicting careers of their two great protagonists: Edward Coke and Francis Bacon. Coke was the leading common lawyer of his day and through most of his life fought to ensure the supremacy of the law and the Parliament in the polity. It was, in fact, his career as a writer, judge, and leader of the Parliamentary opposition that, as much as anything, led to the ultimate victory of both institutions. Bacon, on the other hand, whose whole philosophy was based upon a break with ancient and medieval ideas, gravitated naturally to the royalist view and devoted his public career to increasing the prerogative of the Crown, as the instrument through which the newer concepts of governmental power could be realized.

Coke and Bacon not only stood for opposing conceptions of law and government, but were lifelong rivals in both their careers and personal lives—in the law courts, in Parliament, and even in competing for the hand of the same woman, Lady Elizabeth Hatton (whom Coke ultimately won, though the marriage turned out to be far from a happy one). The bitter competition between the two was something of which their contemporaries were well aware. When Coke and Bacon were both contending for the Attorney-Generalship (a post that Coke gained in 1594), a barrister of Gray's Inn, of which Bacon himself was a member, wrote, when an outcome favorable to Bacon seemed likely, "All is as well as words can make it, and if it please her Majesty to add deeds, *the Bacon* may be too hard for *the Cook*."

In the history of knowledge, of course, the name of Francis Bacon has always stood second to none. Yet, if we follow his own precept "not to intermingle matter of action with matter of general learning," we get a different picture. When we look to the less noble side of Bacon's intellect—to what he once called "the ambition of the will," as opposed to "ambition of the understanding"—the verdict of history becomes far less favorable. In fact, if we leave apart the Baconian contribution to natural science and learning, there is no doubt that history has awarded the palm to his lifelong rival and confirmed Bacon's own estimate early in life (which, alas, he himself was to violate more than observe)—that of "knowing myself by inward calling to be fitter to hold a book than to play a part."

At first glance, it seems paradoxical that the man who had made good his famous boast to Lord Burghley (made when he was only thirty-one) that "I have taken all knowledge to be my province," who, more than anyone else, personified the new ideas of the Renaissance and the Reformation, "the prophet" (in Catherine Drinker Bowen's phrase) "who urged men out of sterile scholasticism into the adventurous, experimental future," should take second place to one whose province was almost entirely limited to the common law, which, with all its great virtues, was essentially a crabbed, medieval system—the very archetype of the kind of learning, rooted in the past, that Bacon sought to supplant.

To the great philosophical innovator, the law and ancient institutions of England were not entitled to sacrosanct inviolability merely because of their existence from what men then deemed time immemorial. Tradition alone, to Bacon, was far from enough to give authority to established rule and doctrine. The very notion of precedent for precedent's sake—the cornerstone itself of the common law—was challenged when he wrote, "Examples which have lain as it were buried in desks and archives . . . deserve less authority."

To Coke, on the other hand, their antiquarian character was the great strength of English law and institutions. For him, the common law was the very culmination of human endeavor—"the perfection of reason," he termed it in a famous passage. "There is no jewel in the world," he also declared, comparable to "the common laws of England."

Some notion of Coke's devotion to "the gladsome light of jurisprudence" and the contrast between his worship of the common law and the newer attitude of children of the Renaissance like Bacon may be drawn from a striking passage in Maitland's Rede lecture: "Perhaps we should hardly believe if we were told for the first time that in the reign of James I a man who was the contemporary of Shakespeare and Bacon, a very able man too and a learned, who left his mark deep in English history, said, not by way of paradox but in sober earnest, said repeatedly and advisedly, that a certain thoroughly medieval book written in decadent colonial French was 'the most perfect and absolute work that ever was written in any human science.' Yet this was what Sir Edward Coke said of a small treatise written by Sir Thomas Littleton."

Coke was precisely the kind of legal scholar who delighted in the obscure language and technical minutiae of the medieval land law, as developed in Littleton's intricate and turgid prose. Littleton's book, which strikes the present-day reader as an egregious example of the dryness of legal immortality, well justifies John Adams' caustic comment that "It contains a vast mass of law learning, but heaped up in such an incoherent mass that I have derived very little benefit from it." But to Coke, the Littleton treatise was "as free from error as any book that I have known to be written of any human learning." For Coke, to read every word, and even the punctuation, in Littleton was to string pearls. "Certain it is," he says, "that there is never a period, nor . . . a word, nor an etc. but affordeth excellent matter of learning."

This, then, was the man whose work did so much to ensure the ultimate victory of both representative government and the common law in the English polity. And if it appears anomalous that one whose whole career was based on looking to the past— Coke's basic attitude had been stated in picturesque phrase: "Let us now peruse our ancient authors, for out of the old fields must come the new corne"—should have contributed more to constitutional progress than the very apostle of scientific and philosophical innovation, the paradox is more apparent than real. The transforming innovation of a Bacon may be appropriate in science and philosophy, but it is out of place in legal and constitutional development. As Justice Frankfurter once put it, "Transforming thought implies too great a break with the past, implies too much discontinuity, to be imposed upon society by one who is entrusted with enforcing its law."

Constitutional development can scarcely prove adequate if it is influenced unduly by mere philosophic speculation. Voltaire, in a famous passage, demanded the total destruction of all existing law: "Do you want good laws? Burn yours and make new ones." Men like Coke, themselves practitioners of the law, knew better. An attempt to write the fundamental law of a people on a *tabula rasa* may turn out favorably in Greek myth. In real life, the successful Constitution must be worked upon an existing political and historical mold. "Experience must be our only guide," John Dickinson once affirmed. "Reason may mislead us."

Even the reason of a Francis Bacon! As Catherine Drinker Bowen points out in her biography of Bacon, there were in the England of the time "two great streams of law, pointing toward two philosophies of government. By inclination or by rearing a man turned to one or the other." First, there was the common law, "which bore the Gothic signature" and exalted individual right and Parliamentary privilege even against the claims of governmental efficiency.

To the philosophical innovator, this backward-looking system lost sight of the prime need for effective government. He was a natural adherent of the newer political theory—which magnified the monarch and believed in strong central authority as the engine for achieving in the political sphere a remaking of the system comparable to that which his new philosophy was to accomplish in the scientific sphere. "No man can say," Bacon was rightly to declare, "but I am a perfect and peremptory royalist."

The personal failings of the Stuarts and the ultimate rejection of their theory of government make it difficult for us today to appreciate the view of those who, like Bacon, so strongly supported the side of absolute prerogative. To them, the real subject of dispute was whether a strong administration, of the type then recently established in countries like France, should be established in England. Their position was well stated by the Victorian constitutional lawyer A. V. Dicey: "Bacon and men like him no doubt underrated the risk that an increase in the power of the Crown should lead to the establishment of despotism. But advocates of the prerogative did not (it may be supposed) intend to sacrifice the liberties or invade the ordinary private rights of citizens; they were struck with the evils flowing from the conservative legalism of Coke, and with the necessity for enabling the Crown as head of the nation to cope with the selfishness of powerful individuals and classes." They wished, at all costs, to give the government the necessary power to accomplish this end.

To Bacon, the will of the sovereign was supreme—his basic doctrine was that the prerogative was beyond and above the ordinary law. His famous assertion that the judges, though they be "lions," yet should be "lions under the throne, being circumspect that they do not check or oppose any points of sovereignty," meant essentially that the judges should, in no circumstances, disturb the action of the administration. The result would have been to place every act alleged to be done in virtue of the prerogative above the law itself, regardless of the effect upon individual rights of property and person.

Bacon sought to accomplish the insulation of government from law by means of the writ *De non procedendo Rege inconsulto,* which prohibited the judges from proceeding with any case in which the interests of the Crown were concerned. "The writ," Bacon wrote to the king, "is a mean provided by the ancient law of England to bring any case that may concern your Majesty in profit or power from the ordinary Benches, to be tried and judged before the Chancellor of England, by the ordinary and legal part of this power. And your Majesty knoweth your Chancellor is ever a principal counsellor and instrument of monarchy, of immediate dependence on the king; and therefore like to be a safe and tender guardian of the regal rights."

It was on precisely the issue of the control of government by law that Coke differed so with Bacon. To Coke, Bracton's celebrated dictum that the king himself was under the law was the lodestar of the constitutional system. And he was willing to stake his entire judicial career upon adherence to this fundamental principle.

Coke's most dramatic assertion of the supremacy of law occurred, in memorable circumstances, on November 13, 1608.

For it was on that day that James I confronted "all the Judges of England and Barons of the Exchequer" with the claim that, since the judges were but his delegates, he could take any case he chose, remove it from the jurisdiction of the courts, and decide it in his royal person. The judges, as James saw it, were "his shadows and ministers . . . and the King may, if he please, sit and judge in Westminster Hall in any Court there and call their Judgments in question."

"To which it was answered by me," states Chief Justice Coke, "in the presence, and with the clear consent of all the Judges . . . that the King in his own person cannot adjudge any case . . . but that this ought to be determined and adjudged in some Court of Justice, according to the law and custom of England." To this, James made the shrewd reply "that he thought the law was founded upon reason, and that he and others had reason as well as the Judges."

Coke then delivered his justly celebrated answer, "that true it was, that God had endowed His Majesty with excellent science, and great endowments of nature; but His Majesty was not learned in the laws of his realm of England, and causes which concern the life, or inheritance, or goods, or fortunes of his subjects, are not to be decided by natural reason but by the artificial reason and judgment of law, which law is an act which requires long study and experience, before that a man can attain to the cognizance of it: that the law was the golden metwand and measure to try the causes of the subjects."

It is hardly surprising that the king was, in Coke's description, "greatly offended." "This means," said James, "that I shall be under the law, which it is treason to affirm." "To which," replied Coke, "I said, that Bracton saith, *quod Rex non debet esse sub homine, sed sub Deo et lege* [that the King should not be under man but under God and law]."

Needless to say, the king's anger only increased. According to one onlooker, in fact, "his Majestie fell into that high indignation as the like was never knowne in him, looking and speaking fiercely with bended fist, offering to strike him, etc." James's indignation was well justified. Coke's articulation of the supremacy of law was utterly inconsistent with Stuart pretensions to absolute authority. In the altercation between Coke and the king, indeed, there is personified the basic conflict between power and law that underlies all political history. Nor does it affect the importance of Coke's rejection of James's claim that, with the king's fist raised against him, Coke was led personally to humble himself. That he "fell flatt on all fower" to avoid being sent to the Tower does not alter the basic boldness of his clear assertion that the law was supreme even over the Crown.

Nor did Coke stop with affirming that even the king was not above the law. In *Dr. Bonham's Case* (1610)—perhaps the most famous case decided by him—Coke seized the occasion to declare that the law was above the Parliament as well as above the king. Dr. Bonham had practiced physic without a certificate from the Royal College of Physicians. The College Censors committed him to prison, and he sued for false imprisonment. The college set forth in defense its statute of incorporation, which authorized it to regulate all physicians and punish with fine and imprisonment practitioners not admitted by it. The statute in question, however, gave the college one half of all the fines imposed. This, said Coke, made the college not only judges, but also parties, in cases coming before them, and it is an established maxim of the common law that no man may be judge in his own cause.

But what of the statute, which appeared to give the college the power to judge Dr. Bonham? Coke's answer was that even the Parliament could not confer a power so contrary to common right and reason. In his words, "it appears in our books, that in many cases, the common law will controul Acts of Parliament, and sometimes adjudge them to be utterly void: for when an Act of Parliament is against common right and reason, or repugnant, or impossible to be performed, the common law will controul it, and adjudge such Act to be void."

Of course, as is well known by now, Coke in *Dr. Bonham's Case* was anticipating the American, rather than the British, constitutional system. It is, in fact, not too far fetched to say that the Coke assertion of judicial power to control the legality even of acts of Parliament was of basic importance in the development more than a century and a half later of American notions of government under a written constitution and judicial review.

Certain it is that to the men of the formative era of American constitutional law, the Coke dictum was of seminal significance. It was as the head of one of the king's courts that Coke stated as a rule of positive law that there was a fundamental law that limited Crown and Parliament indifferently. Had not my Lord Coke concluded that when an Act of Parliament is contrary to such fundamental law, it must be adjudged void? Did not this mean that when the people had reduced the principles of common right and reason to written form in a constitution, the courts were to adjudge any legislative acts contrary to its provisions to be void?

In seeking to subject all of government to law, Coke was moved by the same sentiments that were to motivate American constitution makers. As the legal historian T. F. T. Plucknett has explained the Coke position, "Urged by a presentiment of the coming conflict of Crown and Parliament, he felt the necessity of curbing the arrogance of both." The great common lawyer naturally gravitated toward a legal solution—in the notion of a fundamental law that limited equally both the executive and legislative departments.

Yet, as already intimated, the Coke concept of fundamental law was not destined to prevail in the English constitutional system. Though the dictum in *Bonham's Case* was ultimately to become accepted American doctrine, it gave way in England to the fundamental principle of Parliamentary supremacy—itself the principal legacy of the constitutional struggle against the Stuart kings.

Coke himself, in his later writings, came to see the need for Parliamentary supremacy as the practical means of saving the polity from the opposite extreme of unlimited prerogative. In his *Fourth Institute,* written near the end of his life, he was to declare that, "The power and jurisdiction of the parliament . . . is so transcendent and absolute, as it cannot be confined either for causes or persons within any bounds." But by that time, Coke had become a confirmed "Parliament man."

During the early part of his career, he had, paradoxically, been a zealous advocate of the royal authority. As Solicitor-General and then as Attorney-General (the chief law officers of the Crown), he had been a consistent supporter of the prerogative in the courts and Parliament. All this changed when, in 1606, James I elevated him to the position of Chief Justice of the Common Pleas. Thenceforth, both as a judge and later as a leader of the Parliamentary opposition, Coke stood firm at the head of those who resisted the Stuart attempts to substitute the supremacy of the Crown for the balanced Constitution that had been developing in the English system.

There is no doubt that Coke's attitude toward the royal power underwent a fundamental transformation when he was promoted from chief law officer of the Crown to chief of a common-law court. There certainly seems little in common between the over-zealous Attorney-General whose rancorous ferocity placed a permanent stain on the prosecution of Raleigh and the man who, as Chief Justice, fought for the supremacy of the law and, as Parliament leader, drafted and led the struggle to enact the Petition of Right. The extent of the virtual metamorphosis is indicated in James Spedding's celebrated aphorism about Coke—that the most offensive of Attorney-Generals had been transformed into the most admired and venerated of judges.

Coke's critics have noted with censure the basic inconsistency between his early and later careers—without a doubt, during the early part of his life, he attributed to the Crown arbitrary powers (such as that of indefinite imprisonment) which he was to deny in later years. Certain factors, however, help to explain this inconsistency. The first is the natural tendency of men—and particularly of a congenital advocate like Coke—to favor that point of view which also favors their own position. As an officer of the Crown, Coke could scarcely have been expected to do other than support the prerogative of his royal mistress. His position, then, was after all that of advocate—not judge—and partiality toward one side is usually not considered unseemly in that position.

Nor is it unwonted for one elevated to the bench to become a different sort of man as a judge than he appeared while only at the bar. If there is one thing Americans familiar with the history of judicial appointments, particularly to our highest Court, should recognize, it is how difficult it is to determine in advance how new judges will behave after they don the robe. Felix Frankfurter (himself a prime example of the point just made) once made this point as follows: "One of the things that laymen, even lawyers, do not always understand is indicated by the question you hear so often: 'Does a man become any different when he puts on a gown?' I say, 'If he is any good, he does.' "

Even more important is the fact that it was not necessarily the same thing to be a supporter of the prerogative as an officer of the great Tudor queen as it was as a judge under the first Stuart king. It is this fact, indeed, which makes the supposed inconsistency in Coke's career more apparent than real. The Tudors, with all their proclivity toward arrogation of personal power, were constantly careful to preserve the forms of a balanced Constitution. A partisan of the rights of Englishmen could in Tudor times be a zealous servant of the Crown without violating his fundamental beliefs. The same was no longer true with the accession of an alien dynasty, which neither understood nor professed to adhere to the basic constitutional limitations that Englishmen had come to hold dear. Before he was called to the English throne, James I had reigned for over three decades in a country that had few developed constitutional checks. Parliament, James had remarked, was something he found when he came to England and was obliged to put up with.

The crowning principle of Stuart statecraft was that of the divine right of kings, with its complement that of unlimited prerogative. And this was expressed openly, in a manner that no Englishman could misunderstand. "The state of monarchy," declared James I, in a characteristic passage, "is the supremest thing upon earth. . . . if you will consider the attributes to God, you shall see how they agree in the person of a King. God hath power to create or destroy, make or unmake at his pleasure, to give life or send death, to judge all and to be judged nor accountable to none. Kings make and unmake their subjects; they have power of raising and casting down; of life and of death . . . and make of their subjects like men at the chess; a pawn to take a Bishop or a Knight, and to cry up or down any of their subjects as they do their money."

In the face of such extreme assertion of royal authority— unparalleled in England since the time of Richard II—it is scarcely surprising that men like Coke revised their attitude toward the Crown. Thenceforth, Coke was to transfer to the common law and the Parliament that supremacy which he had ascribed to the Crown when he had been Elizabeth's Attorney-General. Yet, as Holdsworth points out, it was not so much Coke who thus changed in his views: "he stood still. His outlook was always that of a statesman of the latter part of the Tudor period. It was the changing political scene which seemed to place him in constantly fresh positions, and necessarily led him to modify his views as to important doctrines of constitutional law."

Whatever the reasons, it is clear that, just as five centuries earlier the high-living courtier Thomas Becket was transformed into a zealous churchman on becoming Primate, so Edward Coke, till his judicial appointment the avowed official exponent of prerogative, proclaimed an entirely different doctrine after he was elevated to the bench at Westminster. For the rest of his life, Coke lost no opportunity to declare and decide against the prerogative.

In 1606 Coke became Chief Justice of the Common Pleas, and from the central chair of the ancient common-law tribunal, he delivered his affirmations already noted of the supremacy of the law. In other cases, too, he took the occasion to attack the royal prerogative—particularly in the *Case of Proclamations* (1611), limiting the power of the king to legislate without statutory authority, and another decision in the same year restricting the power of the prerogative courts.

Not unnaturally, Coke's pronouncements were viewed with alarm by the adherents of the Crown. Yet, however much he might offend the government, Coke was not a man to be dealt with lightly, for his views certainly represented the increasing popular feeling against the consistent Stuart attempts to expand the prerogative. According to a contemporary writer, indeed, if Coke were to be removed, "he will be honoured as the martyr of the commonwealth." Accordingly, in line with Bacon's advice, in 1613, Coke was removed from the Common Pleas and made Chief Justice of the King's Bench. The hope was that, in Maitland's phrase, "in a more exalted position he would prove more pliant." The hope was to prove vain, for, as Lord Chief Justice, Coke, if anything, intensified his struggle against the prerogative. In *Peacham's Case* (1615), he objected to the judges being asked *ex parte* by the Crown for their opinions as to a matter that was to come before them judicially. Then came Coke's celebrated controversy with the Court of Chancery—which was ultimately resolved by the king himself in Chancery's favor.

The climax came with the *Case of the Commendams* (1616). Coke and his fellow judges received the royal order not to proceed with the hearing of an action in which the king's prerogative was questioned. They answered in a letter that they considered that order (given by Bacon as Attorney-General) "to be contrary to law, and such as we could not yield to the same by our oath." At this, the king sent for the judges personally and all of them but Coke humbled themselves on their knees and promised, in all such cases, to do as the king desired. Coke alone refused to promise that he would obey the royal command in any such case that came before him. Instead, "only the Lord Chief Justice of the King's Bench said for answer, That when the case should be, he would do that should be fit for a judge to do."

Coke's answer—stating in eloquent dignity the immovable duty of the holder of judicial office—still thrills members of the legal profession centuries after it was given. Nor can we overstate the simple courage required to stand for the right, in open defiance of the king himself, in an age when all preferment, and even liberty and property itself, were dependent upon the royal favor.

The very qualities in Coke's conduct that make us admire his actions gave proof to the Crown that he must be humbled, if not broken. Coke was summoned before the Council to defend his conduct and directed to correct the points of impudence and defiance in the eleven volumes of his *Reports*. After a summer's reflection, Coke returned his volumes with a single sheet on which he listed only five trivial mistakes. At this Bacon wrote to the king that "Your Majesty may perceive that my Lord [i.e., Coke] is an happy man, that there should be no more errors in his five hundred cases than in a few cases of Plowden."

Both Coke and the Crown well knew that the offending passages in the *Reports* lay, not in errors of fact or law, but in essential differences of viewpoint—in *Bonham's Case, Peacham's Case* and the other cases restricting the prerogative. These differences could only be resolved by Coke's dismissal from office. The days of judicial security of tenure were still almost a century off, and the king could discharge at pleasure a judge like Coke who refused to be the judicial mirror of the royalist theory of public law.

On November 14, 1616, Coke was discharged from his position as Chief Justice of King's Bench. "The common speech," said an oft-quoted letter written the same day, "is that four Ps have overthrown and put him down—that is Pride, Prohibitions, Praemunire, and Prerogative." The truth, however, is that Coke was overthrown directly because of his consistent judicial efforts to frustrate the royal attempts to place the power of the Crown above the law. James and his advisers were too conscious of the fundamental difference between their own and Coke's views on the relations between law and prerogative to allow him to continue in the highest judicial office. Said Lord Chancellor Ellesmere, at the swearing in of Coke's successor, "Remember . . . the removing and putting down of your late predecessor, and by whom: the great King of Great Britain." For he had sought to "oppose himself against the King that placed him here. . . . [and] dispute the King's prerogative writ when it came to him."

What is of particular interest is that it is the technical expert in the common law—the lawyer's lawyer who delighted in medieval minutiae—who played the leading role in the early opposition to the Stuart attempts at absolute government. In other times, Coke would have been at most an eminent jurist whose whole career would have been devoted to fighting changes in the law. As Samuel R. Gardiner puts it in his monumental *History of England,* "Two hundred years later his name would have gone down to posterity, with Eldon's, as that of a bigoted adversary of all reform. As it was, his lot was cast in an age in which the defence of the technicalities of the law was almost equivalent to a defence of the law itself."

In seventeenth-century England, as in eighteenth-century America, a common lawyer was necessarily involved in politics. In many ways, in truth, the great political struggle that dominated English history from the accession of James I to the expulsion of his grandson eighty-five years later was ultimately a legal struggle over different interpretations of the English Constitution. At such a time, a jurist like Coke, who was both learned in the common law and passionately convinced of its excellence, was all but compelled to take part in politics in order to defend the law and the Constitution from being overthrown by the newer theory of absolute prerogative.

To his contemporaries, Coke, as a discharged Chief Justice at the age of sixty-five, appeared to be at the virtual end of his public career. "A thunderbolt hath fallen on the Lord Coke," reads a letter written five days after Coke's dismissal, "which hath overthrown him from the very roots." What neither Coke nor his contemporaries could know at the time was that the third, and in some ways the most admirable, part of his career—that as Parliament man—still lay ahead. Soon after Coke's fall, his arch-rival Bacon (who had, more than anyone, persuaded the king to remove Coke) was named Lord Chancellor. Yet, even in the realm of personal controversy, the final victory would be with the great common lawyer. It was Coke who was to be a leader of the House of Commons that, in 1621, impeached the Lord Chancellor for bribery and corruption—a proceeding that placed an indelible stain upon Bacon's reputation and led to Pope's famous characterization of him as "the wisest, brightest, meanest of mankind."

The last part of Coke's public career was spent in the Parliament, where he gravitated naturally toward the growing opposition to the Crown. His reputation, learning, and passionate belief in the common law and a balanced Constitution—weighted with age and prestige, he was termed that great *"Monarcha Juris"* by no less a Parliament man than John Selden—all combined to give him an influence second to none among the people's representatives. Coke's reappearance in public life as a Parliamentary leader was a natural development in one who had so conspicuously refused to accede to the Stuart theory of government. For the struggle against that theory was to shift, with Coke's removal from the bench, from the law courts to the Parliament. Thenceforth, the opposition to the concept of absolute prerogative was to be centered almost entirely in the House of Commons, which was ultimately forced to lead the nation in arms to vindicate the principle that even the Crown was subject to law.

In retrospect, it may be said that Coke's emergence as a Parliament man was of primary significance in canalizing the conflict with the Crown along legal lines. It was, in fact, the union of the common lawyers of the day with the Parliamentary leaders that made possible the successful resistance to the Stuart claims. This was true in more than a mere material sense. Without the support of the lawyers, the Parliament would have appeared only as revolutionaries seeking to tear down the established order. Instead, Coke and his confreres in the common law were able to enlist for the opposition that almost superstitious reverence which Englishmen felt for their law and to give to their struggle that note of legal conservatism that was at once its distinguishing characteristic and the cause of its successful issue. "Learned in the law . . . ," Winston Churchill tells us, "they gradually built up a case on which Parliament could claim with conviction that it was fighting, not for something new, but for the traditional and lawful heritage of the English people."

As has already been indicated, James I had a natural attitude of hostility toward the Parliamentary establishment. "I am surprised," he once asserted, "that my ancestors should have permitted such an institution to come into existence. I am a stranger, and found it here when I arrived, so that I am obliged to put up with what I cannot get rid of." As far as James and his advisers were concerned, the Parliament was, without a doubt, an institution with which the country could well dispense. During his reign, James summoned only four Parliaments, and his experience with them proved far from satisfactory. "I have piped unto you," he said to one such assembly, "but you have not danced, I have often mourned but you have not lamented." From 1614 to 1621, the Crown governed without any Parliament.

By 1621, however, want of money made the king convoke his Parliament again; James had not received a subsidy in ten years —"a very long time to live like a shellfish upon his own moisture." The financial problem, which had all but disappeared under the Tudors, became acute again in the face of Stuart extravagance, aggravated by ever-increasing inflation, caused by the decline in the value of the precious metals that was the immediate consequence of the discovery of the New World.

The Parliament of 1621 was called to relieve the financial necessities of the Crown. No sooner had it met, however, than the Commons proceeded to discuss the public grievances. And, in order to ensure that their discussion would have more than academic effect, they proceeded to revive the weapon of impeachment, which (we saw in Chapter 5) had first been used by the Good Parliament of 1376 but had fallen into disuse before Tudor times.

In the Parliament of 1621—the first in which he sat since before his elevation to the bench—Coke found himself, as his biographer, Catherine Drinker Bowen, tells us, "in a position of extraordinary prestige. *Pater patriae,* father of his country, Parliament called him." As chairman of the Committee of Grievances in the Commons, Coke played a leading role in the revival of the impeachment procedure. The supporters of the Crown urged that only a court could exercise the power to judge and punish, to which Coke replied that Parliament was, indeed, a true judicial body, vested with all the authority of a court of record. "He that questions whether this House is a Court of Record," Coke declaimed, "I would his tongue might cleave to the roof of his mouth."

In this respect, it should be noted, the British Parliament has differed from American legislatures. The "High Court of Parliament"—Coke termed it—has always possessed residual judicial as well as legislative powers, and the highest English court, the House of Lords, is, in form, still only part of the upper Parliamentary Chamber. In addition, it has meant that Parliament has had an unreviewable contempt power—which the United States Supreme Court has consistently denied to our Congress.

The impeachment weapon was first employed against the holders of royal monopolies, particularly Sir Giles Mompesson, who was especially hated by the people. Other impeachments followed, notably that of Chancellor Bacon for receiving bribes from suitors in his court. Coke, as one of the managers for the Commons, took a leading role in the proceeding against his old rival. Significantly, it was Coke who objected strenuously when the king sought to transfer the affair from the Commons to a special commission named by him. Coke insisted that such a matter was the proper concern of Parliament alone, saying, "Let us take heed the King's Commission do not hinder our Parliamentary proceedings."

During the Parliament of 1621, too, Coke was vigilant in matters relating to Parliamentary privilege. In his opening-day address as Speaker in Elizabeth's 1593 Parliament, Coke had recited the three traditional privileges of the Commons: freedom of speech, freedom from arrest, and access to the sovereign. These privileges were, by established custom, granted by the Crown at the beginning of each session. James had, nevertheless, indicated that the Houses were not to "presume . . . to meddle with anything concerning our government or deep matters of state." James had made this statement in reply to a petition of the Commons, which Coke had initiated, calling attention to the alarming spread of Popery and expressing the hope of a Protestant marriage for the Prince of Wales.

James's resentment only led to a second petition, similar to the first in terms. Again the king replied that the matters mentioned were no fit subject for Parliaments to consider. As far as the privileges of the Commons were concerned, asserted James, "your privileges were derived from the grace and permission of our ancestors and us, for most of them grow from precedents which show rather a toleration than inheritance." At this, Coke delivered an impassioned address, which may serve as the fundamental statement of principle upon which representative assemblies are based: "The privileges of this House is the nurse and life of all our laws, the subject's best inheritance. . . . When the King says he cannot allow our liberties of right, this strikes at the root. We serve here for thousands and ten thousands."

The Parliamentary institution had thus progressed to the point where it was ready to assert its status as a coordinate department of government. As the representative of "thousands and ten thousands," the Commons could scarcely remain silent in the face of the royal rebuke. Instead, Coke suggested, "Let us make a *Protestation,* enter it in the Journals and present the Journals to the King—but not as requiring an answer."

By candlelight, with Coke's guidance, the Commons drafted their famous Protestation, which was no petition but an unequivocal declaration, "That the liberties, franchises, privileges and jurisdictions of Parliament are the ancient and undoubted birthright and inheritance of the subjects of England; and that the arduous and urgent affairs concerning the King, state and defence of the realm, and of the Church of England, and the maintenance and making of laws and redress of mischiefs and grievances which daily happen within this realm, are proper subjects and matter of counsel and debate in Parliament." In addition, there is a categorical assertion of the privileges of Parliament, particularly that of freedom of speech.

In his *History of the English Parliament,* G. Barnett Smith calls the 1621 Protestation "one of the landmarks in our constitutional history." Certainly, the king himself well realized what the Commons action portended. Sitting in Council Chamber, James sent for the *Commons Journals* and, in the presence of the Lords and judges, tore out the page upon which the Protestation appeared. And Coke and two other Commons leaders were sent to the Tower—Coke to remain there for nearly seven months in close confinement, which was the penalty customary for traitors and murderers.

The Parliament of 1621 marked the end of the first stage in the conflict between Crown and Parliament that dominated the seventeenth century. Clearly delineated were the antagonistic positions of the king and the people's representatives. Those of perception might well foresee that those positions were basically irreconcilable. The Stuart and Parliamentary views of the polity were competing, not complementary. They were so conflicting in their essentials that one could scarcely seek to partition the field between them. In the end, instead, one or the other would have to take over the field and thus resolve the ultimate location of the sovereign power in the British Constitution.

For Edward Coke, the battle for law and Parliament was almost over. Yet, aged though he was—his seventieth birthday came while he was close confined in the Tower—and wearied by his efforts in the public interest, Coke still had one great service to perform that is of particular interest to Americans. His last contribution is a fitting culmination to our discussion of perhaps the greatest of common lawyers.

Coke's last Parliament, that of 1628, had been called by Charles I, who had acceded to the throne on his father's death in 1625. According to Holdsworth, Coke's "labours in that parliament were destined to be a fitting conclusion to his career. They were to result in adding to the statute book the first of those great constitutional documents since Magna Carta, which safeguard the liberties of the people by securing the supremacy of the law."

Much had happened (as we shall see in the next chapter) during the reign of the new king. Under Charles, in fact, the Stuart theory of prerogative was quickly pushed to its ultimate extreme. By 1628, Englishmen had suffered the most serious attacks upon their personal liberties. In the two years that had intervened since the dissolution of the previous Parliament, a forced loan had been demanded, men who refused to pay had been punished, and judges who refused to enforce it had been dismissed. Soldiers had been billeted on the people and men committed to prison by the mere command of the king, with bail refused. Well might Coke plaintively ask the 1628 session, "Shall I be made a tenant-at-will for my liberties, having property in my own house, but not liberty in my person?"

The members of the 1628 Commons were confronted with the basic question of what they should do about the situation. Coke it was who rose to declare that it was the law of the realm that counted, not mere gracious promises from the throne. "Messages of love," he claimed, "never came into a Parliament. Let us put up a Petition of Right! Not that I distrust the King; but that I cannot take his trust but in a Parliamentary way." The result was the landmark Petition of Right—enacted as a law—which declared the fundamental rights of Englishmen.

The details of the Petition of Right will be discussed in the following chapter. Suffice it to say here that its enactment crowned the career of Edward Coke. The Petition declared the fundamental rights of Englishmen as positive law, in language that could admit of but one interpretation. Nor was the declaration weakened by any ambiguous saving of prerogative right. The Lords had proposed an amendment that provided that the Petition "leave intire the Sovereign Power, wherewith your Majesty is trusted for the Protection, safety, and happiness of the People." But Coke and the Parliamentary leaders well saw that the Lords' amendment would virtually nullify their Petition. "To speak plainly," said Coke, "it will overthrow all our Petition. . . . And shall we now add it, we shall weaken the foundation of law, and then the building must needs fall; let us take heed what we yield unto; Magna Charta is such a fellow, that he will have no sovereign. I wonder this sovereign was not in Magna Carta . . . : If we grant this by implication we give a sovereign power above all these laws."

A fitting valedictory for a public career that had been so devoted to the ideal that the law must be supreme! Small wonder then that, over a century later, men on the western side of the Atlantic who also sought to vindicate the rights of Englishmen would follow Coke, both in theory and practice. Again and again, the colonists, from James Otis to the culminating controversy over the Stamp Act, would rely upon the authority of my Lord Coke to demonstrate the invalidity of acts of the mother country that restricted their rights.

And, then, when the conflict over the Stamp Act increased in intensity, the colonists followed Coke's example in the 1628 Parliament. They, too, acted through a measure declaring the rights of Englishmen, as they were conceived to apply in the American Colonies. The 1765 Declaration of Rights and Grievances passed by the Stamp Act Congress was the natural response of men familiar with the constitutional history of Stuart England. As such, it was the direct descendant of the Coke-inspired Petition of Right.

8

FIVE KNIGHTS, SIX MEMBERS, AND JOHN HAMPDEN

In September of 1634, the Lord Coke lay dying at Stoke House, his estate in the southeast of England. "Upon his death-bed," we are told by Roger Coke, his grandson, "Sir F. Windebank . . . by an order of Council came to search for seditious and dangerous papers." The king's men came and took away the manuscripts of the expiring jurist's principal writings and retained them by express order of the king. Alarmed by rumor that Coke was going to publish a book that he suspected might be "somewhat to the prejudice of the prerogative," King Charles directed that the jurist's papers be taken, "as use may be made of them . . . for his Majesty's service, and some suppressed that may dis-serve him. For he is held too great an oracle amongst the people, and they may be misled by any thing that carries such an authority as all things do that he either speaks or writes."

"The fears of Charles," Sir William Holdsworth pungently puts it, "are the best evidence of Coke's reputation." Nor were the king's anxieties about Coke's writings unjustified. In 1641, the seized papers were, upon motion of the House of Commons, delivered to Coke's son and published during the next few years by order of the House. The Long Parliament acted with regard to Coke's manuscripts, "as supposing [they] contain many monuments of the subject's liberties." They were not mistaken in this respect. In particular, his *Second Institute,* which contained a detailed commentary upon Magna Charta and the rights and liberties derived from it, and his *Fourth Institute,* on the jurisdiction of courts, which maintained the supremacy of the common law over the prerogative courts, contained a scathing indictment by the most revered and learned of legal writers of the flagrant violations of the rights of Englishmen, which had increasingly characterized the reign of the second Stuart king.

It can scarcely be doubted that Charles I had pushed the theory of kingship articulated by his father to its logical extreme. His father (we saw in the previous chapter) had enunciated a notion of absolute royal power that was most extravagant in its language. But James I was scarcely the monarch to make more than sporadic efforts to translate that concept into practical reality. His son, on the other hand, not only firmly believed in the theory of divine right, but had the resoluteness of character to devote his whole reign to a never-ceasing effort to put it into effect. Charles, says Macaulay, "had inherited his father's political theories, and was much more disposed than his father to carry them into practice."

From the beginning of his reign, the basic policy of Charles I was to do everything needed to make the Stuart doctrine of absolute prerogative an established part of the English Constitution. To bring about this result, it was essential to disregard—and ultimately to do away with—the fundamental checks upon the royal authority that had thus far developed in the English system. At the beginning of Chapter 3, we quoted Henry Hallam's summary of the two essential checks that had come to circumscribe the power of the Crown by the time of Henry VII. These were the requirement of Parliamentary consent before any new tax could be levied and the requirement of an enactment by Parliament before there could be any new law. It was precisely these limitations upon the Crown authority in the Parliamentary power to tax and to legislate which the second Stuart king found utterly incompatible with his conception of royal power. The one consistent policy of his reign was to do what he could to free himself and his successors from them.

But Charles I did not stop at seeking to eliminate those Parliamentary controls over the purse and the law which are the hallmarks of limited government. He also tried to brush aside the vital safeguards that English law had evolved to secure the liberty of the person itself. As stated by Hallam, "No man could be committed to prison but by a legal warrant specifying his offence; and . . . he must be speedily brought to trial by means of regular sessions of gaol-delivery." The Great Writ of habeas corpus was the effective remedy that the law had developed to ensure that this fundamental principle would not be violated.

The king's need for money was once again the immediate cause of the constitutional conflict. The two brief Parliaments that had sat since Charles's accession had doled out supplies to him most sparingly. The king then resorted to other methods. "To which end," we are told in the report in *Howell's State Trials,* "letters were sent to the Lords Lieutenants of the counties, to return the names of the persons of ability, and what sums they could spare." Those named were assessed amounts ranging from £10 to £20, which they were to contribute to the Crown as a "loan." Commissioners and Lords of the Council were sent to the different counties to arrange the collection of the "loan."

Charles's forced-loan device gave rise to a storm of protest. "On Monday," according to a contemporary letter, "the judges sat in Westminster Hall to persuade the people to pay subsidies; but there arose a great tumultuous shout amongst them: 'A parliament! a parliament! else no subsidies!' " Similar protests were heard from other counties, where "divers persons refused to subscribe or lend at the rate proposed." Those who refused to pay were examined before the Council and, if they persisted, committed to prison. "Many are imprisoned daily," wrote one commentator in March, 1627, "for refusing to lend the king, . . . in divers gaols in the country, remote from their own dwelling."

Five among those who were so imprisoned for refusing to contribute sought to challenge the king's legal authority in the matter. They sought their release by suing out their writs of habeas corpus in the Court of King's Bench. This was done by a writ "directed to the Warden of the Fleet, to shew that court the cause of his imprisonment, that thereupon they might determine whether his restraint were legal or illegal."

In actual fact, as we have seen, the cause of imprisonment in the *Five Knights' Case* was the refusal to contribute to the loan to the king. But it was scarcely to be expected that the Crown would state this cause in the Warden's return, since the right of the king to exact forced loans was not legally defensible. If there was one thing that was settled by the time of the Stuarts, it was that no tax could be legally imposed without Parliamentary authority. Though there had been violations of this principle under the Tudors (particularly Henry VIII), they had not gone so far as to use the benevolence device as a generally imposed substitute for the taxing power of Parliament.

There is no doubt that the contributions exacted by Charles were loans only in a euphemistic sense. To quote Hallam again, "This arbitrary taxation (for the name of loan could not disguise the extreme improbability that the money would be repaid), so general and systematic as well as so weighty, could not be endured without establishing a precedent that must have shortly put an end to the existence of parliaments." Even the Stuart judges could hardly do other than hold the forced-loan procedure illegal, if the question was squarely put before them by the habeas corpus return.

But the return of the Warden in the *Five Knights' Case* did not contain the true reason for the imprisonment. Instead, it sought to justify the imprisonment by stating only that each of the gentlemen detained "was and is committed by the special command of his majesty (*per speciale mandatum regis*)." The focus of the case thus shifted from that of the power of the king to exact a loan to that of the power of the king to imprison without assigning a cause. If anything, the change magnified the significance of the *Five Knights' Case*. For it transformed the crucial issue involved from one of the discretionary power of the king over the pockets of his subjects to that of his discretionary power over their persons.

On November 22, 1627, the five knights themselves were brought to the bar and their case argued at length by some of the most able lawyers of the day. Both sides saw clearly the vital nature of the underlying issue—more important, indeed, than even the question of the royal authority to exact a loan which had originally given rise to the case.

The crux of the case was the arbitrary power claimed by the Crown to imprison whom it chose, for any reason it chose, and for as long as it chose. "If this return shall be good," counsel for one of the knights declared, "then his imprisonment shall not continue on for a time, but for ever; and the subjects of this kingdom may be restrained of their liberties perpetually." On the other side, Heath, the Attorney-General, frankly relied upon the doctrine of absolute prerogative—what he termed "that *absoluta potestas* that a sovereign hath, by which a king commands." His basic argument rested on the claim that where the king himself ordered an act—such as the imprisonment of petitioners—no court could go behind the bare fact of the royal order: "who shall call in question the actions or the justice of the king, who is not to give any account for them? as in this our case, that he commits a subject, and shews no cause for it."

In the Attorney-General's argument was the core of the constitutional controversy that was ultimately to be resolved only by the force of arms. "Shall any say," he asked in another portion of his argument, "The king cannot do this? No, we may only say, He will not do this." It was precisely to ensure that their descendants would be able to say, "The State *cannot* do this," that the men of seventeenth-century England struggled so strenuously against the Stuart pretensions to absolute power.

Yet the judges in the *Five Knights' Case* ruled unanimously in favor of the Crown, and the petitioners were remanded to custody. According to the court, "if a man be committed by the commandment of the king, he is not to be delivered by a Habeas Corpus in this court, for we know not the cause of the commitment." Under the decision, any writ of habeas corpus could be rendered ineffective by the Crown by the simple statement that the individual concerned was being detained by special command of the king.

Though there was some support in Tudor precedents for the *Five Knights'* decision, it was condemned by the Parliamentary opposition and most of the lawyers—as well as by the strongest popular sentiment. For it was all too clear what the decision meant in practice. In an oft-quoted passage, Hallam has asserted that "it was evidently the consequence of this decision, that every statute from the time of Magna Charta, designed to protect the personal liberties of Englishmen, became a dead letter; since the insertion of four words in a warrant (per speciale mandatum regis), which might become matter of form, would control their remedial efficacy. And this wound was the more deadly, in that the notorious cause of these gentlemen's imprisonment was their withstanding an illegal exaction of money. Every thing that distinguished our constitutional laws, all that rendered the name of England valuable, was at stake in this issue."

Hallam was not exaggerating the consequence of the *Five Knights' Case*. When Parliament met a few months later one of its members cried, "This is the crisis of parliaments; we shall know by this if parliaments live or die. . . . Men and brethren, what shall we do? Is there no balm in Gilead?"

The popular feeling against the *Five Knights' Case* was a primary factor in the Parliamentary movement to enact the Petition of Right. In the Parliament of 1628, Coke pointed out clearly just what the *Five Knights'* decision meant to the nation. "This draught of the judgment," he proclaimed, "will sting us. . . . What is this but to declare upon record, that any subject committed by such an absolute command may be detained in prison for ever? What doth this tend to but the utter subversion of the choice, liberty, and right belonging to every free-born subject in this kingdom." Then, summing up in a phrase that illumined for all the impact of the *Five Knights'* judgment, the venerable jurist affirmed that its effect was to "make men tenants at will of their liberties."

One of the primary purposes of the Petition of Right, which Coke induced the Parliament of 1628 to enact, was to reverse the decision of the judges in the *Five Knights' Case*. The great wrongs confirmed by the King's Bench were to be the main themes of the Parliamentary leaders; their principal aim to redress the balance against the asserted royal authority to imprison arbitrarily and exact forced loans. The abuses upheld in the *Five Knights' Case* may thus be said to form the very foundation of the Petition of Right.

The Petition of Right itself starts by seeking to "Humbly shew unto our sovereign lord the king" the various laws that have established the essential liberties of the subject—notably with regard to freedom from illegal exactions and arbitrary imprisonments. It goes on to enumerate violations of such liberties in the forced-loan procedure and imprisonments "without any cause shewed." In conclusion, the Petition prays the king, "That no man hereafter be compelled to make or yield any gift, loan, benevolence, tax, or such like charge, without common consent by act of parliament; . . . and that no freeman in any such manner as is before mentioned, be imprisoned or detained."

When the king finally gave the royal assent to the Petition of Right in the traditional form—he had tried in vain to put the Commons off with a different form of assent—members broke into loud acclamations as soon as the clerk pronounced the ancient formula, *"Soit droit fait comme il est desiré."* According to the *Parliamentary Journal,* "when these words were spoken, the commons gave a great and joyful applause, and his majesty rose and departed." The whole nation echoed their representatives' joy.

The Parliamentary celebration was, however, premature. The Petition of Right—even though it doubtless deserved to be a landmark in constitutional history—was itself only a declaratory document. It did not provide for any enforcement machinery or, as it turned out, really alter the constitutional balance between Crown and Parliament.

Before giving his assent, King Charles himself had questioned the judges on whether the Petition would, indeed, "exclude himself from committing or restraining a subject for any time or cause whatsoever without showing a cause." The judges answered that, "although the petition be granted, there is no fear of conclusion as is intimated in the question."

Armed with this judicial advice, the king proceeded to act as though the Petition of Right had never been added to the statute book. It is plain, says Macaulay, that during the next decade of Charles's reign, "the provisions of the Petition of Right were violated by him, not occasionally, but constantly, and on system; that a large part of the revenue was raised without any legal authority; and that persons obnoxious to the government languished for years in prison without ever being called upon to plead before any tribunal." And the judges, in their decisions on the bench, proceeded to give official confirmation to the advisory opinion they had given Charles intimating that the Petition of Right was a mere declaration of policy, not binding as a practical restriction upon the royal prerogative. This judicial confirmation came, first of all, in the 1629 *Six Members' Case.*

That case arose out of the tumultuous events attending the dissolution of Parliament in 1629. The previous session had declined to grant the king the right to collect the traditional customs tax known as tunnage and poundage. The king had nevertheless continued to collect the tax through his officers, with imprisonment being imposed upon those who refused to pay. "In all this," Winston Churchill tells us, "was seen the King's contempt for the Petition of Right, and his intention to escape from the assent he had given to it."

When the Parliament convened, the Commons prepared to remonstrate against the Crown's illegal acts. The king sought to prevent action by adjournments of the House. When the king tried this a second time, and the Speaker, when asked to put the question, announced, "I have a command from the King to adjourn . . . and put no question," the Commons refused to yield. Instead, the Speaker, "endeavouring to go out of the Chair, was notwithstanding held by some members . . . till a Protestation was published in the house." The Speaker was held down in his chair ("God's wounds!" cried one of the members holding him down, "you shall sit till we please to rise"), while the door of the House was locked to prevent members from leaving and the Usher of the Black Rod from entering, till after the Commons voted their Protestation: "1. Against Popery and Arminianism. 2. Against Tunnage and Poundage not granted by parliament. 3. If any merchant yield or pay Tunnage and Poundage not granted by parliament, he should be reputed a betrayer of the liberties of England."

At this, the king issued an order dissolving the Parliament, asserting that "the undutiful and seditious carriage of the Lower House . . . hath caused this dissolution." Then Charles, in typical Stuart fashion, moved to impose personal punishment upon the leaders of the Parliamentary opposition. Nine members of the Commons, including all the leaders of the House, were committed to prison by the Star Chamber. Six of them sued out their writs of habeas corpus (hence the title of the case); the return stated that they were detained because of "notable contempts . . . committed against our self and our government, and for stirring up sedition against us."

In the habeas corpus proceeding, the imprisoned Parliament men placed great reliance upon the Petition of Right, so recently passed, which the country had assumed would eliminate the royal power of arbitrary imprisonment. But the Attorney-General, adverting to the fact that "the Petition of Right hath been much insisted upon," declared categorically, "the law is not altered by it, but remains as it was before. . . . A Petition in parliament is not a law." The court never decided the question of the legality of the members' detention, for the king simply did not allow them to be produced in court when the judges were ready to give their decision. In this manner, the king managed to keep them imprisoned for over thirty weeks. He then told the judges he was content the prisoners should be bailed, but the latter refused to put up the required security for future good behavior.

The Attorney-General next proceeded to exhibit an information in the King's Bench against the three members who had taken the principal role in the restraint laid upon the Speaker—charging them with criminal conduct based upon their acts in resisting adjournment while the Commons voted their Protestation. In particular, Sir John Eliot, the leading member of the opposition, was prosecuted for seditious speech uttered at the time, while Denzil Holles and Benjamin Valentine, who had actually held the Speaker in his chair, were charged with having "laid violent hands" upon the Speaker, "to the great affrightment and disturbance of the house." The defendants pleaded to the jurisdiction of the court, denying the competence of any court to punish for acts committed in Parliament. The court rejected the plea, ruling unanimously that "the court, as this case is, shall have jurisdiction, though that these offences were committed in parliament, and that the imprisoned members ought to answer."

Despite this ruling, the three members still refused to recognize the court's jurisdiction and declined to put in any other defense. Their refusal was treated as an acknowledgment of guilt and each was ordered to pay a heavy fine and to be imprisoned during the king's pleasure and not to be "delivered out of prison until he give security in this court for his good behaviour, and have made submission and acknowledgement of his offence." Eliot, whom Hallam terms "the most distinguished leader of the popular party," refused to make the required submission and died in the Tower of consumption in 1632 (even on his deathbed, the most he would acknowledge to the king, in a petition to be released because of ill health, was, "I am heartily sorry I have displeased your Majesty"). The other imprisoned members were released after having finally made their submission, except for two, Strode and Valentine, who persisted in their refusals and were not freed until the Short Parliament was summoned in 1640.

The *Six Members' Case* must have been an eye opener to those who had assumed that the enactment of the Petition of Right would restore the constitutional balance to that which had existed in pre-Stuart times. To the Parliamentary leaders, in fact, the case's impact was even more immediate than as an indication that the king would refuse to acknowledge the binding authority of the 1628 Petition. For the arrest and trial of the members for offenses alleged to have been committed on the floor of the House struck at the heart of the privileges of Parliament, without which that assembly could scarcely seek to function as an independent institution of government. Such was, in fact, the intent of the Crown. The whole object of the proceedings against Eliot and the other members, according to one of the king's secretaries, was "to let the world see that Parliament men must be responsible for their words and actions in other courts, and so they will be more moderate and circumspect hereafter."

Perhaps the most fundamental of the privileges of an effective legislative assembly is that of freedom of speech. Without this freedom, in truth, it is difficult to see how the Parliament could have developed into anything more than a rubber-stamp for the Crown. It was concern for the privilege of freedom of speech, which James I had denied in questioning the right of the Commons to discuss certain matters, that, more than anything, led to the Protestation of 1621, discussed in the last chapter.

The information against Sir John Eliot, it will be recalled, charged him with seditious speech in the House of Commons, during the turbulent adjournment session. The actual words he was accused of uttering were "that the Council and Judges had all conspired to trample under foot the Liberties of the Subjects." It is obvious that, if this type of comment could subject a legislator to subsequent arrest and imprisonment, the privilege of freedom of speech itself would soon be rendered meaningless. This was realized as clearly by those directly involved in the case as by us today. "Lastly," concluded the argument of Eliot's counsel, "by this means, none will adventure to accuse any offender in parliament . . . ; for, for his pains he shall be imprisoned, and perhaps greatly fined."

To subject the internal working of the Parliament to the control of courts that were themselves, after Coke's dismissal, subservient to the Crown would be all but to destroy the independence of the representative assembly. As Eliot himself put it, if he had yielded and thus compromised the privilege of Parliament, "All the secrets of the Senate . . . must be subject to the Judges; the most intimate counsells of that conclave obnoxious to their censure."

The Parliament men saw plainly what was at stake in the royal attack upon the privileges of Parliament. "Wee are," a member of the Commons well put it, "the last monarchy in Christendome that retayne our originall rights and constitutions." If the Parliament could be deprived of its basic privileges, it would soon suffer the fate of the medieval representative assemblies in other European countries. If members of the Commons could be prosecuted for words spoken in the House, that fate itself might not be far off.

That was why Eliot chose to die in the Tower, and Strode and Valentine to remain imprisoned for so long, rather than concede the correctness of the king's claims. And that was why also one of the first orders of business of the Long Parliament in 1641 (when the Parliament men were at last to get the upper hand) was to resolve that the imprisonment, prosecution, and decision in the *Six Members' Case* were all breaches of privileges of Parliament—a resolution that was confirmed, after the Restoration, by the Commons in 1667. In addition, in 1668, upon a writ of error, the House of Lords reversed the judgment in the criminal case against Eliot and the other members.

It is not easy for us, hundreds of years later, to appreciate fully the perplexing predicament in which the Parliamentary leaders were placed by the need to resist the royal claims. In the words of one of them, "Wee are in a terrible Dilemma either to forfeit our liberties . . . or to disobey the king's command." In an age in which the king was thought of as God's anointed—"next under Christ Jesus our supreame Gouvernour," Coke once called him— when the whole political and social order, as well as all preferences and dignities therein, seemed to turn upon the royal will, the choice was far more difficult than we can today imagine.

That the Parliamentary leaders would ultimately make the choice they did was due, in the main, to the king's constant efforts to set the Constitution at naught. The *Six Members' Case*, as indicated, showed plainly Charles's willingness to brush aside the most vital privileges of Parliament. But the case showed also that the Petition of Right had proved inadequate in practice to remedy the immediate wrongs that had brought it into being. Despite the Petition, it was now clear, the powers of the king to commit his subjects to prison and to keep them there were exercised as broadly as at the time of the *Five Knights' Case*.

In the opinions delivered in the *Six Members' Case*, one of the judges declared, "You have in every commonwealth a power that hath this superiority, that do they right or wrong, are subject unto no control but of God, and that in this Kingdom is the King." That such an assertion could be made as a statement of positive law just a little more than a year after the Petition of Right was enacted shows how mistaken the Parliament leaders were in assuming that the problems posed by the *Five Knights' Case* could be resolved by the mere legislative declaration of supposedly established rights.

There is no doubt that the king and his councillors treated the Petition of Right as nonexistent during the years between its enactment and the summoning of the Long Parliament in 1641. From a legal point of view, they justified the disregard of its provisions by the theory asserted by the Attorney-General in the *Six Members' Case*—that the Petition merely confirmed the old law and enacted nothing new. As Sir John Finch, himself Speaker at the time the Petition was voted, was to express it in 1637, as Chief Justice of the Common Pleas, "There was no new thing granted, but only the antient liberties confirmed."

As far as the right against arbitrary imprisonment confirmed by the Petition of Right was concerned, the Crown was able, for over a decade, to evade the legislative command for several reasons. In the first place, as Thomas Hobbes was to point out in a striking passage, "Covenants without the sword are but empty words." Mere legislative declaration, without enforcement machinery, is scarcely sufficient to restrain the actions of an Executive determined to make itself the sole source of governmental authority. The right against arbitrary imprisonment—be it confirmed in letters of gold on imperishable tablets—may be truly termed a legal right only if it is enforceable in the courts. But the judges of the law courts were willing, even after the Petition of Right, to recognize very broad powers in the king to commit his subjects to prison.

Even more important, as a practical matter, was the fact that the king had at his disposal the prerogative courts, which would do his will unrestrained by any of the legal restraints that operated in the traditional courts. "In fact," Holdsworth tells us, "so long as he had a court, like the Court of Star Chamber, which he could count upon to obey his commands, opposition on the part of the judges could, to a large extent be disregarded, and the Petition of Right could be evaded in spirit, if not in letter."

In the *Six Members' Case* itself, the original plan had been to proceed against the committed members in Star Chamber. Largely for reasons of what we would now call public relations (to avoid what Gardiner calls "The scandal of calling the offending members before a court composed of Privy Councillors" and to appear instead to appeal to the ordinary guardians of the law), the Star Chamber process in that case was dropped. But nevertheless we should not overlook the fact that the Star Chamber was regularly employed by the Crown to work its will on offenders not as highly placed as the Parliament leaders.

The Star Chamber was the tribunal used against most of those who resisted the government, as in refusing to pay tunnage and poundage. Originally created to check abuses, the Star Chamber developed abuses of its own. King Charles used it increasingly against opponents and critics of Crown and Church. Heavy fines and humiliating punishments were at times imposed. On the floor of the House in 1629, John Selden referred to the fact that "one had lately lost his ears by a decree of the Star Chamber, by an arbitrary judgment." "Next," he declared, "they will take away our arms, and then our legs, and so our lives. Let all see we are sensible of these customs creeping upon us."

A typical case was that of Richard Chambers, a merchant who had refused in 1628 to pay tunnage and poundage on imported goods. Though the Petition of Right had been enacted some months earlier, he was ordered before the Council. There he had defiantly cried that "the merchants are in no part of the world so screwed and wrung as in England; that in Turkey they have more encouragement." For these words, he was committed to the Marshalsea and prosecuted before the Star Chamber. Before that tribunal, says Gardiner, "Chambers had no chance of escape," and he was found guilty and ordered to pay a fine of £2,000 (a tremendous amount in those days) and ordered imprisoned until he made submission admitting that he had committed a wrong. Chambers, a sturdy Puritan, absolutely refused to sign the submission tendered to him. Instead, he wrote at its foot, "I . . . do utterly abhor and detest, as most unjust and false; and never till death will acknowledge any part thereof."

As long as he had the Star Chamber at his disposal to enforce his demands, the king could also readily set at naught that portion of the Petition of Right which declared "That no man hereafter be compelled to make or yield any gift, loan, benevolence, tax, or such like charge, without common consent by act of parliament." Though the immediate cause of this prohibition was the king's use of the forced-loan technique, the language was plainly general enough to restate the broad established principle against the imposition of any tax without Parliamentary permission. But, as we have seen, this Petition of Right provision did not prevent the Crown from continuing to collect tunnage and poundage, even though the Parliament of 1628 had refused to grant it to the king. The fate of Richard Chambers showed clearly what would happen to the ordinary offender who, relying upon the Petition of Right, refused to pay the imposition on imported goods. If he gave in, perhaps he was, in the phrase of the Commons' Protestation of 1629, "a betrayer of the liberties of England." But if he declined to pay the duty, he was sure to be left to the tender mercies of Council and Star Chamber.

Under these circumstances, it is not surprising that the resistance to tunnage and poundage soon died out among most of the merchants. "I have ever said," predicted one of the king's officers in 1629, "that the merchants would be weary of this new habit of statesmen they had put on, and turn merchants again by that time they heard . . . that their store-houses began to grow empty." Most men in commerce soon yielded rather than lose their opportunity to gain wealth for the mere sake of a political principle.

But the Stuart impositions soon affected far more people than those engaged in the importation of goods. For their experience with the first three Parliaments of the reign, particularly the riotous session of 1629, had convinced King Charles and his advisers to attempt the feat, unprecedented for centuries, of seeking to govern without Parliament at all. "From March, 1629, to April, 1640," says Macaulay, "the Houses were not convoked. Never in our history had there been an interval of eleven years between parliament and parliament. Only once had there been an interval of even half that length. This fact alone is sufficient to refute those who represent Charles as having merely trodden in the footsteps of the Plantagenets and Tudors."

Important though the role of the Parliament had become by the seventeenth century, there were still three basic weaknesses in its position that made it possible for King Charles to succeed for over a decade in governing by prerogative alone. In the first place, it was the Crown alone that controlled the force of the nation. This made it possible for opposition to be suppressed by arrest and imprisonment, which (the experience of those who sought to resist tunnage and poundage showed) the Parliament, by the mere enactment of Petitions and protests, had been powerless to prevent.

Second, the king alone had the same exclusive control over the ministers and officers of the government. Nothing like the modern concept of ministerial responsibility had yet developed. Those who exercised governmental authority were responsible only to the king, who had the sole power to appoint and dismiss. The Parliament had, it is true (as was seen in the last chapter), revived the legislative weapon of impeachment. As an instrument for controlling the details of administration, however, impeachment was both too extreme and too cumbersome to be effective. Even more important was the fact that the impeachment power could be exercised only when there was a Parliament in session. Like all Parliamentary powers, that of impeachment went into abeyance when the Houses were not sitting.

And here was the real constitutional weakness of the Parliamentary position: the very existence of the Parliament was still dependent upon the royal pleasure. "The dissolution of a parliament," says Hallam, in the flowery phrase of a century ago, "was always to the prerogative, what the dispersion of clouds is to the sun." Yet it was not doubted that the king had the power at will to dissolve the Houses and so cut short any Parliamentary business, however vital. That power was used to prevent the impeachment of Buckingham in 1626 and to end the Parliament that voted the Protestation over the command to adjourn in 1629.

But it was the king, too, who had the absolute power to convoke the Parliament. Thus, the very coming into existence of the legislative assembly depended entirely upon the royal will. True, the custom had developed of holding Parliaments frequently; yet the actual calling of a new Parliament was up to the king alone. Since the statutes of Edward III (referred to in Chapter 5) requiring annual sessions were no longer considered as legally binding, Charles was within his legal rights when he simply refused to call any Parliament in the eleven years following the dissolution in 1629. Legally, as Charles put it in a 1629 proclamation, it was "presumption for any to prescribe a time to him for parliament, the calling, continuing, or dissolving of which was always in his own power."

From a purely legal point of view, there was no obstacle to the indefinite continuation of government by prerogative, if once the Crown could overcome the constitutional principle that the Parliament alone had the power to legislate and to raise money. To the displacement of that vital principle the Crown councillors devoted a major part of their effort during the years of prerogative rule after 1629.

The need for legislation during the period of prerogative rule was met by exercise of the royal power to issue proclamations. In the famous 1611 *Case of Proclamations,* the judges, led by Coke, had ruled that "the King cannot change any part of the common law nor create any offence by his proclamation which was not an offence before, without Parliament." Such restriction upon the proclamation power was completely disregarded. Indeed, after the dissolution of the 1629 Parliament, royal proclamations were more and more made a substitute for statute. Even Charles himself, in a curious 1641 declaration, conceded that, "since the beginning of our reign, proclamations have been more frequent than in former times, or have extended further than is warranted by law."

The king's control of the government and its officers and the instrument that he had at hand in Star Chamber made it possible for him to secure enforcement of any proclamations issued by him, despite any legal restrictions to the contrary. The situation was well summed up by Clarendon (himself certainly not inclined to be an unfair critic of the Crown): "The council table by proclamations enjoining this that was not enjoined by law, and prohibiting that which was not prohibited; and the Star Chamber censuring the breach, and disobedience to those proclamations, by very great fines and imprisonment; so that . . . those foundations of right, by which men valued their security, to the apprehension and understanding of wise men, [were] never more in danger to be destroyed."

Even more important to the Crown was the assertion of the power to raise money without the need of Parliament. If such royal power could once become established constitutional principle, it might well be possible to govern indefinitely without the people's representatives. As early as 1620, opponents of the Crown had acutely seen that the exaltation of the prerogative "was meant to prepare the way for subsidies without Parliament." The aim of King Charles, after the dissolution of 1629, to rule without calling the Houses again made it absolutely essential for him to find a means of raising adequate "subsidies without Parliament."

As already pointed out, despite the opposition of the 1629 Parliament and of some merchants like Chambers, the Crown had, in practice, made good the claim to collect customs duties on its own authority. With the growth of commerce that characterized the period, these duties furnished about half the revenue needed by the State. In addition, some money was obtained by abuse of the ancient law of the forests and illegal grants of monopolies. There was, however, still the need for a broad-based tax to make up for the general levies that had been granted by Parliament.

The fertile minds of the Crown lawyers now supplied what they felt to be a wholly legal method of meeting the royal need for additional revenue. The method adopted is usually attributed to William Noy, then Attorney-General, who died soon afterwards. "Shaking off the dust of ages," Hallam tells us, "from parchments in the Tower, this man of venal diligence and prostituted learning discovered that the sea-ports and even maritime counties had in early times been sometimes called upon to furnish ships for the public service." Hallam's picture is actually overdrawn. That English kings, from Plantagenet times, required the maritime towns and counties to furnish ships in time of war, and had sometimes allowed the liability imposed to be commuted for money, was widely known. The prerogative to requisition ships, or money in lieu thereof, was exercised at the time of the Armada, as well as in 1619 and 1626. Charles I himself had issued writs for money for provision of a fleet in 1628, but was led by the opposition aroused to withdraw the writs.

Now, in 1634, the royal determination to rule without Parliament led to the adoption of Noy's suggestion that the ship-money device be reemployed. Writs were issued directed to London and the other seaports and ordering them to provide a certain number of ships or their equivalent in money. This first writ of ship money aroused no serious resistance on constitutional grounds, for it was close enough to the earlier precedents to make it appear entirely within the royal authority. There was, nevertheless, one vital modification that opened the way to an attempt to convert ship money into a broad general tax. The nation was at peace in 1634. The old precedents were thus extended to permit the king's demand to be founded on apprehended rather than actual danger.

The next year, 1635, saw an even more important extension. A second writ of ship money was issued that was not limited to the maritime parts of the country. Instead, the whole country was required to contribute. The writ was sent to the sheriffs of every county directing them to assess every landholder and inhabitant according to their means, and to enforce payment by distress. The unprecedented inclusion of the inland counties was sought to be justified by the fact that the entire country benefited from the provision of ships for defense. Lord Keeper Coventry said as much in explaining the new levy, "For since that all the kingdom is interested both in the honour, safety, and profit, it is just and reasonable that they should all put to their helping hands."

Then in 1636, a third writ of ship money imposed a levy on every property owner in the country. This writ made it plain that the king intended to use the ship-money device, freed from its ancient restrictions, as a means of imposing an annual tax without the consent of Parliament. To avert popular opposition, Charles had obtained an opinion, signed by ten out of twelve judges consulted (though issued in all their names), that in time of national danger the king might levy ship money on all parts of the country and "That in such case, your majesty is the sole judge, both of the danger and when and how the same is to be prevented and avoided."

The judges' opinion notwithstanding, there was strong opposition to the collection of ship money throughout the country, and a growing number of people refused to pay. It was out of these refusals that there arose the landmark *Case of Ship-Money*, which was decided by all the judges in 1638.

The refusals to pay placed the Crown in a dilemma. Prosecution for nonpayment would provide the opposition with the national forum that they had lacked since the dissolution of the 1629 Parliament. Not to prosecute, on the other hand, would be to tolerate the defiance of recalcitrant subjects and render the new impost unenforceable. In addition, it was thought, a decision on the law favorable to the king might be expected to deprive the opposition of their strongest arguments on the constitutional issues. At any rate, after at first evading the problem, the Crown decided upon prosecution and chose for the purpose the case of John Hampden.

Hampden was a wealthy country gentleman who refused to pay the sum of twenty shillings assessed upon his estate in Buckinghamshire under the third ship-money writ. As Clarendon describes it, "He was rather of reputation in his own country than of public discourse or fame in the Kingdom, before the business of ship money; but then he grew the argument of all tongues, every man inquiring who and what he was, that durst, at his own charge, support the liberty and property of the Kingdom."

Hampden was proceeded against for nonpayment in the Court of Exchequer, but because of its magnitude the case was heard before all twelve royal judges, sitting in the Exchequer Chamber. The case was argued at great length, with the constitutional and other issues being fully developed by both sides during thirteen days of oral argument. The now-classic argument of counsel for Hampden conceded that the king might, in time of war, require ships to be furnished, but not where he acted merely against "apprehended" danger. If the king alone could determine when an "apprehended danger" existed, he could, in effect, always exact taxation without any Parliament and the liberty and property of all would be in peril: "destroying of the distinction from necessity and leaving the king judge of the necessity; that in judgment so to do it, is all one as to leave it to him arbitrarily, if he will." Counsel for the Crown, on the other hand, relied upon the absolute prerogative of the king. "This power," said the Attorney-General, "is innate in the person of an absolute king, and in the persons of the kings of England."

Thus was the basic issue joined in the *Ship-Money Case*—the issue of whether executive power to deal with emergency is subject to judicial control. That this is still a fundamental issue in the present-day constitutional system is shown by the 1952 *Steel-Seizure Case* decided by the United States Supreme Court. The arguments made on both sides in that case were in many ways but the modern echoes of those heard in John Hampden's case.

The royal judges found for the Crown in the *Ship-Money Case* by a vote of seven to five, though two of the votes for Hampden were based upon the narrow ground of a technical defect in the writ. (One of the judges holding for Hampden was Sir George Croke—leading to the inevitable pun, "The King has ship-money by hook, but not by Croke.") The majority judges in the *Ship-Money Case* confirmed the power of the Crown in the most sweeping terms. According to them, the powers possessed by the king included the following: To "give laws to his subjects"; "To make peace and war"; "To create supreme magistrates"; "That the last appeal be to the king"; "To pardon offences"; "To coin money"; "To have allegiance, fealty, and homage"; and "To impose taxes without common consent in parliament." Truly, under such a view of executive power, prerogative meant absolute prerogative, not subject to any legal limitation.

Nor was it true, under the royal judges' view, that the power of the king was limited even by the authority of Parliament. "No act of Parliament," declared Chief Justice Finch, "can bar a king of his regality." On the contrary, "a statute derogatory from the prerogative doth not bind the king." The same was true of any claim that the king was subject to the law: "The law knows no such king-yoking policy. . . . I never read nor heard, that Lex was Rex; but it is common and most true, that Rex is Lex, for he is 'lex loquens,' a living, a speaking, an acting law."

Under the *Ship-Money* decision, the logical consequence of the Stuart theory of prerogative was reached. In substance, the king was declared to be the sovereign power in the Constitution. In effect, it meant, as one of the judges candidly conceded, that "the king may dispense with any law in case of necessity."

If we sum up the great decisions rendered by the judges during the first part of the reign of Charles I, we may say that they upheld the power of the king, in his discretion, to imprison persons deemed dangerous, to impose customs duties, and to act as he saw fit (including the imposition of taxes) to secure the safety of the country. By the use of these powers, the Crown might well be able to govern indefinitely without any Parliament.

On the face of it, then, the Crown had secured impressive legal victories during the years between 1627 and 1638—which, indeed, appeared to make the position of Charles's prerogative government constitutionally unassailable. The confirmation by the judges of the most extreme royal pretensions could have been of crucial consequence in a nation so concerned with questions of legality and precedent. In a speech in Parliament, Thomas Wentworth well expressed the prevailing sentiment when he affirmed, "That which passeth from White Hall is but a gust which russeth the wether calms: but that which is legally done stinges us."

To the English of the day, it was particularly disquieting that the Crown had used the law itself to deprive the country of its basic rights. "For now," declared Oliver St. John (who had been Hampden's principal counsel) in 1640, "the Law doth not onely not defend us, but the law itselfe is made the instrument of taking all away."

As it turned out, however, the legal victories of the Crown in the courts were not as important in practice as the king's advisers had planned. The main reason for this was the fact that the most significant case of all—that of *Ship-Money*—had been decided in favor of the royal pretensions by a majority of only seven to five. Victory by such a small margin was scarcely the resounding judicial confirmation the government had expected—especially considering the dependence of the judges upon the Crown. And it was mainly that dependence, well understood by the nation, that made most Englishmen unwilling to accept the law as pronounced by the majority judges. After Coke's dismissal, the courts were almost entirely but the mouthpiece of the royal will. With Coke's example before them, the judges, by and large, were careful to act in accordance with the king's desires. To make its authority clear beyond doubt, the Crown altered the formula by which judges were appointed. In King Charles's day, the judges' commissions were changed from appointments *quamdiu se bene gesserint* (during good behavior) to appointments *durante bene placito* (during the king's good pleasure). When Lord Chief Justice Crewe was found "shewing no zeal for the advancement of the Loan" that led to the *Five Knights' Case,* he was summarily removed from office.

The nation well recognized that the judges were really in no position to cast doubt upon the legality of royal assertions of authority. "The courts of justice," as a striking passage by Hallam sums it up, "did not consist of men conscientiously impartial between the king and the subject; some corrupt with hope of promotion, many more fearful of removal, or awe-struck by the frowns of power."

Under these circumstances, the fact that five of the judges voted for Hampden (with two denying in strong opinions the lawfulness of ship money) greatly increased the resolve of those who condemned ship money as unlawful. Consequently, instead of ending the constitutional argument in the Crown's favor, the *Ship-Money Case* only resulted in intensifying the opposition to the royal pretensions. According to Clarendon, when men saw ship money "demanded in a court of law as a right, and found it, by sworn judges of the law, adjudged so, upon such grounds and reasons as every stander-by was able to swear was not law. . . . and no reason given for the payment of the thirty shillings in question, but what concluded the estates of all the standers-by; they had no reason to hope that that doctrine, or the preachers of it would be contained within any bounds; and it was no wonder that they . . . were . . . apprehensive."

To one familiar with American constitutional history, the *Ship-Money Case* has many elements in common with the celebrated *Dred Scott Case,* decided in 1857 by the United States Supreme Court. Both cases were, in many ways, the consequence of the faith that men in a society dominated by the rule of law inevitably place in the legal order as the ultimate arbiter of even the most delicate and crucial political controversies. Both cases could arise only among peoples imbued with a legal spirit and trained to revere the law.

In both Stuart England and pre–Civil War America, the law fell a victim to its own success, which led men to expect too much of judicial power. In both countries, the judges were looked to to resolve basic questions of sovereignty that had come to rend the respective nations asunder. In both cases, the effort of the judges was foredoomed to failure. For we realize now that a controversy that results in a civil war is scarcely one to be settled by judicial decision. It is, to paraphrase Robert G. McCloskey, an essential mistake to imagine that a flaming political issue can be quenched by calling it a "legal" issue and deciding it judicially.

It is clear that both the *Dred Scott* and *Ship-Money* cases had the opposite effect from that intended by those who had hoped by judicial pronouncement to quell the strife that threatened the constitutional structure. If anything, they both intensified the political polarization of the nations concerned and actually proved to be catalysts that helped precipitate the civil conflicts which followed. Soon the extemists on both sides were to dominate the scene. Only bloodshed could settle the fundamental issue of where the sovereignty ultimately lay in the polity and the very nature of the Constitution that that issue placed in the balance.

9

PREROGATIVE AND THE LONG
PARLIAMENT

SUMMING UP his political faith in defense against a charge of
high treason, Thomas Wentworth, Earl of Strafford, declared in
1641: "God, his majesty, and my own conscience, yea, and all
those who have been most accessary to my inward thoughts and
opinions, can bear me witness that I ever did inculcate this, That
the happiness of a kingdom consists in a just poize of the king's
Prerogative and the Subject's Liberty: and that things would
never go well, till they went hand in hand together."

The happiness of a State consists in a "just poize" between
Authority and Liberty. To describe the interplay between Authority and Liberty in these terms requires acute perception. It recognizes that both are essential elements in the functioning of any
polity and that their coexistence must somehow be reconciled.

Yet, if Strafford could thus neatly articulate the theory of a
balanced Constitution—one where there was a "just Symetry,
which maketh a sweet harmony of the whole"—putting such
theory into practice was quite another matter. The difficulty, of
course, was how to secure the "just poize" in the actual operation
of the political system. Despite the theory of governmental
balance that he expressed, the whole of Strafford's career, after
he became a principal minister of the Crown, was devoted to
making the king the predominant partner in the Constitution.
"The Prerogative of the Crown," he declared, "is the first Table

of that Fundamental Law, and hath something more imprinted upon it: For it hath a divinity imprinted upon it, it is God's Annointed: It is he that gives the Powers."

To the Parliamentary leaders and the Whig historians who elevated their views to the plane of established history, Strafford was, in many ways, the arch-villain on the royalist side of the constitutional conflict—the apostate who had forsaken the right for the power and preferment offered by the Crown. "His object," says Macaulay, "was to do in England all, and more than all, that Richelieu was doing in France; to make Charles a monarch as absolute as any on the Continent; to put the estates and the personal liberty of the whole people at the disposal of the crown; . . . and to punish with merciless rigor all who murmured at the acts of the government."

We can now see that the Whig picture of Strafford's villainy was overdrawn. We cannot doubt today that Strafford's transfer of allegiance from the Parliament—he had been one of the leaders of the House of Commons, particularly in the 1628 session—to the Crown was far more a matter of principle than preferment. Like Bacon before him, he sincerely believed that the primacy in the polity properly lay in the Crown. Only through a strong Executive of the Continental type, he felt, could the needs of the rapidly changing economic and social order be met and the State rendered secure. If he supported the royal resolve to rule by prerogative alone, it was because he was convinced that the Commons had sought to usurp the place that rightly belonged to the king.

Strafford, like his opponents, thought he was contending for the correct interpretation of the Constitution. In Gardiner's description, "He was standing in the ancient paths. His knowledge of history told him how a Henry II and an Edward I, a Henry VIII and an Elizabeth had actually guided a willing people. It told him nothing of a dominant House of Commons reducing its Sovereign to insignificance."

But even if we abandon the earlier invidious view of Strafford's motives and objectives and assume that, in absolute good faith, he believed that the Parliament had "upset the sweet harmony of the whole," he was clearly wrong in seeking to redress the constitutional balance by so greatly increasing the power of the Crown. "The authority of a king," he said, "is the keystone which closeth up the arch of order and government." Strafford failed to realize that, whether he willed it or not, the end result of tipping the scales in favor of the royal authority was that stated by Macaulay: to make Charles an absolute monarch of the Continental type. To see in the Stuart polity only an idealized version of the Tudor monarchy was to lose all real appreciation of the state of things in seventeenth-century England.

To be sure, it was not Strafford alone who believed he was seeking to restore the ideal of a balanced Constitution when he was actually working to upset the organic balance in favor of that department with which he was associated. From Tudor times, men had looked to the notion of balanced government as the lodestar of constitutional progress. Clarendon's basic belief at the time, he tells us, was that the Constitution was "so equally poised, that if the least branch of the prerogative was torn off, or parted with, the subject suffered by it, and that his right was impaired: and he was as much troubled when the crown exceeded its just limits, and thought its prerogative hurt by it."

And, on the Parliamentary side, too, it was constantly asserted that the Commons' leaders stood and worked for a proper balance. In her provocative *Crisis of the Constitution,* Margaret Judson refers to a poem in which John Pym, the leading Parliament man after Eliot's death, was praised because:

> He knew the bounds and everything
> Betwixt the people and the King;
> He could the just Proportions draw
> Betwixt Prerogative and Law.

There was, however, a basic lacuna in the concept of a balanced Constitution that made it premature for practical application in Stuart England. The fundamental problem the conflicts of the seventeenth century sought to resolve was that of the location of the sovereign power in the State. As it had actually developed, the Constitution contained two ultimately inconsistent sources of power. First was the king, the head of the Executive and endowed as such with undefined but vast capacities and prerogatives. Particularly in Tudor times, there had been a large development in the legal doctrines which related to the prerogative.

Alongside the royal authority, as we have seen, there had grown up over the centuries the power of the representative assembly, vested with the final authority over the vital areas of legislation and taxation. But the Constitution still left open the question of the interrelationships of the two great sources of governmental power. The position of the Crown in relation to Parliament had not been settled with any precision; more specifically, the question of whether the Crown could control Parliament, or vice versa, had not been definitely raised, much less resolved.

In the event of conflict between Crown and Parliament, it was by no means clear where the ultimate sovereignty lay. Even if either sought to extend its acknowledged authority to its logical extreme, there was no recognized legal means of putting a bound to its claims. Sir Walter Raleigh had pointed this out just before the issue became acute: "If the House press the King to grant unto them all that is theirs by the Law, they cannot, in Justice, refuse the King all that is his by the Law. And where will be the Issue of such a Contention. I dare not divine, but sure I am, that it will tend to the Prejudice both of the King and Subject."

As it turned out, the ideal of a balanced Constitution proved impossible of full attainment in England. Englishmen of the seventeenth century were unable to agree on a proper adjustment between their rights and the prerogative. Instead, they divided into parties that advocated the supremacy of either one or the other. Their failure to agree on a proper adjustment led to both the Civil War and the Revolution of 1688. And that Revolution upset the balance permanently in favor of the legislative branch. Thenceforth, the ideal of a balanced government was to become the basis of the American, rather than the English, system. Montesquieu, as Margaret Judson points out, was thus almost a century too late in picturing the English polity as balanced.

The insoluble dilemma, irresolvable at least by legal means, that presented itself to the England of the 1640's was noted acutely in a 1644 treatise by Philip Hunton. The real question, Hunton said, was "which of the three Estates hath the power of ultime and supreme judicature by Vote or sentence to determine it against the other; so that the People are bound to rest in that determination, and accordingly to give their assistance, *eo nomine,* because it is by such Power so noted and declared?"

In the seventeenth century, there seemed to be no way to resolve the problem of where the ultimate sovereignty resided without making the decider of that issue itself the possessor of supreme authority. As Hunton put it, "to demand which Estate may challenge this power of finall determination of Fundamental controversies arising betwixt them is to demand which of them shall be absolute." When Charles I, in 1629, took it upon himself to resolve the problem of sovereignty by ruling without Parliament, he in effect made himself the sovereign power in the kingdom. When the Long Parliament, which convened in 1641, reversed the royalist trend and assumed the decisive role for itself, it was only shifting the absolute authority to its own hands—arrogating to the Houses, Hunton termed it, that power "which ere while they would not suffer, when the Judges in the case of Ship-money had given it to the King."

In the previous chapter, we had left King Charles in the very fullness of his prerogative power. From 1629, he had governed without summoning the representative assembly and his judges had affirmed his absolute authority to take what measures he deemed necessary for the safety of the realm, including the levying of taxes and the imprisonment of those who opposed his will. From a legal point of view, the royal position appeared unassailable and it must have seemed to many that the last Parliament in Christendom had already gone the way of its Continental counterparts.

That this picture was to change so drastically was due in the main to the king's inability to live within his own, even with the wide powers of raising revenue which the courts had confirmed in the Crown. This inability, in turn, was caused by two factors. The first was the continuing decline in the value of money—one of the constant themes of Western economic history, which was accelerated by the inflow of precious metals from the New World. The revenue that King Charles was able to secure, under his expanded notion of prerogative, would have been more than ample to meet the needs of government a few years earlier. But the ingenuity of the king's advisers proved unable to keep pace with the galloping inflation of the period. This was true, in particular, because of the sudden need for funds brought on by the Scottish rebellion in 1638.

If it was, in the broader view, the decline in the value of money that made it impossible to meet the financial needs of government through prerogative power alone, there is no doubt that the immediate cause of the financial crisis that suddenly confronted the Crown was the Scottish war. That, in turn, was brought on by the king's rash attempt to force his ecclesiastical beliefs upon a people that regarded them with fanatical abhorrence. An attempt was made to put down the insurrection that followed by the sword, but the king's military means proved unequal to the task. Not only were the Scottish forces not defeated, but the Northern counties themselves were invaded. The king was now forced to what he most dreaded. "The game of tyranny," says Macaulay, "was now up. Charles had risked and lost his last stake. . . . No resource was left but a parliament."

Although the Short Parliament met in the spring of 1640, its refusal to grant supplies without a redress of grievances led to its dissolution within three weeks. But because the monarchy had reached the point where it could not deal with the problems confronting the nation without the help of the Houses, a new Parliament was summoned. "In November, 1640," Macaulay tells us, "met that renowned Parliament which, in spite of many errors and disasters, is justly entitled to the reverence and gratitude of all who, in any part of the world, enjoy the blessings of constitutional government."

When the Long Parliament met in the fall of 1640, no one could have anticipated that it would not legally be dissolved until March 16, 1660—though it actually went out of existence when its Rump was expelled by Cromwell in 1653. Winston Churchill refers to it as "the . . . most memorable Parliament that ever sat in England." The first business of the Long Parliament was that of retribution against the ministers who had been the agents of the royal policy of governing by prerogative alone. Of these, the first and most hateful to the Parliament men was Strafford himself—the king's most able minister whom John Pym, in his eloquent speech on the first day the new session met, characterized as one who, "according to the nature of apostates, was become the greatest enemy to the liberties of his country, and the greatest promoter of tyranny that any age had produced."

Nor could the Parliamentary leaders delay, for Strafford was on the point of accusing them of treason because of their negotiations with the Scottish invaders. To secure its own safety, the first act of the Long Parliament was to move, "with an universal approbation and consent from the whole House," to impeach

Strafford for high treason. From a legal point of view, all the same, there can be little doubt that, however obnoxious he had become to the Commons and the country—"A greater and more universal hatred," says a letter just after the opening of the Parliament, "was never contracted by any person than he has drawn upon himself"—he had scarcely been guilty of treason. At his lengthy trial before the Lords, Strafford ably demonstrated his innocence of treason, and it appeared most improbable that a conviction could be secured. The Commons then voted a bill of attainder, which could be enacted like an ordinary bill, without any need for legal proof such as was needed to support a judgment of impeachment by the upper House.

In many ways, the constitutional struggle between Crown and Parliament that culminated in armed conflict was placed in its sharpest focus by the proceedings against the Earl of Strafford. Justice Holmes, in an 1884 address, told his audience that, "In the portraits of those who fell in the civil wars of England, Vandyke has fixed on canvas the type of those who stand before my memory. . . . There is upon their faces the shadow of approaching fate." To the present writer, on the other hand, it is in his portraits of Strafford that Van Dyck has fixed forever the type of man who dominated the period. Who can look at the living canvas in Warwick Castle without having forever before him, in Macaulay's phrase, "those harsh, dark features, ennobled by their expression into more than the majesty of an antique Jupiter"? Even today, we must agree with Macaulay that "the haughty earl overawes posterity as he overawed his contemporaries, and excites the same interest when arraigned before the tribunal of history which he excited at the bar of the House of Lords."

If we look to the law alone, it can scarcely be gainsaid that Strafford was not guilty of the crime of treason with which he had been charged by the Parliamentary leaders. Treason consisted of acts committed against the person or authority of the king. Strafford had hardly been guilty of such acts. If anything, what the Commons sought to condemn him for was exactly the opposite of them. His great offense lay in attempting to magnify the authority of Charles I, which could not qualify as treason in any sense in which that term was understood at the time.

At the same time, it must be recognized that from the point of view of the Parliament men it was imperative that Strafford, as both the most effective and the most hated of the royal advisers, be completely removed from the political scene. More than that, while the detested minister lived, his opponents would never feel safe from his vengeance and his overriding influence on the king. That the accusation against Strafford was framed in the legal terms of a charge of high treason did not change the fact that the real purpose of the proceeding was, not to obtain a verdict of criminal guilt, but to get rid of an odious opponent whom the Commons regarded as a public enemy. "It was," declared Oliver St. John, in arguing for the attainder, "never accounted either cruelty or foul play, to knock foxes and wolves on the head, as they can be found, because these be beasts of prey."

In these circumstances, the legal arguments used by Strafford became irrelevant to the real issues in the proceeding against him. The Parliamentary leaders had become convinced that if they let Strafford go the king would use him to make war upon the Houses. Perhaps the most perceptive comment was the rude saying of one of Strafford's opponents: "Stone-dead hath no fellow."

Strafford's attainder and execution dramatically pointed up the fundamental gap in the English system of constitutional government as it had developed at that time. We can now see that the essential aspect of Parliamentary government is the doctrine of ministerial responsibility, under which the appointment and tenure of ministers are subject to the control of the national assembly. In the modern British system, a minister who loses the confidence of the Commons may be readily dismissed by the people's representatives. Thus, as Gardiner puts it, "In happier times Pym and Strafford need never have clashed together, save in the bloodless contests of parliamentary debate." In the England of 1641, however, it was not yet practically possible for political enemies to realize the ideal stated in Browning's verse drama, where Pym is made to

> . . . think of stealing quite away
> To walk once more with Wentworth—my youth's friend
> Purged from all error, gloriously renewed.

The English Constitution had not yet developed to the point where an unpopular minister of the Crown could lose his job without losing his life. Yet, as we shall see, the Long Parliament was soon to grope toward establishment of a rudimentary version of the doctrine of ministerial responsibility. But the change involved in such doctrine was too far-reaching to be incorporated peacefully into constitutional practice. It was, indeed, the king's refusal to accept what amounted to the surrender of his control over the executive and military arms of government that led directly to the civil conflict that followed.

As already noted, the first business of the Long Parliament was that of vengeance against those who had been the king's chief ministers during the decade of government by prerogative. The impeachment of Strafford was followed by that of Archbishop Laud, Lord Keeper Finch, and the Crown's principal Secretary of State. There followed other impeachments, including those of several judges for their conduct in the *Ship-Money Case.*

On the other side, the Parliament declared that the condemnation by Star Chamber of Prynne, Lilburne, and other Puritans was illegal, and it ordered their liberation—an act that was greeted by great popular acclaim, with, in Clarendon's words, "great herds of people meeting them at their entrance into all towns, and waiting upon them out with wonderful acclamations of joy." In addition, an "Act for the declaring unlawful and void the late proceedings touching ship-money, and for the vacating of all records and process concerning the same" was passed annulling the judgment that had been delivered against John Hampden. And the king's agreement was obtained to the appointment of judges for life *quamdiu se bene gesserint* (though, as we shall see in the next two chapters, the principle of judicial tenure during good behavior was not really secured until after the expulsion of James II).

As a practical matter, there is no doubt that the Parliament was now the master of the situation. For the moment at least, government by prerogative was bankrupt and the king offered virtually no resistance to the flood of reforming legislation that poured forth from Westminster.

It cannot be denied that the legislative record of the first session of the Long Parliament is practically unique in the history of representative assemblies. In the number and quality of important and even landmark enactments, the constructive work of the Long Parliament stands second to none: beside it, even the first hundred days of the New Deal or the first session of the Eighty-ninth Congress seem by comparison virtually periods of legislative inactivity. Certain it is that (as Holdsworth sums up the Long Parliament's first session) "it is not too much to say that some of the statutes regularly passed by it . . . embody some of the most important principles of our modern public law, and still influence the form and contents of that law."

Among the Long Parliament's 1641 statutes that may be said to have fixed the essential outlines of the modern British Constitution, we must consider first those laws which finally gave to the House of Commons the absolute control over all taxation, direct and indirect. The Tunnage and Poundage Act established, "That it is and hath been the ancient right of the subjects of this realm, that no subsidy, custom, impost, or other charge whatsoever ought or may be laid or imposed upon any merchandise exported or imported by subjects, denizens, or aliens without common consent in Parliament." The penalty of a praemunire was imposed on any officer who violated this enactment. A law was also passed outlawing other attempts to avoid the Parliamentary power over taxation, such as ship money.

These statutes closed the constitutional struggle over the right of taxation. Thenceforth there was to be no doubt that the power of the purse was the exclusive preserve of the Parliament, and that it included all forms of indirect as well as direct taxation.

Of even greater practical significance were the statutes regulating the meeting and dissolution of Parliaments. The more than a decade of prerogative rule before the summoning of the Short Parliament had been made possible by the king's unlimited power to summon, prorogue, or dissolve Parliament. "No lawyer," Hallam neatly puts it, "would have dared to suggest ship-money with the terrors of a house of commons before his eyes." It was the complete absence of Parliamentary control that had made possible the excesses of the royal ministers during the late unhappy period of prerogative government.

As was emphasized in the last chapter, perhaps the greatest weakness in the Parliamentary position stemmed from the constitutional fact that it sat only at the pleasure of the king. The remedy was to revive the abandoned statutes of Edward III requiring regular sessions of the Parliament. This remedy was provided, in modified form, in the famous Triennial Act of

1641—"An Act for the preventing of inconveniences happening by the long intermission of Parliaments." By its provisions, not more than three years were to elapse between the dissolution of one Parliament and the holding of another. More than that, machinery was provided for the summoning of the Houses after the three-year period had gone by: by writs of the Chancellor, or, in his default, by the sheriffs, and, in their default, by the electors themselves directly. In addition, no Parliament was to be prorogued or dissolved within fifty days of its meeting without its own consent. Though the Triennial Act itself was repealed after the Restoration, the repealing law specifically provided that Parliaments should "not be intermitted or discontinued above three years at the most." When the Revolution of 1688 finally established the supremacy of Parliament, the object that the Triennial Act sought was also attained—though in a less direct, albeit more certain, manner.

By far the most celebrated measure enacted during the first session of the Long Parliament was the Act of July 5, 1641— "An Act for Regulating the Privy Council and for taking away the Court commonly called the Court of Star Chamber." This law did away at one stroke with the Star Chamber and the other prerogative courts and declared the fundamental principle of the supremacy of the law in the terms that have made it the characteristic feature of the Anglo-American polity: "that neither His Majesty nor his Privy Council have or ought to have any jurisdiction, power or authority by . . . any . . . arbitrary way whatsoever, to examine or draw into question, determine or dispose of the lands, tenements, hereditaments, goods or chattels of any of the subjects of this kingdom, but that the same ought to be tried and determined in the ordinary Courts of Justice and by the ordinary course of the law."

Thus was abolished that tribunal whose very name has remained a synonym of arbitrary injustice—an object of contumely to succeeding generations. With it disappeared the whole structure of prerogative judicature which had been a primary instrument of the Stuart practice of government. The principal rivals to the common-law courts were removed, and the common law was finally enabled to assert its supremacy over every aspect of public and private affairs.

The demise of Star Chamber and the other prerogative courts

was greeted with joy by all except the staunchest supporters of the king, for those tribunals had plainly been misused as engines of royal oppression. Wrote Robert Heath (who, it will be recalled, had stoutly supported the prerogative as Attorney-General in the *Five Knights' Case*) of the statute doing away with the hated court: "I did willingly subscribe to that pt of the act. . . . having Long been of opinion: that the privie Counsell, and that honorable board the Counsell table, should not have meddled with questions of meum and tuum."

But the mere abolition of the Star Chamber, it was realized, was not enough to secure the liberty of the subject. So long as the king possessed the power of arbitrary commitment recognized by the *Five Knights' Case,* he would not really suffer from lack of the additional sanction of a prerogative court. The need was to do away with all authority of arrest beyond the reach of the law courts. This was plainly pointed out by Coke, whose *Second Institute,* which contained the commentary on Magna Charta, had just been published by authority of the House of Commons. Imprisonment at the king's pleasure, Coke showed plainly, was contrary to the principles laid down in the Great Charter.

To eliminate the possibility of such imprisonment, the statute striking down Star Chamber also provided expressly for the abrogation of the rule of law laid down in the *Five Knights' Case.* Thenceforth, all persons imprisoned by the Council or by the king's special command were to be entitled without delay upon application to the King's Bench or Common Pleas, to their writs of habeas corpus. In the return to the writ, the jailer must certify the true cause of commitment (i.e., the mere statement that the imprisonment is by special command of the king will no longer be enough) and, within three days, the court must determine whether the cause specified "be just and legal or not."

Although from a constitutional point of view, these Long Parliament enactments cannot be called revolutionary, this is not to say that they were not far-reaching in their impact. They virtually restored the constitutional balance to what it had been in pre-Tudor times. They were measures that were plainly necessary to protect the position of Parliament or to ensure against governmental abuses and, as such, they were approved by almost the entire nation.

To be sure, restoring the Constitution to its former equipoise could not of itself mean a return to the pre-Tudor polity. Too much had happened to make possible any revival of the balance of earlier days. The Parliament itself was now far from the acquiescent instrument of government it had once been. It had long since ceased being a habitual supporter of the Crown and had developed far in the direction of being a wholly independent repository of sovereign power.

When Clarendon (then Edward Hyde), after he became the king's principal adviser in 1641, worked for the ideal of the king acting in combination with Parliament—a Parliament in which King, Lords, and Commons would cooperate, and in which the king would not allow the Commons to force its will on the Lords, or vice versa, still less to allow both Houses to compel him to give the royal assent to bills of which he disapproved—he was seeking a solution that had become politically unattainable. By 1641, the question of sovereignty could no longer be resolved by a theoretical division between the Crown and Parliament as equals.

It may be doubted whether Clarendon's conception of the Constitution would ever have been possible of practical attainment: "That such a conception of the constitution," asserts Gardiner, "could under any circumstances have been permanently adopted is absolutely impossible." This statement may go too far, but it is certain that affairs had progressed to the point where such accommodation was no longer personally possible between King Charles and the Parliamentary leaders. On both sides, distrust was now the dominant feature of their dealings with one another. In fact, it was their personal mistrust of the king that led the Houses to pass their first measure that may be deemed truly revolutionary in character. "The same distrustful temper," Hallam tells us, "blamable in nothing but its excess, drew the house of commons into a measure more unconstitutional than the attainder of Strafford, the bill enacting that they should not be dissolved without their own consent." On May 11, 1641, there was enacted "An Act to prevent inconveniences which may happen by the untimely adjourning, proroguing, or dissolving this present Parliament." Under it, the Long Parliament could not be prorogued or dissolved "unless it be by Act of Parliament."

This statute in effect made the Long Parliament indissoluble and created the first serious breach in the moderate policy that till then dominated the Commons' leaders. In practical operation, it rendered the Commons at once wholly independent of their sovereign and their constituents and laid down the basic principle of an entirely different polity, which (if it could have been maintained in more tranquil times) might well have converted the House of Commons into an English counterpart of the Venetian Signory.

For Pym and the other Commons men who thought as he did, the time was now past for measures that sought merely to preserve the essentials of a balanced Constitution. The Act making the Parliament indissoluble could be justified on no constitutional or legal theory, but only on the ground of practical necessity. After Strafford's execution, the Parliament men rightly labored under constant fear of the king's intention to overthrow the Parliament, and of the personal danger to the popular leaders that would result from a dissolution. Their fear of the king's intentions led the Parliament men to seek more than the mere removal of the Crown's "evil counsellors." That term was time-honored; since the time of John, opponents had been attacking the "King's evil counsellors." Now, as C. V. Wedgwood tells us, "What they wanted was something more: the transference of effective power from the King's hands into that of the High Court of Parliament."

To justify the revolutionary action by which such transference was to be accomplished, the Parliamentarians had to rely on the dangerous doctrine of necessity—i.e., the very doctrine that they had denounced the royalists for employing. Now, as one member put it in April, 1641, it was essential for Parliament to be able to take drastic action in case of necessity, for "to deny unto that representative Body, the High Court of the Kingdom a liberty to doe anything . . . for the preservation of the greater body it represents . . . is neither agreeable to the Law of Nature, nor of the Land, nor of God." Pym himself was to use the argument of necessity in February, 1641, to justify a forced loan imposed upon the citizens of London, saying that, "in case of necessitie and in pursuance of the truste that is imposed in us for the safety of the commonwealthe wee may assume a Legislative power to compelle such as bee noted riche men to lend ther moneyes."

Though the whole fabric of royalist absolutism had collapsed in less than nine months after the summoning of the Long Parliament, the Parliamentary leaders could not remain secure while the king retained any of the vital prerogatives—control of the armed forces, exclusive authority to appoint and dismiss government officers, and discretion to summon and dissolve Parliament—that had enabled him to rule for so long without the two Houses. Only the last of these key powers had been affected by the legislation enacted during the Long Parliament's first session; the Triennial Act and the law making the Parliament indissoluble without its consent had effectively eliminated the royal ability to govern without the national assembly.

But the king still possessed his authority over the force and government of the nation. Like the power over the sitting of the Houses itself, that authority had belonged to the Crown from time immemorial. To transfer the power to the Parliament meant a revolutionary alteration in the constitutional framework. Yet, revolutionary or not, the Parliament leaders began to see that they must attempt the transfer, or all that they had accomplished might well be set at naught. On October 28, 1641, a member of the Commons "moved touching ill Counsellors that if wee did not take a course to remove such as now remained and to prevent others from coming in hereafter all wee had done this Parliament would come to nothing, and wee should never be free from danger."

When the second session of the Long Parliament opened in October, 1641, the Parliamentary leaders fully recognized that they must wrest control of the Executive from the king. To do this they would have to establish a doctrine like that of ministerial responsibility, under which the Houses would direct the policies and conduct of the government by controlling the appointment of ministers and ensuring that ministers who did not retain the confidence of Parliament would be dismissed.

The Parliamentary leaders had come to realize that only by obtaining such control over the Executive could the constitutional gains that they had made be rendered secure. Already, in June, 1641, they had gotten the Houses to accept Pym's Ten Propositions, which included a demand that the king should put his government into "such ministers and counsellors as his people and Parliament may have just cause to confide in." By November, 1641, Pym was able to move his Additional Instruction, under which His Majesty was humbly beseeched "to employ such counsellors and ministers as should be approved by his Parliament." The adoption of Pym's motion by a substantial majority was a most significant step. "Undoubtedly," says Gardiner, "no proposal of so distinctly revolutionary a character had yet been adopted by the Commons," for the Additional Instruction virtually seized upon the executive power itself.

The next step was to include the demand for control over ministers in the Grand Remonstrance, which was presented to the king at the end of November. That celebrated document recapitulated all the grievances and misgovernment that had been suffered since the accession of Charles I, and included, in its two hundred and four numbered clauses, a plain demand that the king employ only such counsellors and ministers "as the Parliament may have cause to confide in", otherwise, "we cannot give His Majesty such supplies . . . as is desired."

The Remonstrance recognized expressly that it was no longer enough to require ministers only to observe the law, for which impeachment had previously been thought the proper remedy. "It may often fall out," the Remonstrance declared, "that the Commons may have just cause to take exceptions at some men for being councillors, and yet not charge those men with crimes, for there be grounds of diffidence which lie not in proof." The Parliament now sought to control policy and, for that purpose, impeachment was an entirely inadequate instrument.

The Grand Remonstrance, as Holdsworth points out, "foreshadowed the solution ultimately reached by the growth of the Cabinet system." That solution was, nevertheless, not to be accepted for many years. Bitter opposition developed to the Grand Remonstrance itself. The Commons themselves were sharply divided and passed the Remonstrance, after lengthy debate, by a majority of only eleven, at two A.M. To the Commons' leaders, the vote for the Remonstrance was of crucial consequence. How critical the contest was deemed is shown by Cromwell's oft-quoted statement, just after the division: "If the Remonstrance had been rejected, I would have sold all I had the next morning, and never have seen England any more."

Of the greatest significance, however, was the fact that a measure as vital to the Parliament men as the Remonstrance had passed by such a slim majority. The united opposition to the

Crown that had dominated the Long Parliament's first session was no more. Instead, there was a growing reaction in the king's favor on the part of the moderates (who inevitably constitute the inarticulate bulk of any representative assembly), who feared that Pym and his supporters were going too far in seeking utterly to alter the Constitution in favor of legislative supremacy. This reaction was typically English, for the English traditionally sympathize with a weaker party whom they feel is being ill used.

The result was the formation in the Parliament of a royalist party that gave every sign of growing stronger, even attaining a majority, as sentiment continued to turn in the Crown's favor. All depended upon the king's action in reassuring the moderates that he was now prepared to govern as a constitutional monarch. He started out well by using what Clarendon termed "the stratagem of winning men by places," selecting some of the leading moderates to be his ministers and advisers and even offering high positions to the leaders of the Parliamentary party. More than that, he assured his new councillors that he would do nothing affecting the Commons without their advice.

But then came that step which even today fills the observer with amazement at its ill-advised audacity. Had Charles adhered to his assurance to consult the moderate leaders and follow their counsels, he might well have retrieved his position. But "in very few days," says Clarendon, "he did fatally swerve from it." By a renewed appeal to force, the king threw away all that he had gained from the post-Remonstrance reaction in his favor. On January 3, 1642, without giving the slightest intimation to his new advisers whom he had solemnly promised to consult, the king sent his Attorney-General to the House of Lords to impeach Pym, Hampden, and three other leaders of the Commons for high treason. The next day Charles went in person to the House of Commons at the head of an armed force to arrest the five members. But the latter were warned in time and were able to escape to safety before the king's arrival.

There then followed that serio-comic scene in the House which irreparably damaged the Crown's position. The king entered the Chamber and took the chair. He pressed the Speaker to tell him whether Pym and the other accused members were there. Speaker Lenthall, we are told by a contemporary account, "was not a great or heroic man, but he knew what his duty was. . . . 'May it please your Majesty,' he said, falling on his knees before the king, 'I have neither eyes to see, nor tongue to speak, in this place but as this House is pleased to direct me, whose servant I am here.' " The king then saw, with his own eyes, that the five members were gone. "Well," he plaintively conceded, "I see all my birds are flown."

Looking back at it, Charles's attempt personally to arrest the five members appears sheer madness. The king was now, in Macaulay's apt phrase, in the position of "the man who, having attempted to commit a crime, finds that he has only committed a folly." Regardless of the royal protest of good intentions, the entire Parliament felt that they had just escaped a possible massacre. "The orderly D'Ewes," Gardiner tells us, "testified his opinion of the danger by stepping to his lodgings, and immediately making his will."

As far as the constitutional conflict was concerned, the king's attempt to seize the five members was the point of no return. Thenceforth, it was impossible for the Parliamentary leaders to accept the royal protestations of good faith at face value. The only safe course was to reduce the power of the Crown to a point where the king became a mere figurehead. "It was clear," says Macaulay, "that Charles must be either a puppet or a tyrant, . . . and that the only way to make him harmless was to make him powerless." But Charles, with his exalted notions of the kingly dignity, utterly refused to accept this position. The result was the inevitable one of armed conflict to resolve the conflicting conceptions on which neither side would yield peacefully.

The proceeding against the five members may thus be considered the immediate cause of the Civil War that was soon to follow. After the failure of his intended act of strength, the king himself left London, never to return to his capital except as a prisoner on trial for his life. Seven months later, the royal standard was raised at Nottingham and the Civil War officially began.

The key constitutional question upon which the division between king and Parliament turned in the period before the formal outbreak of armed conflict was the control of the force of the nation. While an army was necessary to deal with rebellion in Ireland, the Commons leaders felt that it would have been all but suicidal to leave in the king's hands the military force that might well be used by him for their own overthrow. The Parliamentary movement to control the armed forces had actually begun before the attempt upon the five members. A month before that event, a bill had been introduced to place all military and naval appointments in officers chosen by the Commons. Though the Militia Bill passed its first reading by a small majority, there were then, according to Clarendon, "few men who imagined it would ever receive further countenance." So great an encroachment upon the thitherto unquestioned prerogative of the Crown appeared too extreme a measure to be accepted by the moderates who might soon have the deciding voice in the two Houses.

All this was changed when the king's use of force against the five members showed the Parliament men the danger in which they stood. Now, says Clarendon, "there were very few who did not believe it to be a very necessary provision . . . , so great an impression had the late proceedings made upon them, that with little opposition it passed." But the king absolutely refused to sign the Militia Bill voted by the Houses. He was willing to consent to all the other measures sent to him—even the bill for the exclusion of the bishops—but he refused to relinquish his power over the sword. When it was suggested to Charles that he might yield control of the militia for a short time, he fiercely replied, "By God! not for an hour! You have asked that of me in this, was never asked of a king."

At this point, the Parliamentary leaders resolved to take over the armed forced without the royal consent. They decided not to wait any longer for the king's signature and persuaded the Houses to vote the Militia Bill as an Ordinance issued on the authority of the Parliament alone. "The High Court of Parliament," declared the preamble to the Militia Ordinance, "is . . . a Council to provide for the necessity, to prevent the imminent dangers, and preserve the public peace and safety of the Kingdom."

Here was the logical consequence of the constitutional controversy—the assertion of Parliamentary power to act independently of the king and to take over the defense of the kingdom, as well as its government. This assertion, which went far beyond anything that had till then been claimed, was justified by the Houses on the claim that "the Parliament be the Representative Body of the Kingdom." That being the case, "the Wisedome of this State hath intrusted the Houses of Parliament with a power to supply what shall be wanting on the part of the Prince."

With the passing of the Militia Ordinance, C. V. Wedgwood tells us, the last pretense of conciliation was gone. In May, 1642, the Houses declared that the king, seduced by wicked councillors, was making war on Parliament. In these circumstances, lawful authority for preserving the peace and governing the kingdom devolved upon the two Houses and no order was to be accepted as valid that did not come from them.

The next step was the sending to the king in June of Nineteen Propositions drawn up by the Houses. These were nothing less than a Parliamentary ultimatum to the Crown, for they demanded the virtual surrender by the king of his executive, military, and ecclesiastical powers. For Charles to have acceded to the Propositions would have been to make of him a veritable *Roi Fainéant*—a phantom Merovingian endowed with the mere badge of monarchy while the real sovereignty lay elsewhere. The Nineteen Propositions were a virtual declaration of war, to which the king replied by issuing commissions for the raising of troops. The Houses then voted to raise an army and the civil conflict began in earnest.

From the point of view of constitutional development, however, the history of the period may in many ways be said to stop with the attempt upon the five members. Broadly speaking, the almost two decades that followed—covering the Civil War and the Interregnum—were no more than a constitutional cul-de-sac. Though, as we shall see in the next chapter, they were full of interesting governmental experiments (some of which had profound implications upon developments in the American system more than a century later), they did not really contribute to the mainstream of English constitutional development. It was not until Charles II sat upon his father's throne, taking his place with the freely elected Estates of the Realm, that the ancient Constitution and institutions of government were restored, thenceforth to develop in the historic path from the point that had been attained at the end of 1641.

That meant, we shall see, a return to the basis of government established by the first session of the Long Parliament—one in which the two Houses and the common law could become predominant. As the institutions created by revolutionary experiment gave way, the Parliament reappeared in its historic form, ready to take its destined place as the primary source of sovereignty. Such was the ultimate inheritance left by the constitutional conflicts of Charles I's reign to succeeding centuries, though it may not have been apparent as such until after the reigns of his two sons ended in final disaster for the notion of absolute royal power.

10

INTERREGNUM, RESTORATION, AND REVOLUTION

"The trial and execution of king Charles I," C. V. Wedgwood tells us, "amazed all Europe in 1649." To contemporaries, the death of Charles I marked the visible end of an era—the final overthrow of the ancient Constitution for the preservation of which the conflict with the Crown itself had originally been joined. When the king's severed head was shown to the vast multitude, wrote a diarist, "there was such a groan by the thousands then present, as I never heard before and desire I may never hear again."

The men who brought about the execution of Charles I—"This Man," in Cromwell's phrase, "against whom the Lord hath witnessed"—sought definitively to settle English constitutional development in a new direction, divorced from the monarchical institution that had so long existed in Britain. Paradoxically, however, the killing of the king had only the opposite result, of ensuring a return to the constitutional structure that existed at the end of the first session of the Long Parliament in 1641.

Charles alive was a discredited ex-tyrant, an object of suspicion and mistrust. Charles dead became a martyr, whose memory was associated in the popular mind with the traditional cherished institutions (the drama of his death having all but erased from his subjects the fact that he had once labored so strenuously to destroy those very institutions). From the moment of his death he became far more formidable to his opponents than he had ever been since his days of absolute power. "From that day," says Macaulay, "began a reaction in favor of monarchy and of the exiled house, a reaction which never ceased till the throne had been set up in all its old dignity."

As indicated at the end of the last chapter, the brief period (1649–1660) during which Britain, for the first and only time in her history, possessed a republican polity, was essentially a hiatus in constitutional development, which contributed little, if anything, of permanent significance. This was true even though the period was one of vigorous speculation and experiment throughout the areas of political, legal, and social life. All the ferment in these areas, particularly in that of governmental experimentation, was directly to influence American constitutional development a century and more later, though it played no comparable part in Britain, when once the old institutions were restored with the accession of Charles II.

One who looks at the republican period that followed the death of Charles I with the perspective of American constitutional experience is bound to find striking parallels between the situation of Englishmen who had executed their king and that of the colonists almost a century and a half later who had declared their independence. In both cases, there was the overriding need to reconstruct the fabric of government that had been destroyed. In both cases, too, the need was met in similar fashion. When, in May, 1776, the Second Continental Congress adopted a resolution urging the various Colonies to set up governments of their own, the colonists acted by drawing up written Constitutions establishing the new governments that had been called for. In so doing, they were following the example of Englishmen who acted in a like manner to fill the constitutional vacuum caused by the death of Charles I.

Even before the execution of the king, the Council of the Army, anticipating that event, had presented, in January, 1649, a sketch of a republican Constitution known as the *Agreement of the People*. This document has accurately been called a landmark in the history of constitutional theory. As the first written organic instrument in Anglo-American history, it suggestively foreshadowed many of the fundamentals of later American Constitutions. In particular, it was based upon the essential notion of a

Constitution as laying down significant checks upon the power of government itself.

With the disappearance of the monarchy, it was realized that the chief danger was the misuse of power by a legally omnipotent legislature. To meet that danger, the solution was proposed of a written Constitution that would lay down limits that the Parliament itself would legally be powerless to violate. These limits were specified in the *Agreement* in a manner that anticipated directly the prohibitory provisions of American Constitutions—notably, Article I, sections 9 and 10, and the Bill of Rights of the Federal Constitution.

The *Agreement of the People,* after providing for a Parliament of one House and a system of election based upon an expanded franchise and a more equal apportionment of legislative seats (in both respects, the suggested electoral reforms were not to be accomplished until the nineteenth century), went on to set forth six fundamental "points in the Reserve." These were to be issues beyond the power of the Parliament itself to alter. They included matters of religion (setting forth a principle of freedom of religion, except for "Popery or Prelacy"), military conscription, indemnity "for any thing said or done in relation to the late wars or public differences," sanctity of the public debt, no punishment "where no law hath before provided," and equality before the law.

In addition, during the debates that were held by the army officers before the final draft of the *Agreement* was submitted, other "Particulars were offered to be inserted in the Agreement" as additions to the reserved points beyond the power of Parliament. They included guarantees of the right against self-incrimination, against imprisonment for debt, against restraints of trade, of "punishments equal to offences," of trial by jury, against usury, and against religious disabilities. Though these guarantees were not included in the *Agreement,* they do show the type of radical thinking on the matter that was then current. Too far advanced for its own day, it was to bear fruit in American Constitutions and Bills of Rights.

It should not, however, be thought that the later American achievement in this respect was no more than the mere refurbishing of a constitutional edifice erected by Interregnum Englishmen. One must, in the first place, emphasize the crucial fact that the Framers of American organic documents were the first to put the notion of a written fundamental law that limits the power of the people and their political delegates into practical operation (the *Agreement of the People* itself was quietly shelved by the Rump Parliament to which it had been presented and the *Instrument of Government,* the written Constitution adopted in 1653, contained no real limitations upon the government provided for by it).

Moreover, it should be realized that the concept of constitutionalism embodied in the *Agreement of the People* was at most rudimentary compared to that upon which American Constitution makers were to act. The American Framers well knew that it was not enough only to declare fundamental rights and limitations in an organic document; just as important was the provision of machinery to ensure the enforcement of the document's provisions. The great contribution of the Framers was to establish a polity based upon a system of checks and balances, as well as to provide power in the courts to control the constitutionality of governmental action. Thus was provided the indispensable machinery by means of which the essential rights and restrictions provided for in the Constitution might be enforced. No comparable machinery was provided for in the comparatively crude constitutional documents drawn up in Interregnum England.

As already indicated, the *Agreement of the People* itself never went into effect as a working Constitution. In 1653, Cromwell announced his intention of ruling according to an organic document known as the *Instrument of Government,* which provided for a constitutional government carried on by a Lord Protector and a single House, as well as a Council of State to advise the Protector. It sought to apportion governmental power between the executive and legislative branches and in effect established a limited monarchy without a king in name. In practice, however, the *Instrument* quickly revealed its basic defect—the lack of machinery to ensure its effective enforcement. Thus, a key provision of the *Instrument* provided that legislative acts were to "contain nothing in them contrary to the matters contained in these presents." But there was no institution to ensure that this provision itself would be adhered to.

When the Parliament elected under the *Instrument* met in 1654, it immediately refused to accept the binding force of the

Instrument itself. Instead, it sought to enact a wholly new constitutional scheme, imposing legislative control far greater than that provided for in the *Instrument*. The result was a rapid dissolution of the House by the Protector. Cromwell then governed by naked military force, setting up a system of military government by Majors-General throughout the country. Funds were obtained by vote of the Council of State alone, including the arbitrary imposition of a tithe on the property of royalists. All this was, of course, wholly contrary to the scheme of government set up by the *Instrument of Government* and, in the modern American sense, plainly unconstitutional. Yet there was no legal method provided by which the question of constitutionality could be determined and hence nothing to prevent first the legislature and then the Executive from violating the organic document with impunity.

We can consequently say that the English age of written Constitutions, which began with so striking an anticipation of the American conception of government by law, ended in the very negation of that vital concept. Though Cromwell's wish may have been, in Macaulay's phrase, "to govern constitutionally, and to substitute the empire of the laws for that of the sword," he himself soon saw that it was only by force that he could govern effectively. The result was that "the government, though in form a republic, was in truth a despotism, moderated only by the wisdom, the sobriety, and the magnanimity of the despot."

From this point of view, Sir David Lindsay Keir well characterizes the "restoration of the monarchy in 1660 [as] essentially a return to government by law." The Restoration was essentially the repudiation of the arbitrary rule by Parliamentary and military juntos, which eighteen years of armed force had imposed upon the nation. Instead, there was a return to the ancient institutions of government: the executive authority of the Crown, the legislative and fiscal powers of the two Houses, and the supremacy of the common law. The Restoration established, as it were, that the path of constitutional development was once again to be the traditional path that had been followed before the Civil War.

Thus it was that in 1660 a Stuart king sat once again upon the historic throne of his ancestors. Oliver Cromwell, who had been laid among the sovereigns of England with funeral pomp such as

London had never before seen, had been pulled out of his Westminster Abbey coffin (together with the corpses of Ireton and Bradshaw), drawn through the streets to Tyburn, hanged upon the gibbet for twenty-four hours, and the remains cast upon the dunghill. The period between 1642 and 1660, during which the ancient Constitution had been suspended, appeared all but erased.

Yet, though the constitutional experiments of the Interregnum period played no direct part in molding the future development of the English system, it is wrong to assume that the organic wheel had now swung full circle, as the jubilant Cavaliers of the day doubtless thought. "Ostensibly," S. B. Chrimes tells us, "the Great Rebellion was effaced from the records, but in reality the events of twenty years are irrevocable, and their deletion was fictitious." The result of these years is well stated in Walter Bagehot's now-classic *English Constitution:* "Of course, in seeming, Cromwell's work died with him; his dynasty was rejected, his republic cast aside; but the spirit which culminated in him never sank again, never ceased to be a potent, though a latent and volcanic, force in the country. Charles II said that he would never go again on his travels, for anything or anybody; and he well knew that though the men whom he met at Worcester might be dead, still the spirit which warmed them was alive and young in others."

In form, Charles II had been restored to his father's throne without any conditions or guarantees. The Declaration of Breda, which that monarch issued just before his arrival in England, stated certain principles according to which he intended to govern (general amnesty, liberty of conscience, security of property acquired during the late civil strife, and satisfaction of arrears of pay for the army) but contained no real limitations upon the powers of the Crown.

If, in form, however, there was nothing to indicate any change from the constitutional system that existed before the dissatisfaction with his father's arbitrary rule had begun to lead to armed conflict, in substance, as Charles II himself well knew, the situation was an entirely different one. A profound constitutional alteration, he recognized, had taken place in the country. As Thomas P. Taswell-Langmead puts it, "Although the cause of monarchy was gained, that of absolute monarchy was lost."

Because Charles II constantly acted in realization of this basic fact, his reign, with all its shortcomings, was the most successful of the Stuart kings. Because his brother, James II, foolishly lost sight of it, his reign ended in disaster both for himself and his house. Personal monarchy, as it had been understood both by the Tudors and by Charles I, had been rendered impossible despite the cult of monarchy that was so prominent a part of the Restoration scene.

The Restoration itself was more than the recall of the king to his ancestral throne. "This was," in Winston Churchill's trenchant phrase, "not only the restoration of the monarchy; it was the restoration of Parliament." The Declaration of Breda itself recognized this. The promises of the new king in that document were stated in general terms; the details were all referred to Parliament. The national assembly had, in fact, attained a position that it had never previously possessed—one in which it would become the dominant institution in the State. The king himself now knew that he could not resist the will of Parliament beyond a certain point; by that knowledge Charles II consistently guided his conduct. Nothing could erase the years during which the Parliament, in opposition to the Crown, had conducted the entire business of government. It had become familiar with every facet of the governmental machine and no part of the polity could remain removed from its authority and scrutiny. "The mysteries of kingship," to which James I had been so fond of referring, could no longer be kept beyond the veil that had protected them before the Long Parliament.

The fundamental legal basis upon which the Restoration Parliament acted was the recognition of the validity of every statute to which Charles I had given his royal assent. In practice, this meant that all the laws passed during the first session of the Long Parliament still retained their legal force. And that meant, in turn, that the doctrine of absolute prerogative, which had been overturned by the legislation of 1641, was legally dead. All the statutes restricting the prerogative, which had been enacted just before the outbreak of the Civil War, continued in force under the restored monarchy.

From a legal point of view, Parliament had at last attained the complete supremacy in matters of taxation and legislation. Impositions, benevolences, ship money, forced loans, and other devices fashioned by the prerogative to avoid Parliamentary fiscal control disappeared from English history. The struggle that had lasted from the reign of Edward I was now definitely over: all financial independence of the Crown was at an end. Save for the abortive efforts of James II, no post-Restoration monarch has even attempted to raise a revenue independent of Parliament.

In addition, the judicial jurisdiction based upon the prerogative had also been abandoned. Though a proposal to revive Star Chamber was actually mooted in the House of Lords, it was wisely not pressed. Without the prerogative courts, the Crown could no longer make good any claim to legislate by proclamation beyond the limits recognized by the law courts—i.e., those laid down by Coke in the *Case of Proclamations.* "Arbitrary power," says Keir, "was no longer possible to a king who could neither legislate nor tax out of Parliament, nor do justice outside the courts of Common Law and of Chancery."

Yet, if the constitutional claims put forward against Charles I had thus become settled in the constitutional system established by the Restoration, it should be noted that the internal situation in the Parliament itself was altered from what it had been before the Civil War. The Houses, without a doubt, profited most in the polity from the return to the great principles laid down in 1641. But they profited unequally. Now it was the House of Commons that was plainly the senior Chamber; its predominant influence in the government was coming to be permanently established. The overthrow of the House of Lords during the Civil War and Interregnum had been so complete that that body was never really able to recover its ancient dignity. The outstanding feature of the three centuries of constitutional history that have followed has been the growth in the power and prestige of the House of Commons.

Charles II adapted himself to the changed constitutional situation and was able to prosper as no other Stuart king. James II not only failed to adapt, but actually sought to accomplish the impossible by turning back the constitutional clock to Tudor times, if not to the earlier absolutism of Richard II. The result was the united action of the nation expelling that monarch and his line from the realm.

To the constitutional historian, the reign of Charles II is not nearly as interesting and important as that of his brother, James

II, which, because of that monarch's dramatic though hopeless attempt to remake the Constitution in accord with his father's absolutist theories, constitutes the great watershed in the development of the modern English system. The expulsion of the last Stuart king definitively settled the problem of sovereignty and the essential structure of the British Constitution.

Before we can turn to the drama of James II's attempt to subvert the organic structure, we must say something about developments in the reign of his predecessor—dreary though the petty political squabbles of the period appear to the present-day observer. The reign itself was largely a continuing series of political maneuvers between the king's party and the opposition party in Parliament. The two great parties that were thenceforth to dominate English politics were forming. S. B. Chrimes sums up that process in a sentence: "The old camps of Cavalier and Roundhead had turned into the Party caucases of Tories and Whigs, and the old battlefields were converted into wars of political manoeuvring."

Overhanging all was the depressing state of public and political ability and morality. A nation that had so recently been the foremost power of Europe was reduced to all but a pensioner of the haughty French monarch. The moral tone of the nation was well set by the Court life of the monarch himself, who made one of history's classic understatements in his stated belief that "God will never damn a man for allowing himself a little pleasure."

In an age dominated by what Winston Churchill calls "a life of lust and self-indulgence which disgraced a Christian throne," the caliber of public men was inevitably determined by a political equivalent of Gresham's Law, which left the field to men who, by the standards of any other day, would be deemed indelibly stained by gross perfidy and corruption. Macaulay does not exaggerate when, writing almost two centuries later, he asserts that "the most unprincipled public men who have taken part in affairs within our memory would, if tried by the standard which was in fashion during the latter part of the seventeenth century, deserve to be regarded as scrupulous and disinterested."

And yet, underneath it all, constitutional progress was being made. The party system, which has been so basic in modern British politics, was being formed; the lines were being drawn between the two great parties that have continued, in their broad outlines at least, down to our own day. In addition, under Charles II there began to develop, albeit in rudimentary form, that Cabinet system of government which was ultimately to become a leading feature of the polity. An inner circle of advisers was formed, consisting of a few privy councillors who held some of the highest offices of the state. By a whimsical coincidence, the initial letters of the five men who formed this circle, when it was set up after the fall of Clarendon, made up the word Cabal (Clifford, Arlington, Buckingham, Ashley, and Lauderdale). And it was by that name that the inner body itself was first called, though it soon acquired the name Cabinet (as the council held in the king's own cabinet), which it has since retained.

The Parliament elected in 1661—usually called the Cavalier Parliament—was a reflection of the royalist fervor that dominated the nation during the first years after the Restoration. For some years, it was, in Macaulay's words, "more zealous for royalty then the king, more zealous for episcopacy then the Bishops." It was the longest Parliament in English history, lasting eighteen years before it was dissolved early in 1679. But even the assembly born in the Cavalier zenith of Restoration days was no longer to serve as the rubber stamp that earlier Stuarts had demanded. As time went on the exuberant loyalty of the Houses started to wear off, and they began once again to assume the role acquired before the Restoration of seeking to supervise and criticize the conduct of all branches of government. Corrupt though the Parliamentary leaders doubtless were, their own interests led them to assert to the full the powers of the assembly to which they belonged.

Though the Cavalier Parliament as an entity sat from 1661 to 1679, the individual membership itself changed a great deal during that period. More than three-fifths of the members were replaced at by-elections, and, as time went on, a majority were no longer royalist, reflecting the changing feeling in the country as the reaction from the Civil War abated and misgovernment increased. Ultimately, the Cavalier Parliament confirmed the great constitutional gains that had been made by the Long Parliament's first session; and this is what eventually led to its dissolution, as well as to that of its successor, soon after it assembled, in May, 1679.

The day of the prorogation of the successor to the Cavalier

Parliament is, however, a memorable day in the history of freedom itself, for on that day a statute establishing one of the foundations of personal liberty received the royal assent. "The *habeas corpus*," said Doctor Johnson in 1769, "is the single advantage which our government has over that of other countries." Yet, if that be true, it is largely because of the enactment of the Habeas Corpus Act of 1679. Without the Great Writ, the right of personal inviolability itself may be meaningless. In Lincoln's words, "The benefit of the writ of Habeas corpus is the great means through which the guaranties of personal liberty are conserved, and made available in the last resort." Habeas corpus well deserves its recent tribute by the United States Supreme Court as the "freedom writ," designed to guarantee "man's greatest right—personal liberty."

The development of habeas corpus as the essential safeguard of the sanctity of the person is typically characteristic of English constitutional history. Instead of providing for personal inviolability merely through high-sounding but unenforceable declarations in a paper instrument, the English system has concentrated on the vital procedures by which violations of personal liberty could be immediately corrected. "Throughout the centuries," the Supreme Court tells us, "the Great Writ has been the shield of personal freedom insuring liberty to persons illegally detained."

By the time of the Restoration, habeas corpus was fully established as the means by which personal liberty might be secured. The essential defect in the writ as a security against imprisonments by the Crown, which had been pointed up by the *Five Knights' Case,* had finally been remedied by the 1641 statute abolishing Star Chamber. But the practice during the reign of Charles II showed that there were still important procedural defects that might render habeas corpus ineffective in operation.

The chief abuse was the practice of jailers of transferring prisoners to other places of detention, thus defeating the jurisdiction of courts issuing the writ to them. The practice of even the best of Charles II's officials in this respect is shown by the justified accusation against Clarendon that he had sent imprisoned persons to "remote islands, garrisons, and other places, thereby to prevent them from the benefit of the law." In addition, the *Case of Francis Jenkes,* who had been committed by the Privy Council in 1676 for a Guildhall speech urging the king to call a new Parliament and could not get his writ because the courts were on vacation, showed that a man might unjustly languish in prison many weeks before he could secure his release.

The Habeas Corpus Act of 1679 was intended to remedy these defects. Entitled "An Act for the better securing the Liberty of the Subject and for Prevention of Imprisonments beyond the Seas," it required any judge of any superior court to issue the writ upon application, whether in term time or vacation. A judge who refused to issue habeas corpus was to forfeit £500, an enormous sum in those days. Heavy penalties were also to be imposed upon jailers who did not promptly produce their prisoners in answer to the writ. In addition, no prisoner was to be imprisoned beyond the realm, and habeas corpus was to extend to all previously privileged places to which prisoners had formerly been transferred to avoid the writ.

The Habeas Corpus Act is a landmark of constitutional liberty despite the fact that it made no change of consequence in substantive law. Because it went so far to perfect the procedure by which the legality of detentions could quickly be determined, it made the Great Writ, in Holdsworth's phrase, "the most effective weapon yet devised for the protection of the liberty of the subject, by providing . . . for a speedy judicial inquiry into the justice of any imprisonment."

It was also during the reign of Charles II that there was established the fundamental right of the jury to return an uncoerced verdict, which is, after the right to habeas corpus itself, the true protection developed by the law for personal liberty. In Chapter 4, we touched briefly on the origin of the jury system in the days of Henry II. By the time of the Restoration, of course, trial by jury had become a basic principle of English criminal law. The jury was not yet, however, fully free to hold an impartial balance between Crown and subject, for the power persisted to punish jurors for a false verdict, or, more significantly, for a verdict against the judge's direction. Judges sitting in criminal trials had taken upon themselves the authority to fine and imprison jurors summarily for such verdicts.

Then, in 1670, came *Bushell's Case*—ever since considered a landmark case. Bushell was the foreman of the jury that tried William Penn, who, though forbidden to preach, had delivered a sermon to a Quaker meeting and had then been indicted for disturbing the king's peace "by preaching to an unlawful assembly . . . to the great terror and disturbance of many of his liege people and subjects." The jury was ordered to find Penn guilty of the violation charged, but it persisted in refusing to return the ordered verdict, though the court threatened, "you shall be locked up, without meat, drink, fire, and tobacco; . . . We shall have a verdict, by the help of God, or you shall starve for it." Even after the threat was put into effect and the jurors spent two days and nights without food, water, and heat in Newgate Prison, they refused to find Penn guilty "in the manner and form of the indictment." To this, the court declared, "God keep my life out of your hands, but for this the Court fines you forty marks a man; and imprisonment till paid."

With their fines unpaid, the jurors remained committed in Newgate for several weeks, until Bushell sued out a writ of habeas corpus from the Court of Common Pleas. In ruling that the jurors were entitled to their release, the court definitively decided that it was contrary to law to attempt to control a jury by fine or imprisonment. "Must a juror," asked Chief Justice Vaughan, "merit fine and imprisonment, because he doth that which he cannot otherwise do, preserving his oath and integrity?"

By answering this query in the negative, the king's judges settled forever the freedom of the jury to decide according to their own oath and conscience. The principle that jurors cannot be punished for a perverse verdict or one against the judge's direction is thus fully established. Without this principle, the right to trial by jury itself would scarcely be the vital foundation of personal liberty that it has since remained.

Bushell's Case, it should be noted, fixed the jury's freedom of decision in all countries with systems based upon the common law. When, in the famous 1735 trial of John Peter Zenger in New York, the court tried to limit the jury's power of inquiry, Andrew Hamilton, for the defense, stated that "The rights of the jury to find such a verdict as they in their conscience do think is agreeable to the evidence, is supported by the authority of Bushell's case beyond any doubt." Since Zenger's acquittal, it has never been questioned that the principle laid down in *Bushell's Case* was fully applicable on the western side of the Atlantic.

From the foundations of freedom laid down in the Habeas Corpus Act and *Bushell's Case,* we must turn once again to the recital of other developments during the reigns of the last two Stuart kings. After the dissolution of the Cavalier Parliament in January 1679, Charles II himself appeared at the very bottom of his fortune—at least since the time he had been seated on his father's throne. The government could now rely upon a relative handful of votes in the Parliament and Charles appeared powerless even to prevent the exclusion of the rightful heir from the succession, much less to restore the position of the Crown in the political sphere.

It is unnecessary to recapitulate in detail how Charles II was able, in a few years, to redeem a situation that had seemed virtually hopeless. Suffice it to say that, by consummate political skill and the financial aid of Louis XIV, Charles, by 1681, had become master of the political scene. For the last four years of his reign, Charles was able to govern without any Parliament (a revival of the situation of 1629–1640 made possible by French subsidies) and, at his death, the monarchy seemed stronger than it had been since Tudor times.

"To say of Charles II," says Holdsworth, "that he was the ablest of the Stuart kings would be to damn him unjustly with the faintest of praise." Certainly Charles II was the only Stuart king who was able to leave the Crown in a better position than it had been at his accession. We can best appreciate his accomplishment in this respect when we see how his successor, with more than his father's impolitic obstinacy, so conducted himself as to destroy in three short years all that his brother had been able to secure for his Crown and dynasty.

Paradoxically perhaps, in view both of the controversy that had almost led to his exclusion and the events that so soon resulted in his expulsion, James II acceded to the throne in a climate of popular support that appeared to give his reign the firmest foundation of that of any Stuart king. The vanquished Whigs, who had so bitterly opposed the succession, had been discredited and appeared all but to have disappeared as an opposition party. From all sides, addresses were received that outdid each other in zealous loyalty if not servility. The dominant theme throughout the realm was one of profound veneration for the person and office of the new sovereign.

The enthusiastic support of the nation for the principle of hereditary monarchy was strikingly demonstrated by the manner in which it rallied to support the legitimate heir and crush the attempt at rebellion made by Monmouth, "our beloved Protestant Duke," whom the Whigs had sought to have recognized as next in succession to Charles II. The principle of legitimacy overrode the anti-Popish sentiments of the overwhelming mass of the English people. The Anglican doctrine of passive obedience bound the nation to obey even a monarch who professed the Roman faith, rather than turn the stream of succession out of the ancient channel.

The overwhelming loyalty toward the new king was also shown in the return of a Parliament that was, without a doubt, the most friendly toward the royal pretensions since Tudor times. After the election of 1685, James II is said to have declared that, except for about forty members, the House of Commons was just such as he himself would have named. The Parliament thus assembled appeared almost as subservient to the Crown as any that had sat under Henry VIII. So devoted were the Houses to the Crown that, had James acted even with moderate wisdom, his reign might well have turned out to be eminently successful. In Macaulay's phrase, "There were few things which such an assembly could pertinaciously refuse to the Sovereign; but, happily for the nation, those few things were the very things on which James had set his heart."

For James II (who, in Bernard Shaw's characterization, "became that very disagreeable character, a man of principle") had resolved, with all the obstinacy that dominated his character, on the rash attempt to restore the old faith to the position it had held before the Reformation. In large part, indeed, it was James's unyielding effort for his own religion that led to the ultimate loss of his throne. His bigotry on behalf of his faith, leading as it did to the delusion that he could actually reimpose a Catholic regime, was the very thing that called forth the bitter opposition of all the politically important classes of the nation.

In basing the underlying purpose of his reign upon a restoration of Catholicism, James II took the one course that was sure to result in disaster. Perhaps Leopold von Ranke overstates the matter when he says that James "would have ensured himself a peaceful and perhaps a glorious reign if he could have prevailed on himself to treat his religion as a private matter." But it is certain that the one thing that, rightly or wrongly, united the vast majority of Englishmen of the day was their unrelenting animosity toward the Catholic Church. As Winston Churchill puts it, "The tale of dark designs to subjugate Protestant England to Rome was on every lip." The incredible series of events known as the "Popish Plot," as well as the near-success of the Exclusion Bill, which had come so close to barring him from the throne, should have convinced a prince of even ordinary astuteness of the all but fanatic anti-Catholicism of his subjects.

It is perhaps difficult for the present-day observer to appreciate the extent and significance of religious intolerance in seventeenth-century England. But in fact the great constitutional struggles in Stuart England were both political and religious struggles. It was religious disagreements that aggravated the political controversies of the time and made their resolution impossible except by the sword. (The Framers of the American constitutional system, incidentally, well realized the connection, as is shown by the First Amendment, in which freedom of speech and religion are inextricably linked.) In the previous discussion, the religious side of the story has been minimized to avoid obscuring constitutional developments in doctrinal disputes that have lost their interest in a society of diverse faiths, dominated by the principle of toleration. With the accession of James II, however, the royal attempt to subvert the Constitution is made solely for religious ends. Apart from the bigoted fanaticism that pursues such ends at all cost, in truth, the acts and policies of the last Stuart king virtually defy rational explanation.

To accomplish his purpose, James II turned first of all to the Parliament that had been elected in 1685. But even that assembly, devoted though it otherwise was to the Crown, balked at overturning the solely Protestant character of the English system. The bulwark of that system, to most Englishmen, was the Test Act (1673 and 1678) which, by excluding from civil and military office, as well as from both Houses of Parliament, all who did not take oaths solemnly abjuring the doctrine of transubstantiation, effectively barred all Catholics from public affairs. It was the Test Act, which most of his subjects considered the chief guaranty of Protestantism, that the king now sought to have repealed—as well as the Habeas Corpus Act, itself the essential guaranty of personal liberty. In a letter, Halifax explained his dismissal as Lord President by saying that he was "turned away,

because I could not prevayle with myselfe to promise before hand
to bee for taking away the Test and the bill of Habeas Corpus."

Even the accomplished Trimmer could not bring himself to
yield on the two fundamental laws, and the same was true of the
other members of the otherwise subservient Houses. The laws
involved were not more dear to Whigs than to Tories, and the
question of their repeal was the point at which the devotion of
most members to the Crown gave way to higher loyalty.

When the king found that he could not induce the Houses to
repeal the two statutes, he met their opposition with a summary
prorogation. Parliament never met again during James's reign.
Instead, he tried to accomplish his design of restoring Catholicism by reliance on his prerogative. And, like his father, he
sought to establish the legality of the powers that he asserted by
the decisions of what Holdsworth calls "a packed bench of
judges."

The power by which James II now proposed to attain his end
was, first of all, the dispensing power. Since medieval days, there
had been recognized in the Crown a power, in exceptional
circumstances, to exempt particular persons from the operation
of penal laws. James proceeded to exercise this exceptional
power on a broad scale, using it to exempt members of his faith
from the Test Act and, despite the prohibitions of that law, to
appoint his coreligionists to the highest civil and military positions in the land.

The first step was to secure a judicial decision recognizing in
the king those powers which Parliament had denied him. It
should be borne in mind that the judges were once again subject
to the Crown's will, for Charles II had in 1668 resumed the
practice, which his father had been compelled to give up, of
appointing judges only "during the King's pleasure." Both
Charles and James II made a free use of their power of summary
dismissal to secure a bench made up only of supporters of the
prerogative.

Even judges who were in most ways creatures of the Crown
found difficulty in distorting the law in accordance with the king's
desires. But they were plainly told that they must yield or be
dismissed. "I am determined," said James in a famous statement
to Sir Thomas Jones, the Chief Justice of the Common Pleas, "to
have twelve judges who will be all of my mind as to this matter."

"Your Majesty," Jones replied, "may find twelve Judges of your mind, but hardly twelve lawyers."

Jones's celebrated reply (worthy to stand beside Coke's eloquent statement of the judicial duty in the *Case of Commendams*) led only to his dismissal, as well as to that of other judges who refused to uphold the dispensing power. In less than four years, indeed, James removed no fewer than twelve judges and replaced them with men who would be his tools. The bench thus packed by the king was, without a doubt, at the very nadir of judicial ability in English history. When the 1688 *Case of the Seven Bishops* came before the King's Bench, not one lawyer of eminence sat on that tribunal, while counsel for the bishops consisted of the greatest lawyers in the land (themselves recently dismissed from the scarlet). Truly, in such a situation, as Halifax neatly put it, "Westminster Hall might be said to stand upon its head."

According to a statement attributed to Sir Matthew Hale, the great Chief Justice during the first part of Charles II's reign (one of the paradoxes of the Restoration period—an age characterized by judges like Scroggs and Jeffreys—is the attachment of the amoral monarch to a jurist who, in Holdsworth's phrase, had "a really beautiful character, comparable among English judges, only to that of Sir Thomas More"), "The twelve red coats in Westminster Hall are able to do more mischief to the nation, than as many thousands in the field."

The Hale statement, says Alfred F. Havighurst, "might well be taken as the verdict of history upon the conduct in office of the common law judges under . . . James II." Certainly that was the verdict of the men who made the Revolution of 1688. William of Orange's first declaration asserted that the judiciary had been subverted by the Crown. And, in the House of Commons in 1689, Sir Richard Temple declared: "How has Westminster Hall been tutored, Judges packed . . . so that Westminster Hall was become an instrument of Slavery and Popery, ordinary justice destroyed, . . . in that little and short time of the late King James' reign!"

From his packed bench, James II was quickly able to secure judicial confirmation of the broadside use that he proposed to make of the dispensing power. The test case was *Godden v. Hales* (1686), in which the judges decided that the king had practically unlimited power to dispense with the Test Act. The decision was, like the earlier cases decided by Charles I's judges, replete with language about the absolute nature of royal authority in the matter. Armed with the judicial decision that "there is no law whatsoever but may be dispensed with by the chief lawgiver," James proceeded to exercise his dispensing power to "pack" the government with his supporters—which, to a devout Catholic in an age of intolerance, meant his coreligionists. Within a month after the judges' decision, four Roman Catholic peers were sworn of the Privy Council. The king then began increasingly to appoint Catholics to key civil and military posts, as well as to ecclesiastical and educational positions. In addition, James set up a new Ecclesiastical Commission, intended to control the Anglican clergy, in a manner reminiscent of the hated High Commission that had been abolished by the Long Parliament.

There is no doubt that the royal preferment of Catholics in defiance of express Parliamentary prohibition was bitterly opposed by the overwhelming mass of Englishmen. Nor was such opposition entirely religious. As Macaulay puts it, "Every Protestant who still held an important post in the government held it in constant uncertainty and fear." The common apprehension was that Protestants would soon be as effectually excluded from office, by the dispensing power, as ever Catholics had been by Act of Parliament.

James, however—with, what Shaw terms his talent for making himself unpopular—did not remain content with exercising only the power to dispense with the Test Act for individual Catholics, widespread though his exercise of this power had been. In April, 1687, the king issued his famous Declaration of Indulgence. By it, he suspended all penal laws in ecclesiastical matters, including the Test Act, and all restraints upon liberty of worship.

As a matter of theoretical right, the Declaration of Indulgence may appear commendable to us today, since it seems only to provide for the religious toleration that is now an established part of the Anglo-American society. But in late-Stuart England, the situation was entirely different. Toleration of Papists was something very few Englishmen could accept—even if they could have been convinced that toleration alone was all James desired, rather than the establishment of a religious despotism like that of Louis XIV. More important is the fact that, even if the end sought by the

Declaration of Indulgence was laudable, the means used was indefensible from a constitutional point of view. At stake was the very existence of legislative power in Parliament, for of what avail is the authority of the people's representatives to enact laws if the Executive possesses unlimited discretion to suspend their operation? "If this be once allowed of," said Justice Powell in the climactic *Seven Bishops' Case,* "there will need no parliament; all the legislature will be in the king, which is a thing worth considering."

A 1688 letter quotes James II as saying, in the midst of the crisis caused by the Declaration of Indulgence, "I will go on. I have been only too indulgent. Indulgence ruined my father." Only such blind stubbornness can explain the folly of the king's next moves. In April, 1688, the king reissued his Declaration and followed it with an order directing the clergy to read it in every church of the land. A "humble Petition" was sent by the Primate and six bishops praying that the clergy might be relieved from the duty thus imposed on them, "because that declaration is founded upon such a dispensing power, as hath been often declared illegal in parliament."

To James, the bishops' petition was "a standard of rebellion" and those who presented it "trumpeters of sedition." The bishops were sent to the Tower and, soon after, prosecuted for seditious libel. At the bishops' trial, the leaders of the English bar and the best of the judges dismissed by James appeared for the defense. Overawed by the eminence of defense counsel, as well as by an audience, made up of the greatest peers in the realm, openly hostile to the royal aim, the judges were powerless to prevent a verdict of acquittal. The country now reaped the benefit of *Bushell's Case.* The popular temper against the king was such that, as a letter put it just before the trial, no jury, normally chosen, would find the bishops guilty. The jury, vested with full freedom to decide as they saw fit by *Bushell's Case,* returned the acquittal that caused an outburst of rejoicing throughout the nation.

The *Seven Bishops' Case* and the birth of an heir to the throne while the case was pending were the immediate precipitating causes of the Revolution of 1688. The prosecution of the bishops, Macaulay tells us in a striking passage, united in opposition to the Crown "two feelings of tremendous potency, two feelings which have been generally opposed to each other, and either of which, when strongly excited, has sufficed to convulse the state. . . . Those feelings were love of the Church and love of freedom."

James II had arrayed the entire nation against himself in one huge and compact mass—a combined opposition of Tories and Whigs, Anglicans and dissenters, bishops and nonconforming clergy, united in their determination to prevent a dying dynasty from imposing its religious will. The acquittal of the bishops was, without a doubt, the catalyst that finally caused the Stuart overthrow, for it was the first case of its kind that had gone against the Crown since the days of Coke. On the very day when, to the ringing of church bells and the huzzas of the multitude, the bishops were acquitted, there went forth the celebrated invitation from the leaders of both parties to William of Orange.

11

REVOLUTION SETTLEMENT AND
CABINET SYSTEM

WHAT HAS ever since been termed the Glorious Revolution of
1688 was typically English, both in its execution and effect. In
Macaulay's phrase, it was "of all revolutions the least violent"
and "the most beneficent." It was this which led G. M. Trevelyan, in his leading work on the subject, to say that a more
appropriate title would have been "The Sensible Revolution."

In November, 1688, William of Orange landed with a small
army at Torbay, in Devonshire. Then it was that, as Winston
Churchill puts it, "By one spontaneous, tremendous convulsion
the English nation repudiated James." The courage of the Stuarts
now deserted James II and he fled ignominiously from his capital.
Just after he boarded a ship for the Continent, he was captured
and brought back to London. And here the uniquely English
aspect of the Revolution asserted itself. Instead of seeking the
revenge that has been exacted from all-too-many hated rulers in
James's position, his subjects did all they could to facilitate his
escape. A second flight followed and James left the kingdom for
good on December 22—to spend the rest of his days (after a
brief incursion into Ireland) as the pathetic figure we meet in the
pages of Saint-Simon.

Yet, though its execution was singularly mild, the end of the
last Stuart king's reign did constitute a true revolution, both in its
implications and effects. Nor did those who lived through the

event doubt either its revolutionary or beneficial character. When the almost ninety-year-old Serjeant Maynard led the legal profession in its homage to William of Orange, just arrived at St. James, the prince remarked that the venerable serjeant had outlived all the jurists of his day. To which Maynard made his historic reply that "he had like to have outlived the law if his highness had not come over."

Certainly, Maitland tells us, from a legal point of view "it was very difficult . . . to argue that there had not been a revolution." When James had fled, he did what he could to disrupt civil government and plunge the realm into anarchy. Even the Great Seal—that almost mystic symbol of constitutional continuity—he cast into the Thames on December 11, 1688 (from which date, by legal reckoning, the reign of the last Stuart king has since been deemed ended).

The constitutional difficulty was that from the day when the Great Seal was cast away until February 13, 1689, when William and Mary accepted the Crown, there was no legal government in England. Not only was there no king, but no Parliament either, since James's only Parliament had been finally dissolved in July, 1688. Without a king, it was impossible to assemble a lawfully constituted Parliament and, without the Houses, a legal solution of the problem posed by James's flight seemed just as impossible.

The dilemma was resolved, as it had to be, by extra-legal methods. William called an assembly composed of the peers and members of the Commons during the reign of Charles II, as well as the magistrates of London. Legally, of course, this assembly was quite irregular, but even the lawyers recognized that this was an occasion on which the legal niceties had to yield. When one member said that he could not conceive how it was possible to carry on the government in that way, old Maynard declared, "We shall sit here very long if we sit till Sir Robert can conceive how such a thing is possible."

The assembly called by William advised the prince to summon a Convention Parliament. It met on January 22, 1689, and soon thereafter passed the celebrated resolution "That King James II having endeavoured to subvert the constitution of the Kingdom by breaking the original contract between King and people, and by the advice of jesuits and other wicked persons, having violated the fundamental laws, and withdrawn himself out of the Kingdom, hath abdicated the government, and that the throne is thereby vacant." It was then resolved that the Crown should be settled on William and Mary. The actual tender by Halifax, for the estates of the realm, was made on February 13, 1689. Speaking for himself and his wife, William replied, "We thankfully accept what you have offered us." The Convention thereupon passed an act declaring itself to be (following the precedent of the Restoration) a true Parliament, notwithstanding the want of proper writs of summons.

Thus was effected the Revolution of 1688, which overthrew the last Stuart king and placed upon the throne in his stead joint sovereigns who were plainly not entitled to reign by hereditary right. But the ease with which the governmental change was carried out should not make us lose sight of the fundamental importance of the events of 1688–1689 for English constitutional development. For they finally settled the essential nature of the English polity and, as such, were the constitutional culmination of the struggle between prerogative and law which is the great theme of the seventeenth century.

The 1688 Revolution, says Macaulay, "finally decided the great question whether the popular element which had, ever since the age of Fitzwalter and De Montfort, been found in the English polity, should be destroyed by the monarchical element, or should be suffered to develop itself freely, and to become dominant." Once and for all, it had been settled that the prerogative was bounded by law and the government itself must be conducted only in conformity to the sense of the representatives of the nation. The king himself now reigned by exactly the same right as that by which freeholders chose knights of the shire—by the will of the nation—and not by any prerogative higher than the law.

Above all, the events of 1688–1689 meant the utter demise of the doctrine of monarchy by divine right. The flight of James II ultimately led to a Parliamentary settlement of the succession to the throne, which meant the inevitable rejection of the idea that the king's title depended upon divine right superior to the law of the land. The throne had been vacated by what amounted to the deposition of the rightful king, and the vacancy had been filled by Parliament. The people's representatives had assumed the power to make and unmake kings.

The result was the final establishment of Parliamentary supremacy as the dominant feature of the Constitution. This feature was further emphasized when the Act of Settlement (1701) entailed the throne upon a foreign family that had no real claim upon it except by virtue of such statute. Thenceforth there was no question that the king was king by Act of Parliament alone and that, in the last resort, Parliament was supreme over the Crown. The Revolution, as Holdsworth stated it in a striking passage, "reversed . . . the maxim, 'A Deo rex a rege lex,' and made the crown the creature of the law."

The throne had been offered to William and Mary subject to the conditions laid down in an instrument known as the Declaration of Right, which had been drawn up by a committee of the Convention. After that body had declared itself to be a Parliament, it turned its Declaration into the landmark Bill of Rights, enacted as a statute in 1689. That law may well be considered, after Magna Charta and the Petition of Right, the third great charter of English liberty. As a statement of the basic rights of Englishmen, as well as the limitations upon government that make such rights effective, it is the direct ancestor of the Bills of Rights that form an important part of all American Constitutions.

The 1689 Bill of Rights sought first of all to eliminate the various methods by which the last two Stuart kings had sought to influence Parliament and to suppress opposition therein. It declares that the election of members of Parliament ought to be free, that freedom of speech and debates in Parliament ought not to be questioned in any court or other place, and that Parliaments ought to be held frequently (a provision made more specific by the Triennial Act, 1694, which prohibited the intermission of Parliament for more than three years).

In addition, the Bill of Rights specifically condemned the abuses of the prerogative by James II. It expressly declared "That the pretended Power of Suspending of Laws or the Execution of Laws by Regall Authority without Consent of the Parlyament is illegall." A similar provision outlawed the dispensing power "as it hath been assumed and exercised of late." Thus, to quote Macaulay, "by the Bill of Rights the anomalous prerogative which had caused so many fierce disputes was absolutely and forever taken away." Another royal abuse was dealt with by a provision prohibiting the raising or keeping of an army in time of peace, "unless it be with Consent of Parlyament."

Of particular interest to an American are those sections of the

Bill of Rights which deal with the perversions of justice by the last Stuart kings, for they were to serve as the models for like provisions in American Bills of Rights. These sections provide that "excessive Baile ought not to be required nor excessive Fines imposed nor cruell and unusuall Punishments inflicted" (the direct ancestor of the Eighth Amendment to the Federal Constitution), that jurors should be duly impaneled, and that grants and promises of fines and forfeitures of particular persons before conviction are illegal.

Even more significant in correcting abuses of justice was the final settlement by the Revolution of the problem of judicial independence, which had been acute during most of the Stuart period. From the beginning of his reign, William III abandoned the Stuart practice of appointing judges only during the pleasure of the king. The Act of Settlement (1701) confirmed the changed practice in this respect, providing expressly that "Judges Commissions be made Quam diu se bene Gesserint and their Salaries ascertained and established but upon the Address of both Houses of Parliament it may be lawfull to remove them."

Thus was definitely ended the Crown's power to dismiss judges who withstood the royal will—a power that too often had made the Stuart judges mere servile creatures of the king. Instead there was established that judicial security of tenure that has ever since been an essential feature of the Anglo-American constitutional system. It is this security that has made possible judicial independence and the impartial administration of justice. "In consequence," says Holdsworth, "the supremacy of the law has become the best of all securities for the liberties of the subject, against both the claims of the royal prerogative and the claims of Parliamentary privilege."

Most important of all, however, was the fact that the issue of where the sovereign power resided, which had agitated the country since Tudor times and which had cost one Stuart king his life and another his throne, was now finally resolved in favor of the Parliamentary claim. The coronation oath that William and Mary took contained for the first time an express promise to govern the kingdom "according to the statutes in Parliament agreed on." Thenceforth no English monarch could presume to govern without the support of the legislative assembly. Never again was one even to attempt to recover the lost Stuart prerogative.

Nor, it should be noted, were the effects of the Glorious

Revolution limited to the British Isles themselves. Under the last two Stuart kings, the Crown had sought to eliminate the institutions of self-government that had grown up in the American Colonies. James II had suppressed the assemblies of several colonies. The charter of Massachusetts was withdrawn and the Dominion of New England set up—to be governed in accordance with Sir Edmund Andros' notions of Stuart prerogative. All the colonies north of Maryland were to be combined into a single viceroyalty governed directly by the Crown.

The overthrow of James saved the Colonies from what would have meant an end to the training in self-government that prepared Americans for independence nearly a century later. The colonists resumed their old institutions without waiting to hear London's desires in the matter; their actions were confirmed by the new sovereigns, and the Massachusetts charter was restored in 1691.

Without 1688, there could have been no 1776, not only because the expulsion of the last Stuart king enabled the Colonies to avoid the suppression of local self-government that James II had planned, but also because the establishment of Parliamentary supremacy, with the accession of William and Mary, as the outstanding characteristic of the British polity made the constitutional clash that was to occur with the Colonies practically inevitable. As far as the Colonies were concerned, 1688 was to mean that the divine right of kings was to be succeeded by the divine right of Parliament. The British assembly, now recognized as supreme in the mother country, was soon to be impelled by the needs of empire to extend its sway, in practice as well as theory, to the overseas dominions belonging to the realm. The Colonies, whose own institutions of self-government were now able to grow to maturity, would meet the Parliamentary pretensions by denying that they were subject to the unlimited control of a legislature in which they had no direct voice.

In particular, it was the accession of William of Orange to the British throne that enabled him to form the great coalition against Louis XIV that was ultimately, after years of bloody warfare, to curb the arrogance and ambitions of the Grand Monarch. The financial needs of a nation engaged for the first time in centuries in a great Continental conflict, led, in 1692, to the creation of the national debt—which has since become an all but permanent institution in virtually all countries. The substitution of William III's interventionist policy for the isolationism of his two predecessors—itself a direct result of the 1688 Revolution—led to the origin of that debt which, in Macaulay's phrase, "has since become the greatest prodigy that ever perplexed the sagacity and confounded the pride of statesmen and philosophers."

When the great conflict with Louis XIV finally ended in 1713, the funded debt had grown to some fifty million pounds—an amount that many felt was too great for the nation to bear. Half a century later the debt had grown to a hundred and forty million, and Adam Smith warned that any further increase might be fatal. George Grenville feared that the nation must sink under the load, unless the burden were shared with the Colonies. The attempt to impose part of the burden upon the Colonies led directly to the American Revolution.

In Britain itself the Glorious Revolution finally fixed the fundamental features of the Constitution. In this sense, it was both the summing-up and the final settler of the essential lines of constitutional development. At first glance, this assertion may seem exaggerated, since we are dealing with an event that, after all, made practically no formal alteration in the organic position. If we look at the enacted law establishing the Revolution Settlement—the Bill of Rights (1689), Triennial Act (1694), Act of Settlement (1701)—we are surprised, indeed, by the paucity of substantive changes made in the law of the Constitution.

Legally speaking, the powers of the Crown remained all but unaltered; the authority that the last Stuart kings had validly exercised continued intact, with minor adjustments, in their immediate successors. With Maitland, then, we may say that "it was a goodly heritage that was settled on King William. . . . It was no honorary president of a republic that the nation wanted, but a real working, governing king . . .—and such a king the nation got." Yet if the legal powers of the Crown were not, in the main, formally curtailed, it can scarcely be denied that their whole basis had been transformed. William and Mary and their successors could hardly hope to attain the exact position in the polity held by their two Stuart predecessors. "In outer seeming," J. R. Green observes, "the Revolution of 1688 had only transferred the sovereignty over England from James to William and

Mary. In actual fact, it was transferring the sovereignty from the king to the House of Commons." The institution that unmade and made kings was now the sovereign power in the constitutional system; no post-Stuart monarch could expect to prevail against the united will of the representatives of the nation.

The fundamental question resolved in 1688, says Trevelyan, was: "Is the law above the King, or is the King above the law? . . . if law stood above the King's will, yet remained alterable by Parliament, Parliament would be the supreme power in the State."

It is, of course, true that if we look only at the lawmaking power we find that the Crown itself possesses an important part of that power, in the authority of the monarch to negate any measure voted by the Parliament. Nor was the Crown's veto power formally curtailed by the Revolution. Thus, William III himself did not hesitate to veto laws passed by the estates of the realm on several important occasions.

Since the death of William, as a matter of formal law, the veto power of the Crown has continued in full force. In constitutional theory alone, the queen today retains the same authority to refuse her consent to any law that was possessed by any of her predecessors. But the constitutional reality has become an altogether different thing! The words refusing the royal assent to a bill have actually been pronounced only once since William III's day—and that as long ago as 1707, when Anne withheld her approval from the Scotch Militia Bill. Since that time, the royal prerogative of vetoing laws has all but disappeared from the British Constitution—though, to this very day, constitutional form makes every statute the act of the queen, and, without her assent, no bill even now can ever be inscribed in the statute book.

If we look at English constitutional history since the time of William III, we find that one broad theme is the steady disuse of the prerogatives of the Crown, at least insofar as the personal authority of the sovereign is concerned. The end result is that, like the veto power, the prerogatives soon become mere vestigial survivals—constitutional curiosities, to remind us of an earlier day, when the monarch not only reigned but ruled.

It would very much surprise people, wrote Walter Bagehot in his *English Constitution,* if they were only told how many things the queen could do at present without consulting Parliament. Yet, even in Queen Victoria's day, it was pure fiction to talk of such prerogatives as though they were possessed and exercised personally by the sovereign. The true picture in modern times was stated in a 1913 memorandum written for George V by Lord Esher at the time of the Home-Rule crisis:

"Has the King then no prerogatives?

"Yes, he has many, but when translated into action, they must be exercised on the advice of a Minister responsible to Parliament. In no case can the Sovereign take political action unless he is screened by a Minister who has to answer to Parliament.

"This proposition is fundamental, and differentiates a Constitutional Monarchy based upon the principles of 1688 from all other forms of government."

After 1688, it was all but preordained that the British king would develop into a constitutional monarch, possessed more of the form than the substance of sovereignty. Once the long struggle between absolute and limited monarchy had been settled, the natural development was one in which the prerogatives of the Crown came to be exercised (in accordance with the Esher memorandum), not at the will of the sovereign, but of the responsible ministers, who represent the will of the nation, as expressed through the majority of the House of Commons.

Two fortuitous circumstances contributed to the evolution of the Cabinet system that has become the hallmark of the modern British polity. The first was the fact that the Revolution Settlement was not embodied in a formal organic document. According to *The Autocrat of the Breakfast-Table,* "a written constitution is essential to the best social order." This sentiment is natural in an American. Like most principles of political science, however, it states not eternal truth, but a principle that in application depends primarily upon circumstances of time and place. What was necessary, constitutionally speaking, in the newly independent United States would at best have been inconvenient, if not mischievous, in the England of a century earlier.

An inflexible constitution drawn up after the deposition of James II would have frozen organic development into a rigid mold before the opportune time for constitutional codification had arrived. An organic instrument framed in 1689 would have assigned to the king, in perpetuity, powers that the sovereign soon began to hand over to his ministers, shortly to begin their collective evolution into the more modern Cabinet. In addition, in view of the strong popular support for the so-called Place Bill in the 1690's, it is probable that any formal constitution would have completely excluded the king's ministers from sitting in the Commons—a principle that, if embodied in written organic rule, would have rendered impossible the development of the modern Cabinet system.

Even more significant in enabling the post-1689 constitutional development to occur as it did was the happy accident that, for over half a century after the reign of William III, the throne was occupied by sovereigns who had practically no interest in personally exercising any of the prerogatives still legally possessed by the Crown. Instead, they were all too willing to leave the actual governmental responsibility to their ministers, who now began to exercise (though always in the monarch's name) the substance of power that they have ever since retained.

The royal indifference to the exercise of governmental prerogatives was especially apparent during the reigns of the first two Hanoverian kings. Both Georges were foreigners, wholly unfamiliar with the institutions of the country over which they were called upon to reign. George I could scarcely even communicate properly with his ministers, since he knew no English—his conversations with Walpole, his first minister, had to be carried on in Latin not very fluent on either side. (This tale has recently been branded as apocryphal by J. H. Plumb, though it had been accepted by countless historians as an important factor in explaining the first Hanoverian's lack of interest in the British polity.) It is certain, however, that the first two Georges were all too willing to delegate the burdens of government to their ministers. In Sir Erskine May's description, "left to the indulgence of their own personal tastes—occupied by frequent visits to the land of their birth, by a German court, favorites and mistresses—they were not anxious to engage more than was necessary in the turbulent contests of a constitutional government. Having lent their name and authority to competent ministers, they acted upon their advice."

The first two Georges' lack of interest in English government and politics had most beneficial constitutional results. As Taswell-Langmead puts it, "It allowed the English constitution to develop freely under a kingship from which the element of personal royal power was for the time practically eliminated." This elimination was of the greatest practical importance. Though, with the ouster of James II, the primacy in the polity had passed to the Parliament, the power of the Crown could still be decisive in making its will felt in the unreformed House of Commons. That the Crown, as the fountain of honors and patronage, could tilt the electoral scale as it chose was acutely pointed out in a memorandum prepared for George I on his accession (1714) by Lord Chancellor Cowper: "Give me leave to assure Your Majesty, on repeated experience, . . . that it is wholly in Your Majesty's power to give which of the two parties you please a clear majority in all succeeding Parliaments, by showing your favor in due time, before the elections, to one or other of them."

Had the first Hanoverian king accepted the invitation to personal rule, the constitutional history of England during the past two and a half centuries might well have developed along entirely different lines. But since the first two Georges emphatically rejected the invitation, the substance of power was left almost entirely in the hands of the ministers to whom the authority of the Crown had been delegated.

When George III came to the throne, he sought to recover the ground lost under his immediate predecessors. But it was already too late to restore the balance in favor of personal rule by the Crown. Not even the young George III could now seek to govern contrary to the votes of the House of Commons or other than through ministers who had the confidence of that Chamber. In Trevelyan's trenchant summation, "To bribe Parliament was one thing, to defy it quite another."

By the time of the third George, the system of ministerial government based upon collective responsibility to the House of Commons was already too firmly established to be overthrown and was regarded as an essential part of the polity. The dependence of the Ministry upon the Commons was, indeed, fully recognized when Sir Robert Walpole was at the head of the government during the early part of George II's reign. "When I speak here as a minister," affirmed Walpole in the Commons in 1739, "I speak as possessing my powers from his Majesty, but as being answerable to this House for the exercise of those powers." The "approbation of this House," he declared, "is preferable to all that power, or even Majesty itself, can bestow."

When Walpole made that speech, the Cabinet system was, of

course, well on the way toward being established as an essential institution of the polity. The growth of the system was an almost inevitable development when once the fundamental principle of Parliamentary supremacy was settled in 1688–1689. For Parliamentary government to work, the people's representatives must exercise control over the executive departments. Yet it is obvious that a chamber of several hundred persons can scarcely be expected to perform that function effectively. The answer the British system has developed to resolve the dilemma has been the Cabinet—a committee of the leading Parliamentary members of the dominant party who head the different executive departments, always subject to retention of the confidence of a majority of the House of Commons, upon which the very life of the Cabinet depends.

The Cabinet system itself is the distinctive feature of the modern type of Parliamentary government. It is, Trevelyan tells us, "the key by which the English were able to get efficient government by a responsible and united executive, in spite of the fact that the executive was subject to the will of a debating assembly of five or six hundred men." The present-day concept of Cabinet government is based upon principles that were acknowledged soon after the expulsion of James II. The "noiseless revolution," as Macaulay calls it, by which William III first selected what may be called a Ministry in the modern sense, was effected by the close of 1696. It was not, however, until the first two Hanoverian kings sat on the throne that the system of government by a Ministry—nominally the king's servants, but really representing the will of the majority party in the House of Commons—was fully established. And it was not until the great Reform Bills of the nineteenth century that the Cabinet system really reached its final form.

In peculiarly English fashion, the Cabinet remained unknown to the law long after it had become the efficient engine of the political system. Blackstone in 1765 could write his celebrated *Commentaries on the Laws of England,* containing an account of the public law of his day, without even mentioning the Cabinet. And, as late as 1888, Maitland, in his lectures on constitutional history, could say that the Cabinet was "an organization which is not a legal organization. . . . the law does not condemn it, but it does not recognize it—knows nothing about it."

Even today, the legal picture in this respect is not very

different. "Legally speaking" states S. B. Chrimes in the 1965
edition of his short constitutional history, "there is still no such
thing as the Cabinet, even though statute recognizes the existence
of Ministers of Cabinet rank, and prescribes a salary for them."
That is true even though all students of the British system know
that the Cabinet has long been what Bagehot termed the "efficient
secret" of the Constitution, the "connecting link" by which was
rendered effective "the close union, the nearly complete fusion of
the executive and legislative powers," upon which the very polity
turned.

Before the Cabinet could evolve from the Whig junto of
William III's day to the body of responsible ministers it has since
become, certain basic principles had to be perfected. These had
to do with what Maitland called "the growing solidarity of the
Cabinet. This solidarity (I can find no better word for it) we may
analyze into three principles: (1) political unanimity, (2) common responsibility to parliament, (3) submission to a common
head."

The principle of political unanimity, under which all ministers
are chosen from the same party, marks one of the chief differences between the modern Cabinet and the earlier "council" or
"committees" out of which that body evolved. First applied in the
reign of William III, it became established under the Hanoverian
dynasty, when the Whig Ministry of Walpole set the pattern that
has since (though with occasional aberrations) been followed.
Certainly, by the end of the eighteenth century, except upon the
rare occasions when there may be coalition Ministries, it is
already unthinkable for the bonds of party to be breached in the
choice of Cabinet members.

According to the 1965 edition of the *Encyclopaedia Britannica,*
"The doctrine of collective responsibility is the keystone of the
cabinet arch." It gives the Cabinet the unified cohesiveness that is
necessary for it to govern effectively. It is the Ministry as a whole
that is responsible to Parliament and that implies an obligation
on every minister to support Cabinet decisions in public or else
resign. The principle of collective responsibility was fully established by the end of the eighteenth century. Said Lord North in a
1778 debate on the subject of Cabinet responsibility, "the crimes
or faults, or errors committed there, were imputable to the whole
body, and not to a single individual who composed it."

For the Cabinet as thus developed to function properly, it had to develop a common head, to whom the other members would be, in some degree, subordinate. Like the Cabinet itself, the Prime Minister is known to the law in only the slightest degree. The title began, indeed, as a derogatory term. Sir Robert Walpole, usually deemed the first Prime Minister, was called this only by his opponents, as a term of reproach. "According to our constitution," declared Samuel Sandys, in moving a 1741 address for Walpole's removal, "we can have no sole and prime minister; we ought always to have several prime ministers . . . [each with] his own proper department."

Yet it was apparent by Walpole's time, that a first minister was absolutely essential, if Cabinet government were to run smoothly. Thus, we are told in Lord Hervey's contemporary memoir that George II, who at first desired to conduct things differently, soon arrived at "an opinion that it was absolutely necessary, from the nature of the English Government, that he should have but one minister; and that it was equally necessary, from Sir Robert's superior abilities, that he should be that one."

Since Walpole's day, it has never been doubted that there must be a primacy in the Cabinet. In 1803 William Pitt could categorically affirm that it was "an absolute necessity in the conduct of the affairs of this country, that there should be an avowed and real Minister, possessing chief weight in the Council, and the principal place in the confidence of the King. . . . That power must rest in the person generally called the First Minister"— though it was not until Sir Robert Peel in the 1840's that the position of Prime Minister in the present-day sense was fully established and not until the last quarter of the nineteenth century that the title itself was officially used.

The great theme, then, during the century and a half after the accession of William and Mary was the development of the Cabinet system, through which alone the Parliamentary supremacy established by the events of 1688–1689 could be effectively maintained. For the system to mature, two further principles had to develop. The first was the rule that the king is bound to act on the advice of his ministers—which has, in substance, meant the demise of the royal personal will and pleasure in the government. Except for George III's retrograde effort to govern as well as reign, no post-Hanoverian sovereign has even attempted to violate this essential principle of constitutional monarchy.

This does not mean that the Crown has not been without influence on matters such as the selection of a Ministry. As recently as Victoria, the queen exercised strong influence on the composition of Cabinets. And, even in our own day, there are indications of a royal discretion in some political matters. But the day of active direction of politics by the Crown has been gone for at least the better part of a century. When it was stated that Edward VII was actively opposed to a certain policy, a denial was issued: "The King never expresses any opinion on political matters except on the advice of his ministers, and therefore the statement must be inaccurate."

Most important of all, however, is the development of the principle that the king must choose his ministers—or, to put it more accurately in terms of the more modern practice, his first minister—solely in accordance with the will of the House of Commons. Already in Walpole's day, we saw, the principle that the Ministry depended upon the support of the Commons was recognized. Yet even after that time, the Crown has sought at times to support Ministries that did not have the confidence of a majority of the House. In 1804, George III, we are told by a contemporary, declared "that he had taken a positive determination not to admit Mr. Fox into his councils, even at the hazard of civil war."

The most important modern incident of the Crown's supporting a Ministry not supported by the House occurred early in Victoria's reign. In 1839, the queen refused to appoint Sir Robert Peel as Prime Minister because of his insistence upon changes in Household appointments, and instead entrusted the administration to Lord Melbourne, whose Ministry lasted two years, despite the fact that his party had only a minority in the House. But the Melbourne Cabinet had to resign when Peel carried a resolution in the Commons that "it is at variance with the spirit of the Constitution for a ministry to continue in office without the confidence of the House."

Since that time, it has never been gainsaid that the principle for which the Peel resolution contended is constitutionally correct. Though there were other minority governments during Victoria's reign (notably in 1846–1852, 1858–1859, and 1866–1868), as well as a coalition (in 1852–1855), that was true only because no party had a decisive majority during those years. When clear electoral verdicts were given, even the imperious queen could not resist them. However personally distasteful Gladstone may have been to her, she had no choice but to call him to power whenever he was given a workable majority in the Commons. And, during the present century, of course, the principle that the Prime Minister should be chosen in accordance with the will of the House of Commons has never been questioned, much less violated.

Perhaps even more significant to an American observer than the evolution of the Cabinet system during the century and a half following James II's ouster was the development of many of the essential guarantees of personal liberty during the same period. It was these guarantees, as they were developed by English law during the eighteenth century, that served both as the basis for Americans' resistance to encroachments upon personal liberties (throughout the first part of their struggle against the mother country it was their claim to "the rights of Englishmen" upon which the colonists rested their case) and the foundation for the subsequent elevation of these liberties to the constitutional plane by American Constitution-makers.

The primary requisite for the development of legal guarantees for individual liberties was the independence of the judiciary, which was a principal feature of the Revolution Settlement. As already pointed out, since William III's time, English judges have been appointed during good behavior. The security of tenure so provided was strengthened by a 1760 statute under which neither judicial office nor salary was to be affected by the demise of the Crown. Judicial independence has made it possible for the English judges to develop the fundamental principles of personal right in their case-law, even without the establishment of such principles by a written organic document. Since the Revolution Settlement, no English judge has come even close to staining the bench with the obloquy associated with those Stuart judges who had been the mere instruments of the royal will.

Foremost among the rights of the individual is, of course, that of the sanctity of the person itself—that right of personal freedom in the physical sense upon which all other rights, in the last resort, depend. In *Sommersett's Case* (1772)—almost a century before the same rule became part of American law—Lord Mansfield declared the basic principle that slavery was contrary to the law of England. According to perhaps the greatest of English judges, "The state of slavery is of such a nature, that it is incapable of being introduced on any reasons. . . . It is so odious that nothing can be suffered to support it."

To be sure, it is not enough merely to state the principle of personal liberty. Even more important is the provision of legal machinery by which that principle is made effective in practice. In the writ of habeas corpus, the English system has provided the most effective legal machinery ever developed for giving practical meaning to the physical liberty of the person. The Habeas Corpus Act of 1679 was the landmark statute that established the procedure by which the Great Writ might be speedily secured in actual cases of detention. Even after the 1679 statute, however, habeas corpus procedure was still subject to two defects: (1) there was no limit on the amount of bail that might be demanded; and (2) the court could not go behind the fact of the return so that a false return could not readily be attacked. The first defect was dealt with by the prohibition against excessive bail in the Bill of Rights, 1689, the second by an 1816 statute that authorized the judges "to examine into the Truth of the Facts set forth in such Return," and in all cases of doubt to bail the prisoner.

One matter of great consequence to personal liberty had not been settled by the 1679 Habeas Corpus Act, namely, the practice of arresting persons by general warrants (i.e., warrants not specifically describing the person or things to be seized, or the place to be searched). Though this practice was declared illegal by the House of Commons in 1680, it persisted until the matter was finally resolved by the courts in the middle of the eighteenth century.

The general-warrant issue was brought to a head by the publication by John Wilkes in 1763 of the celebrated No. 45 of the *North Briton,* with its offensive attack upon the king's speech. A general warrant was issued for the discovery and arrest of the authors and printers (not named) of the newspaper. "Armed with their roving commission," says Sir Erskine May of the officials who executed the warrant, "they set forth in quest of unknown offenders; and unable to take evidence, listened to rumors, idle tales, and curious guesses. They held in their hands the liberty of every man whom they were pleased to suspect."

No less than forty-nine persons, including Wilkes himself, were arrested on suspicion under the general warrant. Wilkes and his printer brought separate actions for damages for false arrest and recovered verdicts. In both cases, the general warrant was ruled illegal, the court asserting in one of them, "If such a power is truly invested in a secretary of state, and he can delegate this power, it certainly may affect the person and property of every man in this kingdom and is totally subversive of the liberty of the subject."

Then, in 1765, came what the United States Supreme Court in 1959 said "is properly called the great case of Entick v. Carrington." That case, the American high bench tells us, "announced the principle of English law which became part of the Bill of Rights and whose basic protection has become imbedded in the concept of due process of law. It was there decided that English law did not allow officers of the Crown to break into a citizen's home, under cover of a general executive warrant, to search for evidence."

Entick v. Carrington also arose out of a general warrant against the suspected author of several numbers of another newspaper, directing his seizure, "together with his books and papers." An action was brought against the officials concerned and a verdict was again recovered. This time, the ringing opinion of Lord Camden set the matter at rest by holding conclusively (a holding never since challenged in Britain itself) that the general-warrant practice was absolutely beyond the pale of legality.

Under Lord Camden's analysis, the very structure of arbitrary authority of arrest and search and seizure collapsed. He completely denied that any Cabinet member could order arrest on his own authority, save in cases of treason, and certainly not by any general warrant. In addition, he ruled that the seizure of books and papers under a general warrant (not specifying the things to be taken, but giving authority to take all books and papers in their discretion) was completely contrary to law. What *Entick v. Carrington* established is the fundamental principle that a person may not be seized, nor his house ransacked, on mere suspicion. "If this point should be determined in favour of the jurisdiction," Lord Camden affirmed, "the secret cabinets and bureaus of every subject in this kingdom will be thrown open to the search and inspection . . . , whenever the secretary of state shall think fit to charge, or even to suspect a person."

Dr. Johnson, Boswell tells us, "would not admit the importance of the question concerning the legality of general warrants. . . . 'It is a matter of such indifference, a matter about which the people care so very little, that were a man to be sent over Britain to offer them an exemption from it at a half-penny a piece, very few would purchase it.' " But, like too many of the great Panjandrum's political observations, this sentiment scarcely shows an understanding of the crucial constitutional issue. The men who made the American Revolution knew better. The practice that Lord Camden outlawed in *Entick v. Carrington* continued in full force on the western side of the Atlantic and was, indeed, one of the primary causes of the breach that took place between the Colonies and the mother country. When Britain sought to enforce the increased revenue imposts upon the Colonies that followed the French and Indian War, the principal instruments of that enforcement were general warrants and writs of assistance (which were virtually blank search warrants).

Four years before *Entick v. Carrington* itself, James Otis delivered his landmark attack in Massachusetts against general warrants and writs—an attack that has been described as the first step on the road toward American independence. The Otis oration, exclaimed John Adams, "breathed into this nation the breath of life," and "Then and there the child Independence was born."

When the Framers had finally won the struggle for nationhood, they did not forget the abuses in the general-warrant practice from which they had suffered. They sought instead to ensure that such abuses would not recur in the polity they were creating. To that end, the Fourth Amendment provides expressly for "The right of the people to be secure . . . against unreasonable searches and seizures" and demands that all warrants shall be ones "particularly describing the place to be searched, and the persons or things to be seized"—a provision that Justice Frankfurter once described as central to enjoyment of all the other guarantees of the Bill of Rights.

Thus it was that English law had, by the end of the eighteenth century, developed the protection of the individual and his property from unjustified governmental intrusion to the point where William Pitt the Elder could make his celebrated declaration: "The poorest man may in his cottage bid defiance to all the force of the Crown. It may be frail; its roof may shake; the wind may blow through it; the storm may enter, the rain may enter—but the King of England cannot enter; all his force dares not cross the threshold of the ruined tenement."

The development just described, culminating in the general-warrant cases in England, and a quarter century later in the Fourth Amendment in this country, would scarcely have occurred when it did, but for the establishment of freedom of the press, which enabled men like Entick and Wilkes to write and publish newspapers. The first newspapers actually began to appear late in the reign of James I. Under the first two Stuarts, nevertheless, the press was anything but free; publication was closely controlled, in Sir Erskine May's phrase, "by the licensor, the Star Chamber, the dungeon, the pillory, mutilation, and branding."

The fall of Star Chamber did not mean the end of a controlled press. The Long Parliament continued a stringent system of licensing and censorship. Milton's *Areopagitica* is eloquent testimony both of the contemporary suppression of truth by the licensor—the slaying of "an immortality rather than a life"—and of the need to end "this authentic Spanish policy of licensing" and to guarantee instead "the liberty to know, to utter, and to argue freely according to conscience, above all liberties."

Milton's plea for press freedom had little influence in his own day. Under both the Commonwealth and Restoration, strict licensing of the press was continued. Within a half century after he wrote, however, the Milton view was vindicated. Freedom of the press was one of the early benefits from the expulsion of the Stuarts. In 1695, the House of Commons refused to renew the Licensing Act, "Because that Act prohibits any Thing to be printed till licensed; . . . by Colour thereof, great Oppression may be, and has been, practised."

The system of compulsory licensing of all publications that had been rigorously enforced since Tudor times, consequently expired. Since 1695, overt censorship of the press has formed no part of English law (at least in time of peace). The press, in Macaulay's phrase, "was emancipated from the censorship soon after the Revolution; and the government immediately fell under the censorship of the press."

By the middle of the eighteenth century, Blackstone could categorically declare that "The liberty of the press is indeed essential to the nature of a free state." By Blackstone's day, freedom of the press had already come to mean what it meant to the men who wrote the First Amendment into the American Constitution—the right of every free man to lay what sentiments he pleases before the public without being required to obtain a license to be able to publish and the prohibition of prior restraints upon publication by anything akin to a censorship system.

If we look at the Constitution that developed as the fruit of the Revolution Settlement, we must conclude that, with all its defects, it was by far the best organic system that had till then evolved. Certainly, foreign observers of the time looked to the English system with admiration, if not envy. To them, the British Constitution was (to paraphrase Madison in *The Federalist*), what Homer has been to the didactic writers on epic poetry.

A typical foreign admirer was Voltaire, who, in 1717, was sent to the Bastille for a poem that he had not written, whose author he did not know, and with whose views he did not agree. When he visited England a few years before Blackstone delivered his eulogy of English law, it is scarcely surprising that his predominant feeling was of having left the realm of despotism for a land where, though the laws might sometimes be harsh, men were ruled by law and not by caprice. Here, said Voltaire, the very air that one breathes is free, for there is no place for arbitrary power.

The encomium of so acute an observer is perhaps the best commentary on the Constitution that had developed in Britain as a result of the Revolution Settlement. Compared to other systems of the time, the British polity was remarkably well balanced— one of the few systems of the day to recognize the truth of the famous Madison maxim, "that where the *whole* power of one department is exercised by the same hands which possess the *whole* power of another department, the fundamental principles of a free constitution are subverted."

Blackstone, typical son of his century that he was, used the analogy of mechanical science to illustrate the principle of constitutional balance: "Like three distinct powers in mechanics, they jointly impel the machine of government in a direction different from what either, acting by itself, would have done; but at the same time in a direction partaking of each, and formed out of all; a direction which constitutes the true line of the liberty and happiness of the community."

The eighteenth century—the age of etiquette and overrefinement, when every activity, however practical, was embarrassed by ceremonial and checks—has since given way to an age dominated by supposedly more practical considerations. In the mid-twentieth century, the attitude expressed by Edmund Burke toward the institutions of his country—"We ought to understand it according to our measure; and to venerate where we are not able to understand"—appears as quaint as the costume of his time. To the changing English Constitution since Burke's day and especially to the dominant features of the contemporary Constitution we must now, in conclusion, turn.

12

REFORM AND THE CONTEMPORARY
CONSTITUTION

IN 1780, JOHN DUNNING moved his now famous resolution in the House of Commons, "that the influence of the crown has increased, is increasing, and ought to be diminished." In 1937, another Commons resolution was moved. "In the opinion of this house," it asserted, in almost the very words of Dunning's motion, "the power of the Executive has increased, is increasing and ought to be diminished."

During the century and a half between the Dunning resolution and its more recent counterpart, the problem of abuse of power in the British system changed drastically. The Revolution Settlement had, it is true, shifted the entire sovereignty to the national legislature, and particularly to its elective Chamber. Yet, as pointed out in the previous chapter, an assembly made up of several hundred persons can scarcely perform efficiently the task of controlling, much less directly exercising, the multifold powers of government.

In Dunning's day, the Parliament was controlled through that system of "management" which the Duke of Newcastle had converted into a fine art. During the first part of George III's reign, the king himself was able to "manage" the House of Commons and ensure a majority for his policies and those through whom he chose to govern. Hence, when Dunning moved his resolution, the primary constitutional complaint was that against the "influence" of the Crown. The growth of this influence, at a period in English history when government by prerogative had so recently been subverted and popular rights and freedoms enlarged, is, indeed, the starting point for Sir Erskine May's treatment of constitutional history during the century after the accession of George III.

By 1937, when the more recent Dunning-type resolution was moved, the constitutional situation had become completely altered. The problem of royal influence gradually disappeared during the eighteenth and nineteenth centuries. With the accession to power of the Whigs in 1830 and the enactment of the great Reform Act of 1832, government became directly responsible to the majority; the controlling element came to be less and less "influence" and more and more public opinion.

For influence by the Crown, the more modern British polity has substituted as the dominant factor control by political party. And that, in turn (as we shall see), has tended to make responsibility of the Cabinet to the House of Commons more a matter of theory than reality most of the time. Supervision of the Executive by the people's representatives has become increasingly less effective in the face of ever-tightened party discipline. The result, is that, in Sir Ivor Jennings' neat phrase, "the House does not control the Government but the Government controls the House."

In the present English polity, the dominant development is that of the expansion of executive power. The twentieth century has seen a constant increase in the authority of the Executive and a correlative decrease in the effectiveness of Parliament as against Her Majesty's Government. Consequently, for the "influence of the Crown," against which Dunning's motion was directed, the 1937 resolution substituted "the power of the Executive," for it is the department that has "waxed fat" in the contemporary Constitution.

The growth of executive power in the twentieth-century sense was not, however, the development that the men of the eighteenth century—which Sir David Lindsay Keir terms "the Classical Age" of the English Constitution—anticipated or directed their energies to control. Once the influence of the Crown had been minimized, the principal political problem appeared to be the legally unlimited power of an omnicompetent legislature. With Madison, political thinkers of the day came to see that "The legislative department is everywhere extending the sphere of its activity, and drawing all power into its impetuous vortex. . . . It is against the enterprising ambition of this department that the people ought to indulge all their jealousy and exhaust their precautions."

In the American system, of course, the problem of the over-weening legislature was dealt with by the written Constitution, which set up a system of checks and balances between the three branches. In Britain, the solution was along different lines, for the problem of legislative power was intimately related to the un-representative character of the national assembly, even in its elected Chamber.

In the last two chapters, we saw how the Glorious Revolution had preserved Englishmen from the dangers of unlimited pre-rogative. Thenceforth, both liberty and property were secure from Stuart-type attacks by prerogative. No government after 1688 even ventured to infringe upon any of the rights guaranteed in the 1689 Bill of Rights. But, as Macaulay puts it, "The Revolution had saved the nation from one class of evils, but had at the same time—such is the imperfection of all things human—engendered or aggravated another class of evils which required new remedies." During the long seventeenth-century struggle against the Stuarts, the aim of the opponents of prerogative had been to shift the constitutional balance in favor of the House of Commons. Now, the Parliamentary victory had been won and the Commons were legally supreme in the polity. The next line of development, we saw, was the evolution of the Cabinet system, which made the heads of the executive departments directly responsible to the lower House.

The difficulty arose from the fact that, while the Executive was thus becoming fully responsible to the House of Commons, it was becoming apparent that the House of Commons itself was not really responsible to the nation. That was true because the composition of the lower House had, by the latter part of the eighteenth century, become only a parody of a representative assembly, insofar as the apportionment of seats among the actual population of the country was concerned. The reality of the period's Parliamentary representation was pointed out in Paine's *Rights of Man*: "The county of York, which contains nearly a million of souls, sends two county members; and so does the county of Rutland, which contains not an hundredth part of that number. The old town of Sarum, which contains not three houses, sends two members; and the town of Manchester, which contains upward of sixty thousand souls, is not admitted to send any. Is there any principle in these things?"

What was clear was that an astonishingly small minority of the nation could elect a majority of the House of Commons. It was estimated in 1793, when the country had a population of some eight and a half million, that 257 members (an actual majority of the Commons) were returned by only 11,075 electors. In 51 constituencies at the time, there were actually less than 50 voters, and in 130 boroughs less than 300. Worse still was the fact that many of the constituencies were under the absolute control of individuals and/or for sale to the highest bidder (such as the "sale" to the Prince of Wales in 1749 for £3,000 of the right to nominate every member to be elected at Old Sarum). In 1793, it was shown that the Lords of the Treasury, 71 peers, and 82 commoners could together nominate 306 out of 558 members—a decisive majority.

It was thus plain by the latter part of the eighteenth century that most members of the House of Commons did not represent their constituencies and even plainer that their constituencies did not represent the nation. Macaulay sums it up: "while the ministry was accountable to the Parliament, the majority of the Parliament was accountable to nobody."

The obvious remedy was, of course, to make the House of Commons responsible to the nation by making it a truly representative body—i.e., by reforming its constitution so that the number of members from any district was proportionate to the number of people (or at least electors) in that district. This obvious step, despite its clear necessity by the middle of the eighteenth century, took the better part of a century to achieve.

The slow progress of the Reform Movement can be explained by the innately conservative nature of the polity established by the Revolution Settlement, reinforced as it was by the convulsions caused by the French Revolution and the Napoleonic wars. To Englishmen of the day, the expulsion of the last Stuart king and the accession, in his place, of William and Mary had saved them from the type of despotism that prevailed across the Channel. At any moment, such fate might still befall the realm should the pretending heirs of the ousted monarch succeed in recovering their inheritance. Therefore, the dominant aim of both Whig and Tory alike was to preserve unaltered the Revolution Settlement that shielded them from a Jacobite upheaval.

In this state of affairs, it is perhaps not surprising that the system of government fashioned in the crucible of constitutional conflict came to be regarded as (to use what Doctor Johnson once said of the law) "the last Result of Publick Wisdom, acting upon publick Experience." The reaction against James II's attempts at radical revision made men only too ready, for a century and a half, to desire only the continuation of institutions in their existing form. To all too many Englishmen, who looked upon their institutions with the veneration of an Edmund Burke (we are told by G. M. Trevelyan), "the year 1689 seemed the last year of creation, when God looked upon England and saw that it was good."

And what of the indefensible defects like the "rotten boroughs," which plainly could not be justified on any rational grounds? Most men of the day answered with the elder Pitt that they were "the natural infirmity of the Constitution," which he feared "could not be removed without endangering the whole"— "Amputation might be death."

The refusal to make any alterations at all in the Constitution was at its most uncompromising during the quarter century following the French Revolution. The dominant classes of the day, convinced and alarmed by Burke's "choice words and measured phrase," wanted nothing less than to make the slightest alteration in that system which, they were firmly convinced, preserved them from the perils that beset other peoples. Particularly during the Napoleonic wars, all efforts to bring about necessary reforms were severely repressed. "For 15 years," Sir Charles G. Robertson says, "Great Britain lived in the hurricane of a European convulsion, and Wyndham's phrase as to the folly 'of repairing your house in the hurricane season,' for all its shallowness, correctly summed up the mood of three-fourths of Great Britain."

The situation changed drastically with the final defeat of Napoleon. In the words of Henry Brougham after Waterloo, "the *gag* is gone, which used to stop our mouths as often as any reform was mentioned—'Revolution' first, and then 'Invasion.' These cries are gone."

As it turned out, the great reformer was oversanguine in this

1814 statement. Resistance to change was still able to stifle reform legislation for almost two more decades. By the 1830's, nevertheless, the Reform Movement could no longer be blocked. The existing system of representation could no longer be anything but condemned by men whose eyes were not clouded by revolutionary panic and war fever. The Industrial Revolution was every year pushing forward a new and unrepresented urban population, creating a new middle class, which paid the vast bulk of the taxes but under the existing electoral order had no political rights. By 1830, the pressure for reform had become all but irresistible. As William Cobbett wrote at the time, it is as "clear as daylight that reform arose out of the will and resolution of the people."

When Parliamentary reform came, it came in typically English fashion by legislative enactment voted by the Parliament itself. At the general election of 1831, public opinion in support of the Reform Bill was so overwhelming that a large Commons majority was returned in its favor. Thus it was that, as Trevelyan puts it, "The unreformed House of Commons reformed itself. There was no need of a second Revolution."

Nor is the Trevelyan statement mere hyperbole. It was seen at the time that Parliamentary self-reform was the alternative to the revolution that might well break out if all reform were denied. "If this bill should be rejected," asserted Macaulay in the House of Commons debate, "I pray to God that none of those who concur in rejecting it may ever remember their votes with unavailing remorse, amidst the wreck of laws, the confusion of ranks, the spoliation of property, and the dissolution of social order."

The great achievement of the Reform Movement was the Reform Act of 1832—that memorable statute which produced effects that, in Keir's words, "constitute a veritable revolution." The 1832 Act brought about a reform both in the distribution of Parliamentary seats and in the electoral franchise itself, but its main accomplishment was the redistribution of seats. All the fifty-seven "rotten boroughs" were abolished, and thirty more were divested of half their seats. Twenty-two boroughs, till then unrepresented, received two seats each and twenty-one one representative apiece. Furthermore, the members to be returned from substantially underrepresented areas (notably in London) were increased.

In addition, the great Reform Act placed the elective franchise upon an entirely new basis, essentially by extending the vote to the middle class—to those in boroughs paying rent of £10 yearly and those in counties who were copyholders, leaseholders, or tenants at will paying a rent of £50 a year. The extension of the franchise thus provided was far from revolutionary. As a whole the electorate was increased by some 217,000 or 50 per cent. Five-sixths of the adult male population was still left voteless, including the entire working class. But the process of enfranchisement begun by the great Reform Act could not stop at the line drawn in 1832. On the contrary, the prevailing theme during the century that followed was that of consistent further extensions of the right to vote (by statutes of 1867, 1884, 1918, 1928, and 1948) until in our own day, the stage of suffrage for all adults—and not confined to males alone—has been reached.

As it turned out, then, the Tory opponents of the 1832 Reform Act were right when they asserted that it was only the first step toward establishment of a democratic system. More than that, during the present century, there have been realized in the British polity all three of the great electoral ideals of the original Reform Movement: universal suffrage, "one man, one vote," and "one vote, one value." Today, every adult is entitled to vote; all plural voting, whether university or business, has been abolished; and the electoral map has been recast into single-member constituencies, each embracing substantially equal populations.

It is thus the democratic principle, Sir Ivor Jennings tells us, that is now the fundamental principle of the British system: "The King, the Cabinet, the House of Commons and even the House of Lords are the instruments which history has created as, or political conditions have converted into, instruments for carrying out the democratic principle." Americans, too often dazzled by the venerable façade of government—Queen, Lords, Black Rod, tradition, ceremony, and the like—tend to overlook that all, from the royal prerogative down, have been subordinated to public opinion. All serve as the means for giving effect to the expressed will of the electorate. Not all the ancient panoply of Her Majesty's Government can mask the fact that demos is really now king in the British polity.

Before continuing our discussion of the development of the democratic principle in Britain and its implications for the contemporary constitutional system, a word should be said about another important aspect of the movement to reform existing institutions, which had as its principal product the great electoral reforms already discussed.

On June 6, 1832—the day before the royal assent was given to the great Reform Act—Jeremy Bentham died. The coincidence was fitting, for the name of Bentham is intimately connected with the Reform Movement, though primarily in the legal, rather than the electoral, field. The year before he died, he was characterized by Brougham (himself the leader in translating Bentham's ideas into the statute book) as "the father of law reform."

It should be borne in mind that the English legal system during the first part of the nineteenth century was essentially what it had been in the days of Sir Edward Coke. The three great common-law courts (which were described, during their early development, in Chapter 4) continued unaltered as the repositories of the law in civil cases, to which individuals looked for redress of their ordinary legal grievances. But their procedure was anti-quated and overtechnical, permeated with archaic survivals that had lost their meaning centuries before. The whole was a maze of intricate fictions and technicalities entirely unsuited to the needs of the modern industrial society. Worse still was the inevitable inefficiency involved in the existence of three wholly independent courts with concurrent jurisdiction, each engaged in unseemly competition for business with the others—the result being a deplorable waste of judicial time, with the King's Bench so busy that arrears piled up, while the Common Pleas and Exchequer had much lighter calenders.

Alongside the three common-law courts had grown up the separate Court of Chancery. Originally developed to correct the inadequacies of the common law, the Chancery had, by the nine-teenth century, become the type of tribunal described in *Bleak House*—one in which innumerable *Jarndyce v. Jarndyces* were doomed to drag their dreary length, perennially hopeless.

Worst of all perhaps were the barbarities of the criminal law. The frequency of capital punishment—every felony, even the stealing of a loaf of bread, was punishable by death—was the great blot on English law. The severity of the English criminal code in this respect continued even after the work of Beccaria had its beneficial effects upon the Continent.

In some ways, law reform was even harder to secure than

Parliamentary reform. The view expressed by the Chancellor in *Iolanthe* was all but too characteristic of the manner in which Englishmen (particularly those connected with the legal profession) regarded their law. All too many Englishmen of the day had the attitude toward reform that Bagehot ascribes to the great conservative Chancellor, Lord Eldon: "He believed in everything which it is impossible to believe in—the danger of Parliamentary Reform, the danger of Catholic Emancipation, the danger of altering the Court of Chancery, the danger of altering the Courts of Law, the danger of abolishing capital punishment for trivial thefts, the danger of making landowners pay their debts, the danger of making anything more, the danger of making anything less."

Despite the attitude of men like Eldon, however, reform in the law could not be kept back indefinitely, any more than could reform in the Parliamentary and electoral systems. The nineteenth century, indeed, saw the adoption of the most far-reaching reforms in all branches of English law. "After a long interval of various fortune," declared Brougham in his great Commons speech on law reform in 1828 (itself the great Parliamentary catalyst in the giving of practical effect to the Benthamite philosophy), "and filled with vast events, but marked from age to age by a steady course of improvement, we are called again to the grand labour of surveying and amending the laws." Brougham's address led to the appointment of several royal commissions which, Holdsworth tells us, "effected more for the reform of the law than any royal commissions or reports of Parliamentary committees had ever done before."

What was accomplished was nothing less than a wholesale transformation of the law, retaining the essentials that have always made the English legal system the cynosure of jurists the world over, while, at the same time, eliminating those defects and antiquated anomalies that had earned the deserved strictures of Dickens and other writers. First, there was a complete recasting of the court structure. In the place of the three common-law courts and the wholly separate Court of Chancery, there was established by an 1873 statute one Supreme Court of Judicature (consisting of a High Court, in which cases are tried, and a Court of Appeal). All cases, whether sounding in common law or equity, are instituted in the High Court. Moreover, the separate substantive law, previously administered by the separate common-law and Chancery court systems, was unified.

In addition, the old procedure, encrusted with antiquated technicalities that made every action a running of the formalistic gantlet, was eliminated. In its stead, there was adopted the modern system of pleading and practice, which, even though at times it may appear technical to the layman, is, compared to the earlier procedure, a very model of simplicity and efficiency.

There has been a comparable reform in criminal law and procedure. Most striking was the elimination of the unmitigated harshness of criminal punishment. The appalling frequency of capital punishment was the immediate object of reformers like Romilly and Brougham. So successful were their corrective efforts that they led, during the nineteenth century, to the elimination of the death penalty from all but the most serious offenses and to the abolition of capital punishment in our own day. Also accomplished were improvements in criminal procedure (notably those protecting the adjective rights of those accused) and basic reforms in the penal system.

It may be said that the task of the English constitutional system during the past century and a half has been to adapt itself to the changed conditions brought about by the transition to an urbanized industrial society. By the Parliamentary, electoral, and legal reforms discussed in this chapter, the necessary adaptations were made. The development of the democratic principle, through a century's gradual process—extending political rights to all by the type of steadied progress ("seldom hastening and never turning back," to use Trevelyan's phrase) that is characteristically English—and the establishment of a modern legal order, capable of meeting the needs of the present-day community, have been the great changes that have made for a viable Constitution in a Britain so different from what it was only a generation ago.

Because the Reform Act of 1832 was the inevitable first step toward implementation of the democratic principle, which is now the fundamental principle in the British system, it can be said that the modern history of the British Constitution commences with that statute. That Act, by making the Parliament a truly representative body, finally put an end to the "influence" which had till then served as the main method of securing harmony between the executive and legislative branches. "The representation of 'interests,' " as Keir puts it, "has been abandoned in favour of proportioning representation to population." The Burke doctrine of "virtual" representation has given way to one in which the House of Commons is directly representative of and responsible to the will of a democratic electorate. Thenceforth, as the process of democratization proceeded, political power came more and more to rest upon popular election. The Cabinet became the great link between the Executive and legislature. Hence, Holdsworth can say, "The modern history of the cabinet begins with the Reform Act."

A Chamber that is the constitutional means of giving effect to the will of the people comes naturally to be considered the supreme power in the polity. Legally there can be no restraint upon the body that is the direct reflection of the electoral will, expressed at a general election. Parliamentary supremacy attains its apogee in the constitutional omnipotence of the House that is the political mirror of the entire nation.

The powers of the Crown and of the House of Lords must be exercised in subordination to the will of the elective Chamber. The House of Lords, once in fact as well as name the upper House, inevitably becomes only a mere second Chamber, which may delay but scarcely prevent any change that the Commons is determined to effect. What Coleridge said of the Lords in 1832— that "its supremacy as a co-ordinate estate of the nation" was destroyed—has certainly proven to be true since that time.

Paradoxically, however, the century that has seen the constitutional culmination of the power of the House of Commons (capping the development that had begun so long ago when Simon de Montfort caused writs of summons for the 1265 Parliament to go to knights and burgesses as well as the prelates and barons of the realm) has also seen increasing questioning of the ability of the people's representatives to preserve and maintain their position of supremacy in the polity in a practical sense. In a 1929 broadcast, Bernard Shaw declared, "Our present parliament is obsolete: it can no more do the work of a modern State than Julius Caesar's galley could do the work of an Atlantic liner." This statement may be too extreme, but one familiar with the British government in operation must admit that there is a growing gap between the supreme position of the House of

Commons in constitutional theory and its actual position in the polity.

This gap may be attributed to two vital changes that have largely occurred during the present century: (1) the changed relationship between the House of Commons and the Government, which has increasingly tended to make the latter more the master than the servant of the former; and (2) the changing role of government itself in the modern society—a role that cannot be performed without the delegation by Parliament of the broadest powers to the Executive. These two changes must be briefly discussed so that we can understand the great transformation that has taken place in the contemporary position of Parliament.

It is, of course, an elementary proposition of British constitutional theory that the Government of the day is collectively responsible to the people's representatives, assembled, in collegiate form, in the House of Commons. For a Ministry to be formed, it must have the confidence of the Commons, expressed in the form of a majority vote in its favor by that Chamber. To remain in power, it must retain such majority support. So far as constitutional theory is concerned, the Commons retain complete control over any Government, for they can, at any moment, dismiss that Government by an adverse vote.

The reality of control, as between the Parliament and the Government is, nevertheless, an altogether different matter. This reality has tremendously increased the powers of the Executive, while, at the same time, reducing the effectiveness of Parliament as against Her Majesty's Government. The present century has, in fact, seen a growing ascendancy of the Government in Parliament which has all but made the House of Commons the mere instrument for working the will of the leaders of the majority party.

Perhaps the primary reason for the growth of the *real* power of the Government at the expense of the theoretical Parliamentary hegemony has been the development of party organization and discipline. When Burke delivered his celebrated defense of party in 1770, the party system was after all only rudimentary by present-day standards, and parties could still be deplored by many as mere divisive factions. In our own day, no one can doubt the vital place of party in the British political machine. Sir Gilbert Campion has gone so far, in truth, as to assert that

"Parliament is an engine which seems to require the fuel of party spirit to make it work."

Within limits, the party organization in Britain is plainly necessary if the political system is to work effectively, without being fragmented into splinter groups such as have been the bane of Parliamentary government in too many countries. Yet, as L. S. Amery well states, "The danger lies in the growth of the notion that such an organization, instead of being a useful and, indeed, indispensable adjunct to the work of the party system in Parliament, should in effect supersede it, . . . using Parliament merely as an instrument for carrying through policies shaped without reference to it."

The outstanding fact that dominates the operation of Parliament in the mid-twentieth century is that of party discipline and the strictness of party control over the votes of members. The result is that a Government majority in the House of Commons (almost no matter how slight, as is shown by the experience since the last war when both Labour and Conservative Governments have succeeded in governing with the very slimmest margins) continues for virtually all practical purposes for the life of the Parliament, unless the Ministry chooses for strategic reasons to appeal to the electorate at an earlier date.

Party discipline has ensured the progressive decline of the risk of Government defeat in the House of Commons and has relegated the right of the House to dismiss a Ministry to the status of an all but unused weapon in the Parliamentary armory. "Owing to the intensity of the Party system . . . ," we are told by G. W. Keeton, "such a right has become almost as formal as the royal veto." Party discipline not only all but frees the Government from the danger of defeat by vote of the Commons, it also has increasingly enabled the Government to control the operation of the House itself. In the first place, the Government has acquired a virtual monopoly of the initiative in legislation. Practically all the Parliamentary time available for legislation is now taken over by bills introduced by the Government. In Keeton's phrase, "Bills promoted by private members which eventually reach the statute book have the scarcity value of freaks."

It should also be borne in mind that the time of the House of Commons is controlled by the Government to an extent that is most striking to the American observer. Ministers not only now have precedence over other members for their business but almost completely monopolize the time of the House for such business. Drastic powers are now possessed by the Government for curtailing debate by means of closure, for excluding amendments, and for forcing bills through their different stages in accordance with fixed timetables.

There are to be sure, still the opportunities of "question time" for the individual M.P. who desires to air objections against the Government. One who is familiar with the House of Commons in actual operation must, however, conclude that too many Americans, from Woodrow Wilson down, have overstated the practical importance of the question asked in the House. The question, like so many other Parliamentary weapons, has become less important in controlling the Executive. The characterization of it as "largely ineffective" by so informed an observer as Sir Gilbert Campion, when Clerk of the House of Commons, is significant in this respect. The casual observer cannot help but feel that there is truth in Ellen Wilkinson's 1932 conclusion that "it is the job of the skilled answerer of the questions to produce an answer which will (a) soothe the House of Commons, and (b) give the impression that the questioner is rather a fool, and then everyone is perfectly satisfied."

In some ways, the greatest difficulty from the point of view of effective functioning of the modern legislature is the ever-increasing pressure on Parliamentary time. Since the beginning of the century, the bulk of the statute book has grown from an average of some 350 to an average of over 1,000 pages each session. This means that ever more of the time of the Houses and of members must be devoted to enactment of detailed Government programs. The result, says L. S. Amery, is that "The 'best club in London' has become an overworked legislation factory, with a working day from 10:30 A.M. to 10:30 P.M. or later."

Added to the problem of time is the fact that even the best-informed M.P. is not capable of mastering the vast amount of technical knowledge needed for an informed judgment on modern legislation. "A permanent official," to quote Miss Wilkinson again, "always speaks about the matter coming before Parliament as though that were in fact a real safeguard, but when the average Member of Parliament is expected to have expert knowledge on all subjects from the Charing Cross Bridge to diseases in potatoes, all in the same day, is it not a fact that all this so-called criticism is in fact a farce?"

Thus, the time of the Commons is completely controlled by the Government, and members are all but wholly dependent upon the Executive for the technical information needed to perform their functions. Even if a member is able, despite these handicaps, to take an independent position, he will almost never feel free to refuse to abide by the direction of his party's "whips." And all of this to the end that the Government may be able efficiently to enact its legislative program and defeat any Opposition attempts to delay or amend such program, as it winds its inevitable way from the Queen's Speech to the statute book.

One may wonder, however, whether the transformation of the national assembly into a "legislation factory" is necessarily consistent with the proper position of the legislature in a democratic system or whether it does not, on the contrary, signal a significant decline in Parliamentary status. An assembly is scarcely worthy of the proud name of Parliament (or even Congress, for that matter) if it simply grinds out statutes, as a sausage maker grinds out sausages.

The changed position of the Parliament in relation to the Government that is nominally only its servant is of particular interest to an American in view of recent proposals to extend the terms of Congressmen to make them coincide with that of the President—a proposal endorsed by President Johnson in 1965. This proposal, if elevated to the plane of constitutional amendment, cannot help but make the Congressman more like his counterpart in Britain, insofar as his dependence upon the Administration will be concerned. Though there are doubtless undesirable aspects of the present Congressional independence vis-à-vis the President and party discipline (an independence that has been lessening in both respects in recent years), it is doubtful whether a substitution of the British-type Government and party-controlled legislature would be a solution that Americans, familiar with the actual working of the present-day Parliament, would endorse.

All that has been said about the changed position of Parliament in relation to the Government should be taken together with the great change that has taken place in the role of government itself in the modern society. This change may be traced, in part at least, directly to the progressive extension of the franchise during the past century. The theory enunciated by Burke in his famous 1774 Speech to the Electors of Bristol—that "Your representative . . . betrays instead of serving you if he sacrifices [his judgment] to your opinion"—has given way to the view of the modern voter that his M.P. is less a representative of the broad national interest than a delegate sent to redress his constituents' grievances and further their direct interests.

With the Parliament directly responsible to an electorate co-extensive with the entire nation, public opinion is able to make itself felt in the legislature to a degree never before possible. Nor is it surprising that modern public opinion seeks to have government do ever more for those who make up the vast bulk of the community. The result is that to an ever-increasing extent the modern society is made up of clients, as well as constituents, of the State. The tendency during the present century is the same as that which a Chancellor of the Exchequer spoke of as long ago as 1899: "to look to the Exchequer and the central Government for superintendence, for assistance, for inspection, and for control in all kinds of departments of life, in all kinds of relations between individuals, in which, in the old days, the Government of the country was never deemed capable of action at all."

Much of the present century, in Britain as on the western side of the Atlantic, has been devoted to the expansion of governmental authority—both of the power to regulate the activities carried on by private individuals and that to dispense benefits to individuals and groups. The field of benefactions, in fact, has become increasingly important and today occupies a large proportion of the efforts of government, even more so in Britain than in the United States. The geometric growth of government largess is amply demonstrated by the fact that the political order itself is now compendiously called the Welfare State.

The increasing development of the Welfare State, as well as the dangers inherent in it, were well described in 1931 by a royal commission headed by Lord Macmillan: "The most distinctive indication of the change of outlook of the government of this country in recent years has been its growing preoccupation, irrespective of party, with the management of the life of the people. A study of the Statute Book will show how profoundly the conception of the function of government has altered. Parliament finds itself increasingly engaged in legislation which has for its conscious aim the regulation of the day-to-day affairs of the community, and now intervenes in matters formerly thought to be entirely outside its scope. This new orientation has its dangers as well as its merits. Between liberty and government there is an age-long conflict. It is of vital importance that the new policy, while truly promoting liberty by securing better conditions of life for the people of this country, should not, in its zeal for interference, deprive them of their initiative and independence which are the nation's most valuable assets."

From a constitutional point of view, among the greatest problems posed by the changed role of the State is the need for the legislature to delegate more and more powers to the Executive. Such delegation is an all but inevitable concomitant of the newly positive role of government which causes it to intervene more and more in the day-to-day life of the society. That positive role can hardly be performed by mere prohibitions enacted by legislative fiat. "Much of our social and economic legislation," L. S. Amery tells us, "covers so vast and detailed a field that no statute, however cumbrous . . . could possibly provide for all contingencies." Since the representative assembly is peculiarly unequipped to perform the continuous tasks of regulation and benefaction that are increasingly demanded by the nation, it has had to delegate their performance to the Executive, through its different departments and agencies. "The truth is," reads the 1932 conclusion on the subject of the famous Lord Chancellor's Committee on Ministers' Powers, "that if the Parliament were not willing to delegate law-making power, Parliament would be unable to pass the kind and quantity of legislation which modern public opinion requires."

The constitutional problem arises from the fact that powers are delegated to the Executive in the very widest terms—amounting, in many cases, to a virtual grant of legislative authority coextensive with that of the Parliament itself. The tendency in modern statutes is for the legislature to lay down only the broadest principles—with power given to the Executive to work out all the details of the given legislative scheme. Such statutes are aptly denoted "skeleton legislation," under which the flesh and the blood—not to mention the soul—of the schemes of legislative regulation or benefaction are left entirely to administrative discretion. All too often, as Sir William Graham Harrison put it before the Committee on Ministers' Powers, Parliament has "given the rule-making authority a blank cheque to do anything it thought proper for securing a certain object."

Any observer of the British statute book is bound to note the increasing frequency of wholesale delegations to the Executive. So common has such delegation become that, not too long ago, an M.P. could declare, in the debate on a proposed grant: "Indeed, if only Moses could have known this technique, he would never have committed himself to anything so precise, and occasionally so inconvenient as the Ten Commandments. When he came down from Mount Sinai, he would have taken powers to make regulations."

To what has been said about delegated legislation, which has transferred much of the substance of legislative power from Parliament to the Executive, should be added another crucial factor—the development of the permanent civil service. Such corps of public employees had to be created for government in Britain to be able to perform effectively the multifold functions demanded of it by modern public opinion. The British bureaucracy is, in the main, made up of permanent officials, for whom the public service is a lifetime career and who perform the actual task of carrying out the vast statutory complex of regulation and social services which is the major part of government in the modern State. Only at the very apex of the departmental hierarchy is a change in personnel brought about by a change in Her Majesty's Government, caused by a political shift in the composition of the Commons. The stability of the British administration is, indeed, most striking to an observer from a country where the percentage of public officers appointed by patronage remains surprisingly large.

When we speak of delegation of vast powers to the Executive, we are really referring to the grant of authority to the permanent civil service, who, in practice, perform almost all the actual work of administration carried on by the Government. According to Bernard Shaw, in fact, "The nearest thing to a puppet in our political system is a Cabinet minister at the head of a great public office. Unless he possesses a very exceptional share of dominating ability and relevant knowledge, he is helpless in the hands of his officials. He must sign whatever documents they present to him, and repeat whatever words they put into his mouth."

Shaw's seemingly exaggerated sentiment has been increasingly echoed by serious students of political science. Thus, the same conclusion was reached by Ramsay Muir, in his *How Britain Is Governed:* "The Cabinet has arrogated to itself, half blindly, a series of colossal responsibilities which it cannot meet, which it will not allow Parliament to tackle, and which are not met at all except in so far as they are assumed by the bureaucracy behind the cloak of Cabinet omnipotence."

The changed position of the Parliament and the increased delegation of broad powers (to be exercised, in practice, by the virtually anonymous officials at the head of the permanent civil service) have raised, in modern form, questions not unlike those upon which the great constitutional conflicts of the seventeenth century turned. The two great questions in Stuart times (as G. W. Keeton has recently summarized them) were, first, whether the Crown possessed legislative power, independent of Parliamentary control, and second, whether the ordinary law of the land, administered by the common-law courts, governed all cases and all men.

In today's terms, the first question becomes a very real one in view of the delegation of vast powers to the Executive, delegation so broad that the administrator may in substance be given virtual *carte blanche* upon which he may scribble what he pleases in the delegated area of authority. The paramount position in the Parliament now possessed by the Government, which is still the nominal servant of the House, tends all too often to make Parliamentary control over delegated legislation no more than a mere euphemism.

The second question—that of the supremacy of the common law—may be stated today from two points of view. First is the control by the courts of exercises of delegated power—a control that remains central to the Anglo-American conception of the rule of law. This judicial control, based upon the doctrine of *ultra vires* (under which the courts will annul administrative action beyond the limits of the delegated power), continues as a matter of constitutional theory. Its practical effectiveness is, however, diluted by the breadth of actual delegations. Under the typical modern statute, the *vires*—the limits—of the authority delegated have become so broad as to cover almost all administrative action within the area of governmental function involved.

In addition, the principle that all cases are to be governed by the ordinary law of the land is being put in question by a virtual renaissance of executive justice. "The distinctive development of our era," said Charles Evans Hughes in 1931, "is that the activities of the people are largely controlled by government bureaus in State and Nation. . . . A host of controversies as to private rights are no longer decided in courts." This development has if anything been more striking in Britain than in the United States. The consistent trend there during this century has been one of delegation of the authority to decide cases involving private rights to the Executive. Such cases are increasingly decided, not by the courts of law, but by officials in the relevant Ministry or administrative tribunal. The conferring of judicial-type powers upon Ministries and tribunals has, in truth, proceeded so far that the Executive has replaced the courts in the decision of disputes in ever wider fields of right and obligation. In the extended Executive that it has created, Parliament has thus brought into being a rival, not only to itself, but to the ordinary law.

The developments described here have been strongly censured by distinguished British observers themselves, who see in them a grave peril to the free government that has developed over the centuries. In 1929, Lord Chief Justice Hewart went so far as to write a blistering attack against the growth of executive power, unjudicially titled *The New Despotism*. More recently, there have been books like that of G. W. Keeton, somewhat hyperbolically entitled *The Passing of Parliament*.

One who is himself only an outsider should speak with the greatest diffidence in seeking to evaluate the validity of strictures such as those referred to. The peril of misunderstanding should put a warning finger to the lips of one who is, after all, not himself British. At the same time, one may wonder if those who point to the passing of Parliament and other essential features of the British system do not mourn prematurely. Like the report of Mark Twain's death, it may be said that the predicted demise of the British Constitution has been grossly exaggerated.

If we look at the near-millennium of English constitutional history, as its broad outlines have been summarized in this volume, we can see that Macaulay did not really exaggerate when he wrote, with characteristic Victorian exuberance, "The history of England is emphatically the history of progress." The great theme of English constitutional evolution is the development of free representative institutions—with government more and more coming to be conceived of as the means to an end: liberty under law. To quote Macaulay again, "The Charter of Henry Beauclerk, the Great Charter, the first assembling of the House of Commons, the extinction of personal slavery, the separation from the See of Rome, the Petition of Right, the Habeas Corpus Act, the Revolution, the establishment of the liberty of unlicensed printing, the abolition of religious disabilities, the reform of the representative system—all these seem to us to be the successive stages of one great revolution."

Yet though there has thus been a seemingly inexorable development toward the modern British Constitution, we must not make the mistake of assuming that, with its attainment, the last stage of organic evolution has been reached. On the contrary, we should, with de Tocqueville, recognize that "what we call necessary institutions are often no more than institutions to which we have grown accustomed, and that in the matter of social structure the field of the possible is much wider than men who live in each society imagine."

All we can say with assurance is to repeat, with Albert Camus, that "the wheel turns, history changes." To suppose that one's contemporary system is the ultimate stage of the evolutionary process is as supercilious as it is short-sighted. The fact that the British, like the American, constitutional system is continuing to evolve beyond the "perfection" that Victorian historians (who looked upon all of constitutional history as only a dress rehearsal for the stage reached in the great queen's day) assumed it had attained is scarcely surprising. The problems of the present day— essentially those posed by the twin facts of accelerating urbanization and explosive scientific revolution—can hardly be resolved by the exact institutions and principles that served an age confronted by different difficulties. If the governmental role has altered and the power of the Executive augmented, it has been to enable the State to meet the needs of the industrialized urban society of the mid-twentieth century.

Despite the 1937 resolution quoted at the beginning of this chapter, it is not the growth in the power of the Executive as such that threatens free government. Power canalized within banks that keep it from overflowing is an instrument to allow the State to fulfill its role in the world of today. It is the growth of *uncontrolled* executive power that threatens the constitutional polity.

Those who point only with alarm at contemporary developments in Britain lose sight of the recent efforts made by the British themselves to control the power of the Executive—the impartial investigations by the Committee on Ministers' Powers (1932) and the Committee on Administrative Tribunals and Enquiries (1957), the establishment in the House of Commons in 1944 of a select committee to scrutinize all delegated legislation, the enactment of the Tribunals and Inquiries Act, 1958 (laying down certain procedural essentials for executive justice, providing for judicial control, and the setting up of a Council on Tribunals to review the composition and procedure of administrative tribunals), and, most recently, the appointment of a so-called *ombudsman,* a Parliamentary Commissioner to deal with citizens' complaints against any administrative action.

Perhaps the attempts to control what some deem the inexorable onrush of executive power will prove as futile as the effort to hold back the inevitable attributed to King Canute. One familiar with the great thrust of English constitutional history should, however, take a more optimistic attitude. Certainly, all that has been said in this volume bears out the truth of the de Tocqueville dictum that "It is impossible to think of the English as living under any but a free government." One who knows how seventeenth-century Englishmen met and mastered the challenge posed by the executive power of their day cannot help but feel that somehow their present-day descendants will do no less than follow their example.

REGNAL YEARS OF ENGLISH AND
BRITISH RULERS

WILLIAM I	1066–1087	ELIZABETH I	1558–1603
WILLIAM II	1087–1100	JAMES I	1603–1625
HENRY I	1100–1135	CHARLES I	1625–1649
STEPHEN	1135–1154	OLIVER CROMWELL	1649–
HENRY II	1154–1189	(*The Commonwealth*) 1660	
RICHARD I	1189–1199	CHARLES II	1660–1685
JOHN	1199–1216	JAMES II	1685–1688
HENRY III	1216–1272	WILLIAM III	
EDWARD I	1272–1307	*and* MARY	1689–1702
EDWARD II	1307–1327	ANNE	1702–1714
EDWARD III	1327–1377	GEORGE I	1714–1727
RICHARD II	1377–1399	GEORGE II	1727–1760
HENRY IV	1399–1413	GEORGE III	1760–1820
HENRY V	1413–1422	GEORGE IV	1820–1830
HENRY VI	1422–1461	WILLIAM IV	1830–1837
EDWARD IV	1461–1483	VICTORIA	1837–1901
EDWARD V	1483	EDWARD VII	1901–1910
RICHARD III	1483–1485	GEORGE V	1910–1936
HENRY VII	1485–1509	EDWARD VIII	1936
HENRY VIII	1509–1547	GEORGE VI	1936–1952
EDWARD VI	1547–1553	ELIZABETH II	1952–
MARY	1553–1558		

BIBLIOGRAPHICAL NOTE

THE FIELD of English constitutional history is so vast that any attempt to give a list of all the works relevant to that field would only result in a bibliography too long to be of real value. Instead of such an exhaustive list, the present note is intended as a selective indication of those books which were of particular value or interest to the author in the writing of this volume.

Among the general constitutional histories, the author found most useful: Stubbs, Bishop William, *The Constitutional History of England in Its Origin and Development* (3 vols., 1874–83); Hallam, Henry, *The Constitutional History of England from the Accession of Henry VII to the Death of George II* (2 vols., 5th ed., 1846).

It is recognized that modern research has cast doubt on many of the facts and conclusions in both Stubbs and Hallam. These classical constitutional histories still remain, however, the indispensable tools for study of the subject, Stubbs for the period up to 1485, Hallam from that date to the accession of George III. Both also have the virtue of being written as works of literature, pleasures to read even with their sometimes anachronistic Victorian style.

May, T. Erskine, *The Constitutional History of England Since the Accession of George III* (3 vols., 1912), intended as a sequel to Hallam, covers the period 1760–1860 and 1860–1911 (Vol. III by Francis Holland covers the latter years).

Maitland, F. W., *The Constitutional History of England* (1908). Originally delivered as a series of lectures, this is, in many ways, the most useful work, because of its readable style and its author's unchallenged mastery of the subject.

More modern constitutional histories of value: Taswell-Langmead, Thomas P., *English Constitutional History* (11th ed., 1960, by T. F. T. Plucknett); Keir, David L., *The Constitutional History of Modern Britain Since 1485* (6th ed., 1960); Jolliffe, J. E. A., *The Constitutional History of Medieval England from the English Settlement to 1485* (4th ed., 1961); Chrimes, S. B., *English Constitutional History* (3rd ed., 1965), a survey even briefer than the present volume.

240

Among English constitutional histories by Americans are: Adams, George B., *Constitutional History of England* (rev. ed., 1934), the standard American text; Marcham, F. G., *A Constitutional History of Modern England, 1485 to the Present* (1960); Smith, G., *A Constitutional and Legal History of England* (1955).

To a constitutional lawyer, in some ways the best detailed treatment of the subject is in Sir William Holdsworth's monumental *History of English Law* (15 vols., 1903–65, with Vols. I–XII by Holdsworth himself).

Other legal histories of value are: Plucknett, T. F. T., *A Concise History of the Common Law* (5th ed., 1956); Pollock, F., and Maitland, F. W., *A History of English Law Before the Time of Edward I* (2 vols., 2nd ed., 1911), the classic account of early legal history; E. Jenks, *A Short History of English Law* (5th ed., 1938); Radcliffe, G. R. Y., and Cross, G., *The English Legal System* (4th ed., 1964).

For collections of constitutional documents and other source materials, see: Stephenson, C., and Marcham, F. G., *Sources of English Constitutional History* (1937); Stubbs, W., *Select Charters and Other Illustrations of English Constitutional History from the Earliest Times to the Reign of Edward the First* (9th ed., 1913), with invaluable commentary; Tanner, J. R., *Tudor Constitutional Documents* (1922); Elton, G. R., *The Tudor Constitution* (1961); Tanner, J. R., *Constitutional Documents of the Reign of James I* (1930); Gardiner, S. R., *Constitutional Documents of the Puritan Revolution* (3rd ed., 1906); Kenyon, J. R., *The Stuart Constitution* (1966); Costin, W. C., and Watson, J. S., *The Law and Working of the Constitution: Documents 1660–1914* (2 vols., 1961); Williams, E. N., *The Eighteenth-Century Constitution 1688–1815* (1960).

Works covering a particular period which were found of special value include:

I. McKechnie, W. S., *Magna Carta* (2nd ed., 1914), still the classic work on the subject, though subject to criticism by more recent writers; Holt, J. C., *Magna Carta* (1965); Thompson, F., *Magna Carta: Its Role in the Making of the English Constitution, 1300–1629* (1948); Painter, S., *The Reign of King John* (1949); Warren, W. L., *King John* (1961).

II. Ilbert, Courtenay, *Parliament: Its History, Constitution, and Practice* (3rd ed., 1948); McIlwain, Charles H., *The High Court of Parliament and Its Supremacy* (1910); Pollard, A. F., *The Evolution of Parliament* (2nd ed., 1926); Smith, G. B., *History of the English Parliament* (2 vols., 1892).

Bémont, C., *Simon de Montfort* (1930); Costain, T. B., *The Magnificent Century* (1951); *The Three Edwards* (1958); Jenks, E., *Edward Plantagenet (Edward I) The English Justinian* (1902); Tout, T. F., *Edward I* (rev. ed., 1909).

Chrimes, S. B., *English Constitutional Ideas in the Fifteenth Century* (1936); Clarke, M. V., *Medieval Representation and Consent* (1936); White, A. B., *Self-Government at the King's Command* (1933).

III. Pickthorn, K. W. M., *Early Tudor Government* (2 vols., 1934); Elton, G. R., *The Tudor Revolution in Government* (1953); Maitland,

F. W., *English Law and the Renaissance* (1901); Neale, J. E., *Elizabeth 1 and Her Parliaments, 1559–1581* (1953), *1581–1601* (1957).

Gardiner, S. R., *History of England from the Accession of James I to the Outbreak of the Civil War 1603–1642* (10 vols., 1889–93), these famous volumes, though in part outdated, contain the most detailed history of the period; Trevelyan, G. M., *England Under the Stuarts* (21st ed., 1965); Bowen, Catherine D., *The Lion and the Throne* (1956), a superb biography of Coke; *Francis Bacon* (1963); Wedgwood, C. V., *The King's Peace* (1956); *The King's War* (1958); *A Coffin for King Charles* (1964), the most readable account of the Civil War; Judson, M., *The Crisis of the Constitution: An Essay in Constitutional and Political Thought in England 1603–1645* (1949), with valuable insights into the constitutional conflicts of the period.

Tanner, J. R., *English Constitutional Conflicts of the Seventeenth Century* (1928); Hexter, J. H., *The Reign of King Pym* (1941).

Jenks, E., *The Constitutional Experiments of the Commonwealth* (1890); Pease, T. C., *The Leveller Movement* (1916); Wolfe, D. M., *Leveller Manifestoes of the Puritan Revolution* (1944).

Trevelyan, G. M., *The English Revolution 1688–1689* (2nd ed., 1946); Turner, G. C., *James II* (1948); Macaulay, T. B., *History of England from the Accession of James II* (best ed., 6 vols., Firth, C. H., ed., 1913–15), with all the criticisms more recently directed against it, still the most detailed and vivid account of the period 1685–1702.

IV. For the modern period, the works are so numerous that even an illustrative list would be too long. The following were, however, of particular value to the author: Bagehot, W., *The English Constitution* (1913 ed.); Amery, L. S., *Thoughts on the Constitution* (1964 ed.); Jennings, I., *Cabinet Government* (2nd ed., 1951); *Parliament* (1939); Laski, H., *Parliamentary Government in England* (1938); Allen, C. K., *Law and Orders* (2nd ed., 1956); Friedmann, W., *Law and Social Change in Contemporary Britain* (1952); Wiseman, H. V., *Parliament and the Executive* (1966).

INDEX